Praise for *People Analytics in the Era of Big Data*

"This book provides easy-to-understand processes for drawing competitive information out of Big Data and turning it into applicable knowledge. In short, this book is both a compelling argument and a framework for the reader on which to build a talent management strategy and work plan." —**Dr. Jac Fitz-enz, CEO, Human Capital Source**

"Talent is one of an organization's greatest assets, and analytics must be part of the overall talent strategy. This book provides the business leader and hiring manager with a compelling framework to leverage analytics across the entire talent life cycle." —**Chip Smith, Chief Marketing Officer, Sears Home Appliances and Services**

"*People Analytics in the Era of Big Data* is a practical guide that's an essential read for any HR professional who wants to get a handle on the landscape of People Analytics and how it can increase workforce return on investment." —**Rathin Sinha, Founder and CEO, JobFindah Network, and former CEO, America's Job Exchange**

"People are the most valuable asset in an enterprise. Jean Paul and Jesse have given us seven pillars that transform how we attract, develop, and retain people. Forward-thinking leaders should read this book." —**Michael C. Krauss, @ C Level columnist, Marketing News, and President, Market Strategy Group**

"The topics covered in *People Analytics in the Era of Big Data* touch the core of what we as HR people should be preoccupied with. People Analytics are the prerequisite foundation for any real talent strategy." —**Mieke Van de Capelle, Chief HR Officer, Perfetti Van Melle**

"Companies live and die by their ability to attract and develop high-value talent. *People Analytics in the Era of Big Data* provides a key framework to help companies leverage analytics to get the most from their talent investments." —**Neil Costa, Founder and CEO, HireClix**

"Talent analytics is a must for any organization to ensure that investment in talent is well targeted and delivering the desired results. *People Analytics in the Era of Big Data* provides HR leaders with important building blocks to develop an effective People Analytics practice." —**Kathy Andreasen, Chief People Officer, Endurance International Group**

"Without question, talent is the essential ingredient in an organization's success or failure. Unfortunately decisions about talent are typically dependent on gut feelings and immeasurable interpersonal relationships. Finally there is a playbook on how to collect, interpret, and act on the talent data so organizations can recruit and retain talent better." —**RD Whitney, Group Vice President, Diversified Communications**

"Whether you call it the "War for Talent" or the "Talent Tsunami," there is no debate that the ability to acquire a world-class workforce will be *the* competitive differentiator for companies that want to out-think, out-innovate, and simply beat their competition. *People Analytics in the Era of Big Data* provides organizations with revolutionary thinking and the prescriptive tools on how to leverage Big Data to significantly improve the quality of their workforce." —**Steve Pogorzelski, CEO, Avention OneSource, and former President, Monster.com**

"The authors have found a compelling way to bring together two of the most important focus areas for any business leader: analytics and recruiting. *People Analytics in the Era of Big Data* is essential reading not just for HR professionals but for entrepreneurs like me who recognize the importance of talent, team, and culture." —**John Kelly, CEO, CoachUp**

"Big Data and analytics are hot topics in all areas of business these days, and talent management is no exception. This book provides a solid foundation for leaders who want to use analytics to drive ROI across their entire talent life cycle." —**Wayne Cooper, Executive Chairman, Chief Executive Group, and CEO, The Chief Executive Network**

"This is a must read for anyone looking for a practical and actionable approach to leverage people analytics in their organization." —**Matt Gough, CEO, Echovate**

"*People Analytics in the Era of Big Data* contains an easy-to-apply framework to one the hottest topics in analytics today. Leaders who wish to improve the ROI from their workforce management practices should take heed of the advice and techniques in this book." —**Roger Baran, Ph.D., Associate Professor of Marketing, and Director, Asian Programs, DePaul University**

"Thorough research, incisive analysis, and well-chosen case studies are the hallmarks of Isson and Harriott's work. They weave all of that together with clear, cogent arguments about why and how data analytics will permeate every aspect of the HR, talent management, and recruiting life cycles. Best practices based on anecdotes or instinct will no longer satisfy line management. It's time for corporate talent managers to get on board. If you don't quite get how to apply data in these ways, this book will be your primer." —**Glenn Gutmacher, Vice President, Diversity Talent Sourcing, State Street Corporation, and Founder, Recruiting-Online.com**

"In today's Big Data explosion, it's imperative for every business leader to leverage analytics to optimize their talent management. JP and Jesse's book provides the framework and actionable insights every leader needs to compete and win with People Analytics." —**Stephane Brutus, Interim Dean, John Molson School of Business, Concordia University**

"Human capital is the number one source of competitive advantage in the twenty-first century. Like finance, product, and marketing before it, the field of human capital is now flooded with data but deprived of frameworks, processes, and methodologies to make sense of it. This is what this book provides: a practical guide to applying data science's best practices to the field of human capital. My hope is that it helps HR departments across industries take their legitimate seat at the business strategy table. The world needs this—badly." —**Louis Gagnon, CEO, Ride.com, and former CMO and CPO, Audible**

"People Analytics is a new territory for most HR managers, which is enabled by more systematic data collection and advances in machine learning and analytics. This book shows how to apply analytics across an entire life cycle of employee management. With many real-life examples, this is a must-read for HR practitioners and managers." —**Minha Hwang, Analytics Consultant/Expert, Double Ph.D. (MIT and Stanford)**

People Analytics in the Era of Big Data

Changing the Way You Attract, Acquire, Develop, and Retain Talent

Jean Paul Isson
Jesse S. Harriott

WILEY

Published by John Wiley & Sons, Inc., Hoboken, New Jersey.
Published simultaneously in Canada.

For general information on our other products and services or for technical
support, please contact our Customer Care Department within the United
States at (800) 762-2974, outside the United States at (317) 572-3993 or fax
(317) 572-4002.

Wiley publishes in a variety of print and electronic formats and by print-on-
demand. Some material included with standard print versions of this book
may not be included in e-books or in print-on-demand. If this book refers to
media such as a CD or DVD that is not included in the version you purchased,
you may download this material at http://booksupport.wiley.com. For more
information about Wiley products, visit www.wiley.com.

Library of Congress Cataloging-in-Publication Data:

Names: Isson, Jean Paul, 1971– author. I Harriott, Jesse, author.
Title: People analytics in the era of big data : changing the way you
    attract, acquire, develop, and retain talent / Jean Paul Isson, Jesse S.
    Harriott.
Description: 1 I Hoboken : Wiley, 2016. I Includes index.
Identifiers: LCCN 2016001834 I ISBN 9781119050780 (hardback) I
    ISBN 978-1-119-23315-2 (epdf) I
    ISBN 978-1-119-23316-9 (epub) I 978-1-119-08385-6 (obook)
Subjects: LCSH: Personnel management. I Employees—Recruiting. I BISAC:
    BUSINESS & ECONOMICS / Human Resources & Personnel Management.
Classification: LCC HF5549 .I687 2016 I DDC 658.3—dc23 LC record available
at http://lccn.loc.gov/2016001834

Printed in the United States of America

10 9 8 7 6 5 4 3 2 1

I dedicate this book to my daughters, Roxane and Sofia, who have been my inspiration for so many things I do. Daddy was not available as usual to play with you and hopes when you read this book you will be proud of your patience. A special thanks to my wife, Marjolaine, for her love and support taking care of our little Sofia to give me more time to write.

—JP Isson

This book is dedicated to all the unsung analytical heroes, working tirelessly to uncover new insights, predict future business trends, and drive business impact. Keep pushing forward and never give up.

—Jesse Harriott

Contents

Foreword

People Analytics in the Era of Big Data does a great job of melding analytic processes and methods with the mass of data that is growing exponentially every day. Future success in talent management will be largely dependent on an organization's ability to mine that database. The days of scanning job boards, college recruiting trips, open houses, and advertising are obsolete. Organizations' main problem is twofold. One, there is no competitive advantage in applying these recruitment processes. Everyone can and does use them, and the results are similar rather than unique. Two, these methods are all behind the competitive curve. Nothing within them speaks to the special demands of the future because they do not uncover and express true future talent demands. At best, they are simply common tools.

The good news is, as the authors so clearly explain, that diving into the Big Data ocean with predictive analytics fishing gear virtually ensures that you will catch exactly what you're fishing for. First, think about the talent pool. In truth, there is no shortage of qualified people for any one company. The talent ocean has not been overfished for the needs of your company. The problem is that there are many boats fishing. You need a world-class talent acquisition system. This is where predictive analytics comes to the rescue.

There is a shortage of twenty-first-century talent acquisition strategies. Recruitment doesn't start in the employment section of the human resources department. Employment methods, by whatever label is in vogue, are simply functional tools. Everything starts with the organization's purpose, goals, and strategic plans. It has been clear for decades that issues of organizational purpose are often not fully addressed. Statements that the goal is to increase market share by *x* percent next year are accepted as purpose statements. Not true. They are nothing more than wishes. Management must first be absolutely clear regarding the purpose of the organization expressed in terms of its role in society. Books have been written about this, yet seldom is there a deep dive into purpose.

Once purpose is clear, then data and analytics can be brought to bear in forming a strategy. One more time, Big Data is the talent ocean. Analytics is the fishing gear. Analytics helps management find the school of fish that it seeks to fulfill its unique purpose.

Analytics comes in three levels: descriptive, predictive, and prescriptive. *Descriptive* speaks to what has happened up to the present. *Predictive* reveals what must be done to achieve future goals. *Prescriptive* tells how to do it. When a patient tells a doctor that he has sinus congestion, that is descriptive. The doctor applies her knowledge to determine what type of treatment will alleviate or cure the condition. That is predictive. The paper that the patient takes to the pharmacy explains how the treatment is to be administered. That is the prescription.

This book provides all three analytics: the description of the talent market and its shortcomings (Big Data), what types of analytics tools are available and are under development that should be used to reveal where the talent is, and finally how to use predictive analytics to solve the talent needs of the organization.

The basis of this book stems from real-world examples from the authors' years of talent acquisition experience. They provide easy to understand processes for drawing competitive information out of Big Data and turning it into applicable knowledge. In short, this book is both a compelling argument and a framework for the reader on which to build a talent management strategy and work plan.

Dr. Jac Fitz-enz, CEO, Human Capital Source

Preface

Talent is top of mind again as leaders struggle with how to capitalize on the opportunities of a changing postrecession economy while at the same time keeping workers happy and engaged. Even though many parts of the global economy are still struggling, there continues to be a talent shortage and many companies still struggle to hire and hold key talent. At the same time, younger workers continue to enter the workforce while older workers retire. These younger workers have a different expectation for the pace of feedback, career development, promotion, and what it means to be an employee. Also, the world of work has changed, with social media providing new ways to connect, engage, and find candidates. This enables candidates to promote their skills, while at the same time leaving a gold mine of talent data to be harnessed as a competitive edge for hiring managers.

At the same time, executives are putting pressure on their human resources (HR) departments to produce fact-based insights and strategies for critical talent issues such as: Do we have the right talent mix to achieve our objectives? Can we predict who are going to be the best leaders for the future? What development should we give these potential leaders? How engaged are our top performers in our key business strategies? Do we know which talents are at risk of leaving? What are we doing to keep them?

Workforce dynamics have always been complex during business cycle changes. However, what's different in this economic cycle is that human capital executives and hiring managers now have Big Data analytics to leverage in attracting, acquiring, and advancing the right talent through the organization. The amount of available data on your employees and business processes is exploding, and Big Data is now everywhere, including the workplace. Real-time information on employee engagement, actions, sentiment, productivity, location, quality, and aspirations is everywhere, making it possible to tie talent to business outcomes in ways that were almost impossible before.

The implications are significant because talent management in many businesses has traditionally revolved around interpersonal relationships or decision making based on educated experience, rather than deep analysis. Advanced People Analytics provides a unique opportunity for human capital professionals and hiring managers to position themselves as fact-based strategic partners of senior executives, using analytically proven techniques to recruit and retain those top employees who drive superior value in companies.

People Analytics is a new domain for most HR departments. However, with the application of new techniques and new thinking to talent management, the field of People Analytics is becoming more mainstream. Leading companies are increasingly leveraging sophisticated methods to analyze employee and business data to enhance their competitive edge. The old approaches of gut feel and "that's worked in the past" are no longer enough.

We wrote this book to be different from the other available books on People Analytics, and we are glad you have chosen to read it. The focus of this book is on practical approaches that can help a business leader create value from and make the most of the organization's analytical assets. Also, unlike other books, we outline how to inject data analytics at every stage of the talent management process, from talent acquisition through retention. Furthermore, we have included real-world examples of what other companies are doing, both what's working and what's not working.

This book will help you think about People Analytics across your organization, evaluate whether you are doing People Analytics well, and provide you with frameworks to take your efforts to the next level, creating business value for your organization in the process. This is not a technical book; it is written to be relevant to someone with no analytical experience as well as to the person with a great deal of analytical experience.

The focus of this book is on effective People Analytics and how companies can create business value from their Big Data assets. By effective People Analytics, we mean analytics that start with a strategic human capital business goal or question, integrate disparate data sources together, create a prediction for the future, and lead to business actions with measurable results. We provide numerous People Analytics examples throughout the book with an eye toward those real-world examples that will be of interest to a business leader as well as practicing analytical professionals.

To support different workforce analytics covered here, this book will also provide you with interviews and frontline stories from leading People Analytics organizations, including: Accenture, Adobe, AOL, Best Buy, Black Hills, Bloomberg, Bullhorn, CareerXroads, CGB Enterprise, CVS Aviation, Deloitte, Dow Chemical, Facebook, FedEx, General Electric, General Motors, Goldcorp, Google, Harrah Entertainment, Hewlett-Packard, hiQ Labs, Johnson & Johnson, Lockheed Martin, Microsoft, Monster, Omnitracs, Pfizer, SAS Institute, Société de Transport de Montréal, Sprint, Starbucks Limited Brands, Transcom, The Container Store, Wells Fargo, Workplace Safety and Insurance Board, and Xerox.

Big Data continues to be touted as the next wave of technology and analytics innovation. From our perspective, the next wave of innovation is not just about Big Data, but more about how companies leverage Big Data analytics to take action and optimize their business. Having data is not enough; it needs to be leveraged effectively to drive and optimize business action that is coordinated at all levels of the organization. As it relates to People Analytics, Big Data is critical to providing real-time insights to businesses regarding how to maximize the value of the talent for the organization as well as maximize the organization's value for the talent it intends to retain and develop. Throughout the book, we review our Seven Pillars of People Analytics Success in the context of Big Data, providing examples for each pillar to help illustrate the key concepts to effective People Analytics.

This book is written where each chapter builds on the preceding one, but each chapter can be read by itself as well. You will get more out of the book if you read it from beginning to end, but if you are interested in quickly learning about employee engagement analytics, for example, you can jump right to that chapter. Regardless, we encourage you to start with Chapters 1 through 3, which provide the foundation for the book as well as outline one of our key frameworks, the Seven Pillars of People Analytics Success. Throughout the course of this book, we explore each pillar of the People Analytics framework, offering insights on how to successfully leverage analytics for every pillar, and we provide frontline stories from companies that have successfully leveraged the framework to improve business outcomes. We will also share best practices and takeaways at the end of each chapter.

We are confident that if you follow the principles contained in this book you will develop high-impact People Analytics and generate business value from the Big Data and little data available to your organization. Some of the practices we outline are not easy to accomplish, but whether you are in a large company or a small one, you can apply your vision of People Analytics and create business value from your data.

Acknowledgments

We engaged hundreds of business leaders to help in the writing of this book. Whether through interviews, formal contributions, or informal collaboration, we are indebted to many for helping to complete the book. We would especially like to thank Kim Lascelles, who not only reviewed our previous book but was very helpful to review the first proposal of this book, as well as most chapters of the manuscript. Despite his busy schedule, his support and feedback were invaluable. Kim, you are definitely a key pillar of the writing of our book.

A special acknowledgment goes to Melissa Fernand, who has done a terrific job reviewing every chapter of this book, including case studies. Melissa's review helped a lot to make the book easier to understand for all readers. Despite having a full-time job, she was instrumental in providing fast-turnaround reviews and insightful feedback. Melissa's input was critical in making this book relevant and insightful for our readers. Thanks, Melissa, for being *the* reviewer of this book; your assistance was invaluable to us.

Writing a book on People Analytics would not be possible without the input of other professionals: industry leaders and experts and, more important, the contributions of hundreds of people and companies who were generous enough to participate in our research for this book and share their People Analytics journeys. You will see many of their contributions throughout the book in the form of great insights in their quotes and concrete examples of how they make People Analytics work. They gave us some of their precious time for interviews (despite time zone differences), provided case studies, and even contributed writing for some chapters in the book. So we would like to thank all of you because your contributions helped to provide readers with frontline stories and also actionable insights that they can quickly leverage in their organizations. The list is endless, as we engaged hundreds of companies. Just to name a few, we would like to thank:

Foreword to the Book

- Dr. Jac Fitz-enz: The father of human capital strategic analysis and measurement, he published the first human resources (HR) metrics in 1978 and introduced benchmarking to HR in 1985. In 2007, he was cited as one of the top five "HR Management Gurus" by *HR World*, and the Society for Human Resource Management chose him as one of the 50 persons who in the past 50 years has "significantly changed what HR does and how it does it." Dr. Fitz-enz has published 13 books and over 400 articles.

Contributions to Chapters

- Pasha Roberts, Chief Scientist at Talent Analytics, Corp., for his contribution to the Employee Lifetime Value and Cost Modeling chapter.

- Amel Arab, Senior Manager at Deloitte Consulting, LLP, for her contribution to the Employee Retention chapter.

- John Houston, Deloitte Partner at Deloitte Consulting, LLP, for his contribution to the Employee Retention chapter.

Interviews and Case Studies

- Jeanne Harris **(Accenture)**, Global Managing Director of Information Technology at the Accenture Institute for High Performance. Jeanne is the coauthor with Tom Davenport of the well-known book *Competing on Analytics*, as well as the *Harvard Business Review* article "Competing on Talent Analytics." Jeanne was the first person JP interviewed for this book, and provided insights that helped to reshape some of the content of the book.

- Michael Housman **(hiQ Labs)**, Workforce Scientist in Residence, and former Chief Data Analytics Officer at Evolv. Thanks, Michael, for your time and great insights.

- Allison Allen Durrell Robinson **(Bloomberg).** Thanks so much for the firsthand insights on talent acquisition and talent retention you shared with JP.

- Kathy Andreasen **(Endurance International Group)**, Chief People Officer.

- Art Papas (CEO, **Bullhorn**). Despite his busy schedule, Art spoke with JP and provided actionable workforce analytics insights from the front lines as well as from a C-suite perspective.
- Dawn Klinghoffer **(Microsoft Corporation)**. Thanks for your input for the case study and discussion with JP.
- Gerry Crispin **(CareerXroads)**. JP spoke to Gerry several times to gather his invaluable insights on talent acquisition and overall workforce analytics. Thanks, Gerry, for sharing your experience and expertise.
- Ian Bailie **(CISCO)**, Global Talent Acquisition and People Planning. Despite the time zone difference, Ian was flexible enough to provide JP with actionable applications of analytics for talent acquisition at CISCO.
- Jenn Mann **(SAS Institute)**, Vice President and Chief Human Resources Officer. Thanks so much for sharing with JP your firsthand experience in the successful implementation of the SAS Employee Wellness and Health Program.
- Gale Adcock **(SAS Institute)**, Chief Health Officer. Thanks so much for sharing with JP your firsthand experience in the successful implementation of the SAS Employee Wellness and Health Program.
- Suzanne Sprajcar Beldycki (**SAS Institute**). Thanks, Suzanne, for your help connecting JP with the right people at SAS for this research.
- Arun Chidambaram **(Pfizer)**, Director of Global Workforce Intelligence. Thanks for your time for the case study and the insightful People Analytics discussions you had with JP.
- Mark Berry **(CGB Enterprises, Inc**.), Vice President, Human Resources (Chief Human Resources Officer), and former Vice President, Human Resources Workforce Analytics Planning, at ConAgra Foods. Mark spoke with JP several times and provided him with invaluable inputs and frontline experience in People Analytics. Thanks so much for your contributions.

- Glenn Gutmacher **(State Street)**, Vice President, Diversity Sourcing Team. Glenn was generous enough to provide JP with invaluable talent sourcing references and help him to connect with the best minds in talent acquisition in the industry. Thanks, Glenn, for our multiple chats and exchanges.

- Josh Bersin **(Bersin by Deloitte)**. Despite his hectic schedule, Josh managed to provide us with invaluable inputs and expert advice on talent retention and overall people analytics. Thank you.

- Robin Erickson, PhD **(Bersin by Deloitte)**. Thanks for your inputs on talent retention.

- Greta Roberts **(Talent Analytics Corp.)**. Thanks, Greta, for your time and the insightful feedback you provided at the beginning this journey.

- John Callery **(BNY Mellon)**. Thanks for the insights on talent retention.

- Rob Macintosh **(ERE Media).** Thanks for providing insights on the quality of hire.

- Christophe Paris, Josée Gauvreau, and Cedric Lepine **(Société de Transport de Montréal, STM)**. Thanks so much for sharing your workforce planning analytics success story with JP.

- Eugene Wen **(Workplace Safety and Insurance Board, WSIB),** Vice President and Chief Statistician. Thanks so much for the interview and for sharing your workforce safety and insightful success story with JP. Enjoyed our talks.

- Chad Harness **(Fifth Third Bank)**. Thanks for the insightful exchange on overall workforce analytics, human resources, and quants.

- Marina Byezhanova **(Pronexia)**, Cofounder of Pronexia—New Generation Headhunters.

- Jean-Baptiste Audrerie **(SPB Organizational Psychology),** Director of Marketing.

- Nathalie Carrenard **(L'Oreal)**, Talent Acquisition Manager.

- Heather Johnson **(IBM)**, Advanced Analytics Consultant for Performance Marketing. Thanks, Heather, for your help with this project and great exchanges with JP.
- Shirley Farrell **(Human Resources Call Centre)**, Principal Consultant and Chief Executive Officer. Thanks for the interview with JP despite the time zone difference. Your input has been very helpful, offering a global perspective to the research for this book.
- Michael Bazigos **(McKinsey)**, Vice President for OrgSolutions. Thanks for sharing your experience and success stories delivering People Analytics solutions.
- Haig Nalbantian **(Mercer)**, Senior Partner.
- Dan DeMaioNewton **(ACT)**.
- Louis Gagnon **(Audible/Amazon)**, Chief Marketing Officer.
- Fanta Berete **(CCI France)**, Manager of Human Resources Projects and Communication.
- Meredith Lazar **(Constant Contact)**, Human Resources Manager.
- Matt Gough **(Echovate.com)**.
- Paul Zikopoulos **(IBM)**, Vice President for Analytics Customer Success.
- Ramesh Karpagavinayagam **(CapitalOne)**, Senior Director and Head of Human Resources Analytics.
- James Gallman **(General Electric)**, Leader of Strategic Workforce Planning.
- Ian O'Keefe **(Google)**, People Analytics Leader.

Thanks to members of the Monster team—Joanie Courtney, Matt O'Connor, Matt Mund, Ajith Segaram, John McLaughlin, Eugene Robitaille, Kareen Emery, and Marlene Lasgoutte—for their support and assistance with some content for this book. Also, thanks to members of the Constant Contact team: Lisa Pimentel, Bob Nicoson, Sue LaChance, Marcus Tgettis, Harpreet Grewal, and Amy Guiel.

Writing a book while holding a full-time job would never be possible without the love and support of family and friends: Nathalie de

Repentigny and her parents, Yvan and Michele de Repentigny, as well as Eric de Larminat and Mario Bottone. JP would like to thank his mom Martha and his father Samuel for nurturing his passion for mathematics as well as great hard work values at an early age. He would also like to thank his brother Faustin (Moise), sister Betty, and Cousin David for their support. Special thanks to our families, especially our young children and our wives for their patience while we were in front of our laptops writing this book. You all helped us to finish the book and are key pillars to this achievement—thanks for your love and support.

About the Authors

Jean Paul Isson is Global Vice President for Predictive Analytics and Business Intelligence at Monster Worldwide, Inc., where he has built his global predictive analytics team from the ground up and successfully conceived and implemented global customer scoring, customer segmentation, predictive modeling, and web mining applications and talent analytics solutions across North America, Europe, and the Asia–Pacific region. Prior to joining Monster, Mr. Isson led the global customer behavior modeling team at Rogers Wireless, implementing churn models and pioneering customer lifetime value segmentation to optimize services, marketing, and sales activities.

Mr. Isson is a worldwide expert and an evangelist in Big Data and advanced business analytics. He is an internationally acclaimed speaker and a thought leader who specializes in helping organizations create business value from their Big Data or little data. Mathematician and statistician by training (he holds a master's degree in mathematics and statistics), he loves helping executives to apply data science to business questions to tell the data story, and was named among the 180 leading data science, Big Data, and analytics bloggers in the world by Data Science Central.

Mr. Isson is frequently invited to be the keynote speaker at executive events on advanced analytics, human capital management, human resources analytics, and innovation in the United States, Canada, the United Kingdom, Germany, France, Denmark, the Netherlands, Poland, the Czech Republic, Australia, and China. He has more than 22 years of experience in advanced business analytics, focusing on predictive analytics, workforce analytics, behavior modeling, market segmentation, and sales coverage optimization. He teaches classes for the Executive Certificate in Advanced Business Analytics at Concordia University. He has delivered business analytics workshops at executive programs in the United States, Canada, Europe, Asia, and Australia.

He is the author (with Jesse Harriott) of *Win with Advanced Business Analytics* (John Wiley & Sons, 2012), a reference business analytics book that was translated into several languages, including Chinese, and is a contributor to several local and international newspapers and online magazines, including the *Journal of the American Management Association*, the *Wall Street Journal*, the *New York Times*, *MIT Sloan Management Review*, the *Guardian*, *Financial Post*, *National Post*, *Les Echos*, *Liberation*, *Wich50* (Australia), *Le Journal du Net Silicon*, *Challenges, le Monde*, the *Gazette*, and the *Globe & Mail*. Mr. Isson has appeared in various media outlets, including TV, to cover Big Data analytics, talent analytics, and employment conditions.

■ ■ ■

Jesse S. Harriott, PhD, has been a research and analytics professional for more than 20 years and has held various client- and supplier-side global analytics leadership positions. He is currently Chief Analytics Officer at Constant Contact, a technology company that helps more than 600,000 organizations generate repeat business and referrals through online marketing solutions. Prior to Constant Contact, Dr. Harriott was Chief Knowledge Officer at Monster Worldwide, where he helped drive annual revenue from $300 million to over $1.3 billion. Dr. Harriott started an international analytics division at Monster and created the Monster Employment Index that was tracked by millions of people in more than 30 countries in North America, Europe, and Asia. He also led web analytics, business intelligence, competitive intelligence, data governance, marketing research, and sales analytics departments for Monster.

Prior to Monster, Dr. Harriott created an analytics consulting practice for e-commerce company Gomez (now Compuware), where his team led projects for Internet start-ups and well-known brands, including Orbitz.com, WebMD, and Fidelity. He has advised many private and public organizations regarding analytics and labor market issues, including the White House, the Department of Labor, the European Commission, the Federal Reserve, the National Governors Association, and the Clinton Global Initiative, and various U.S. senators. He is the author or coauthor of several publications, including the books *Win with Advanced Business Analytics* (John Wiley & Sons, 2012) and *Finding Keepers* (McGraw-Hill, 2008), which has been published in North America, South America, Europe, and Asia.

Dr. Harriott has taught at the University of Chicago and holds an MA and a PhD in experimental psychology from DePaul University. He has appeared in various media outlets, including CNBC, the *Wall Street Journal*, the *New York Times*, CBS radio, Bloomberg, and Reuters. Dr. Harriott has won several awards, including the Hardin Award from the American Marketing Association, the Platinum Award from PR News, and an Ogilvy Award from the Advertising Research Foundation, and he was named by the *Boston Business Journal* as one of Boston's top 40 under 40. He lives in the Boston area with his family.

List of Case Studies and People Interviewed

Chapter 1

Interviews: Jeanne Harris, Global Managing Director of Information Technology Research, Accenture; Michael Housman, Workforce Scientist in Residence, hiQ Labs; and former Chief Data Analytics Officer, Evolv

Chapter 2

Interview: Mark Berry, Vice President, Human Resources (Chief Human Resources Officer), CGB Enterprises; former Vice President, People Insights, ConAgra Foods

Chapter 3

Case Study: Bloomberg

Chapter 4

Interviews: Art Papas, CEO, Bullhorn; Christophe Paris, Human Resources Business Intelligence Manager, Société de Transport de Montréal
Case Studies: Dow Chemical and Black Hills

Chapter 5

Interviews: Gerry Crispin, Principal and Cofounder, CareerXroads; Pete Kazanjy, Founder, TalentBin
Case Studies: Monster Worldwide, Inc.; General Motors

Chapter 6

Interviews: Dawn Klinghoffer, Senior Director of HR Business Insights, Microsoft; Ian Bailie, Director of Talent Acquisition Operations, CISCO
Case Studies: Google; Xerox

Chapter 8

Interview: Kathy Andreasen, Chief People Officer, Endurance International Group

Chapter 9

Case Studies: General Electric; Goldcorp

Chapter 11

Interviews: Arun Chidambaram, Director of Global Workforce Intelligence, Pfizer; John Callery, People Analytics Director, AOL

Chapter 12

Interviews: Jenn Mann, Vice President of Human Resources, SAS Institute; Gale Adcock, Chief Health Officer, SAS Institute; Eugene Wen, Vice President and Chief Statistician, Workplace Safety and Insurance Board

CHAPTER 1

The People Analytics Age

War is 90 percent information.

—Napoleon Bonaparte

rganizations are in a worldwide war—a war to acquire a diminishing resource, an asset that is more valuable than oil and more critical than capital. The resource can be bought but not owned. It is found in every country but is difficult to extract. Leaders know that without this resource they are doomed to mediocrity, yet most of them use outdated methods to measure and understand it.

The resource is skilled workers. In the United States alone, employers spend more than $400 billion a year locating, securing, and holding on to them.[1] Internationally, companies large and small devote a similarly significant amount of money (as well as staff and executive time) to bringing in skilled workers and keeping them happy. Just one part of the process, help wanted advertising, costs employers almost $20 billion per year.[2] Whether they're called employees, talent, human capital, or personnel, these are the people with the skills, work habits, knowledge, experience, and personal qualities that drive your organization to meet its goals. Top talent is rare by definition—the ones you want on your team whether you are on a hiring binge or managing layoffs.

Top personnel create the best new products, make the most revenue, and find the greatest efficiencies. They build great workplaces, delight customers, and attract others like themselves to join the organization. They adapt to changing business conditions. Finding, managing, and holding that top talent is the key to your future.

It takes a ton of work to maintain top talent in your workforce. The underlying dynamics of locating, hiring, and retaining all employees—especially the best ones—call for a continuous give-and-take between employer and employee, and analytics is a must for understanding those dynamics unique to your organization. Your talent strategy, and People Analytics, must go beyond your current workforce to include people at every stage of the employment cycle. It includes understanding potential employees who work elsewhere, candidates (those who might work for you), current employees, and former employees (alumni, including retirees who have left employment altogether). If talent mattered less in the modern economy, the quest to find it would be less urgent. Today, it's the only long-term path to greater profits.

THE PEOPLE ANALYTICS ADVANTAGE

If you are reading this book, we assume you see the importance, as we do, of using People Analytics to positively impact your organization. You may be a human resources (HR) business leader who wants to learn more about how companies use data effectively. You may be an analytics manager who wants to understand pitfalls to avoid that can lead to failure when undertaking People Analytics. You may be motivated to learn some of the latest techniques and best practices of how to use different types of people-related information across the enterprise. You may be an analytical professional and want to learn how to take your organization's People Analytics to the next level. You may be an HR leader who wants to learn about data across the enterprise so you can decide how best to use it to make strategic human capital decisions. Whatever your motivation for reading this book, we assume your organization has business challenges that you hope data and the practice of People Analytics will help you overcome.

In 2015, Deloitte's Global Human Capital consulting group conducted a global survey among more than 3,300 HR and business leaders in 106 countries. It's a great resource and one of the largest global studies of talent, leadership, and HR challenges. The findings revealed many challenges facing human capital, not the least of which are related to People Analytics. For example, the number of HR and business leaders who cited engagement as being "very important" approximately doubled from 26 percent the previous year to 50 percent in 2015. Sixty percent of HR and business leaders surveyed said they do not have an adequate program to measure and improve engagement, indicating a lack of preparedness for addressing this issue. Only 12 percent of HR and business leaders have a program in place to define and build a strong culture, while only 7 percent rated themselves as excellent at measuring, driving, and improving engagement and retention.[3]

According to Deloitte, organizations are also missing the growth opportunities presented by analytics. The Deloitte report revealed that analytics is one of the areas where organizations face a significant capability gap. Seventy-five percent of respondents cited talent analytics as an important issue, but just 8 percent believe their organization is "strong" in this area—almost exactly the same as in 2014.

"HR and people analytics has the potential to transform the way we hire, develop, and manage our people," said Jason Geller, principal at Deloitte Consulting LLP and national managing director of the company's U.S. human capital practice. "Leading organizations are already using talent analytics to understand what motivates employees and what makes them stay or leave. These insights help drive increased returns from talent investments, with huge consequences for the business as a whole."[4]

It is gradually becoming clear that in today's cutthroat business climate where the employee is gaining power, failing to leverage People Analytics effectively in your organization can mean the difference between thriving and slow death.

PROFILE

▼ Interview with Jeanne Harris, Global Managing Director of Information Technology Research, Accenture Institute for High Performance

JP Isson had a chance to interview Jeanne Harris, the coauthor with Tom Davenport of the well-known book *Competing on Analytics* (Harvard Business Review Press, 2007), as well as the October 2010 *Harvard Business Review* article "Talent Analytics."

Isson: How will analytics change the HR world in the future?

Harris: In some ways, the book *Moneyball* [by Michael Lewis (W. W. Norton, 2004)] is really about analytics for talent management and its net impact. And that is really a good way to show people the potential analytics holds for every industry. Ironically, most companies leverage analytics in certain aspects of their business; however, HR tends to be the one they wait to look at later in the process. It just seems to me we need to be getting started earlier. But the important thing to keep in mind is this is not a one-size-fits-all situation, and all answers will vary depending on the business.

The impact of analytics will depend on your business model: If your strategy is customer intimacy, you're going to focus initially on your customers' analytics. For example, if your business is in retail, you will find that it's equally important that your employees focus on those customers, too. By setting up and managing your customer analytics, you will be able to develop insights on customer relationships and determine the best strategies for improvement.

However, these strategies will vary if you are an investment banker. Instead of your primary focus being on creating a tight relationship with your customer, you might instead want to better understand how you can quickly identify, manage, reward, and motivate your employees who do the best job of investing money—in other words, how you best manage your star performers.

Isson: Do you believe HR is ready to embrace People Analytics?

Harris: Companies that I have talked with about People Analytics tend to be in the very early stages of implementation. Sometimes, they themselves are not clear on what information they want to collect and how they will leverage it. This is an important issue we need to address.

Many times, HR leaders have the sense that so much of what they have to do is reporting for regulatory or legal purposes, and they want to become more of a strategic partner with the business by managing and developing the right talent needed to drive the organization forward. While they may know analytics is the vehicle for accomplishing this, oftentimes they are not exactly sure how to do so.

I think that in many organizations, there is the perception that the most interesting issues are not addressed by HR, but instead they occur in other parts of the business. This is an interesting wrinkle: As an HR professional, you don't want to try to lift away from the business, but you want to add value. It is all about striking the right balance between

(Continued)

(continued)

HR and the business. I think this really is the core issue most executives struggle with sometimes.

Isson: How can companies leverage HR analytics or People Analytics?

Harris: One of the ways HR teams are starting to get involved in analytics is through applying the customer life cycle management (CLCM) model to their own employees. This is an idea that goes back to a *Competing on Analytics* case study, where a company (at the time, Nextel), had used CLCM to study their own employees from the time they heard about Nextel to the time they resigned. It's about marketing and tracking your internal resources as much as you do your external ones.

Developing a model that enables you to track your candidates and new hires from the first time they hear about your company through the employee life cycle will help you keep your fingers on the proverbial pulse of your talent and enable you to better manage your retention activities. For instance, if a hiring manager has an employee who says he or she is leaving, that manager can look at the expected lifetime value of that specific employee before deciding whether or not to make a counter offer.

Companies will be successful if they manage their HR teams the same as they manage their sales or marketing teams. They can leverage the HR team as a strategic department that can provide cost-containment insights and help them best manage their overall employee life cycle, much in the same way they do with their own customers. Using hard data points, they will be able to build models to react in real-time and better manage employee attrition through deciding what actions can be taken to keep high-potential and high-value employees.

Isson: What impact will Big Data have on HR teams looking to embrace analytics?

Harris: I constantly think Big Data just means more data that you now need to know how to analyze. I have always thought that way even before big data was "Big Data." It's one of those things that you want to do properly, but that you couldn't quite technologically handle. And now, all those barriers are all gone.

My message for HR executives is to approach Big Data as a sky's-the-limit opportunity. There is a lot of value that can be unearthed just by mining the data you already have in your system. Once you've explored your data, you can add other data from other resources, such as publicly available talent data, labor market data, and benchmarked data from other companies. The limit that we historically had to deal with regarding massive data does not exist anymore, and this is a mind-set change that we must all learn to adapt to and embrace. Big Data will help us bring our organizations closer to achieving our collective company mission and associated goals.

Isson: What advice would you give to a company beginning to make use of People Analytics?

Harris: My advice is twofold:

1. The important thing is just to get started. Start by engaging your business partners throughout the company and gain a comprehensive understanding of their talent issues, gaps, strengths, and goals. In many ways, that is the first hurdle for HR executives to overcome because the business side of companies aren't typically used to thinking about HR in these terms. It's a reeducation process, and it comes down to establishing an open dialogue between business units.

2. The second thing is to think big, start small. Choose a high-impact area where you can add demonstrable value to your internal customers. Take the data you collect, learn from it, and use it to improve processes. HR analytics is in its infancy stage, and it's going to take some time to figure many things out, but there is no doubt that People Analytics will become the *Moneyball* for HR.

Companies are getting smarter about using People Analytics to acquire, advance, and retain top talent—and, in the course of doing so, to improve their return on human capital investment. Some of the conclusions that companies are coming to are sometimes counterintuitive. For example, according to a *Wall Street Journal* story,[5] when looking for workers to staff its call centers, Xerox Corporation used to pay lots of attention to applicants who had done the job before and had a lot of experience. Then, an analytics algorithm told Xerox that experience doesn't matter when seeking a top performer. The algorithm said that what does matter in a good call-center worker—one who won't quit before the company recovers its $5,000 investment in training—is personality. Data showed that creative types tended to stick around for the necessary six months. Inquisitive people often don't. After a half-year trial that cut attrition by 20 percent, Xerox now leaves all hiring for its 48,700 call-center jobs to analytics software that asks applicants to choose between statements like: "I ask more questions than most people do" and "People tend to trust what I say." The Xerox example is a brief illustration of the insights that can be gained through leveraging Big Data in an effective People Analytics practice.

As People Analytics is rapidly evolving and often indicates different things to different people, we think it is important to outline what we mean by the term for the purpose of this book. We define People Analytics as the integration of disparate data sources from inside and outside the enterprise that are required to answer and act upon forward-looking business questions related to the human capital assets of an organization. We realize this is a fairly broad definition; however, our experience in practicing People Analytics, as well as that of the hundreds of companies that have provided input for this book, indicate to us that People Analytics is moving away from an isolated reporting and dashboard mentality inside the HR department toward an integration of various types of people-related information across the organization in tighter alignment with the business goals of C-level executives.

Even though People Analytics is a relatively new field, we see it as having the potential for great organizational impact and importance, far beyond that of the more traditional and isolated HR reporting function. Actually, the practice of People Analytics is beginning to have meaningful impact in many companies, some of which we profile in this book.

There are several key components worth noting in our definition of People Analytics that may differ from more traditional definitions of HR reporting or analysis. First, in our view, effective People Analytics must be grounded in key business questions. The amount of data available to businesses is overwhelming and growing at an exponential rate, and it's easy to enter analysis paralysis or drift into intellectual curiosities. Therefore, organizations must articulate and prioritize the key questions they want People Analytics to answer.

Second, we believe that People Analytics has the most impact on the organization when it is forward-looking—not backward-looking. In other words, it is most useful when it is predictive and provides a lens into the future regarding likely business outcomes.

Third, to us, the new age of People Analytics requires the integration and synthesis of various information disciplines across the organization such as employee research, employee behavior, web analytics, business reporting, competitive intelligence, economic and labor market research, and outside data sources, among others, in order to be effective. If you recall from our definition, all effective People Analytics should be grounded in key business questions and objectives. Those business questions and objectives do not care about your organizational structure, that some of the employee data is in finance, some is in HR systems, and some resides in the information technology (IT) department. Those business questions just demand answers, and whichever organization can answer them consistently with speed and accuracy will win. Will that be you or your competitors?

So, how do you unleash the power of People Analytics to address the business challenges that are most critical to your organization while overcoming typical pitfalls inside your company? If you could only find one brilliant data scientist and woo them into your organization, then everything would be all right and your company could do brilliant things with its people data. That one genius could help you identify your at-risk employees effectively, learn how to increase your employee productivity, reduce employee turnover, predict what will make new employees likely to succeed, and increase your organization's talent return on investment (ROI) by 30 percent, right?

Wrong. Certainly smart and knowledgeable staff is critical to making good use of your data—but that is nowhere near enough. There are several other challenges your organization needs to be aware of before you can most effectively leverage People Analytics. This book is designed to help you address those challenges, but first, let's outline a few of them.

THE WORLD OF WORK HAS CHANGED

There are many factors that are setting the stage for People Analytics' rise to importance. We see labor market and societal forces that are leading up to the newfound focus on People Analytics. Some of these have been occurring gradually over the course of decades, and some are more recent phenomena. However, they're all coming together to make People Analytics a necessary capability for any organization that wants to remain competitive in the future.

Let's start by considering the economy. We all know that over the past eight years or so the global economic environment has been more intense and challenging than ever before. At the time we write this book, the U.S. economy is showing fits and starts of positive growth and the labor market is again tight in many areas with the war for talent raging. In a 2015 press conference, Janet Yellen, chair of the Federal Reserve Bank, indicated that "the U.S. economy hit a soft patch earlier this year. Real gross domestic product looks to have changed little in the first quarter. Growth and household spending slowed, business fixed investment edged down and net exports were a substantial drag on growth."[6] Those companies that identify with the Fed's moderate outlook are trying to hold market share, keep their current customers happy, and keep their employees engaged. Despite the lack of dramatic growth in the economy, finding new talent and holding on to existing talent continue to be a struggle for most companies.

In addition, much of the global economy is still on unsure footing in many parts of the world. Consumers are still being conservative about their spending in places like Europe and Asia. The global real estate market has not fully recovered, and global businesses are struggling to understand how to grow effectively, yet profitably.

However, business and consumer confidence have shown signs of improvement and the long-term payroll data trend from the Bureau of Labor Statistics indicates that companies are creating new jobs again.

Therefore, optimistically minded companies are eagerly trying to be smart about staying ahead of business trends as well as capturing some of the economic growth.

With this as a backdrop, let's consider some of the other forces that are changing the world of work and paving the way for the rise of People Analytics, including:

- Impact of digital technology on the labor market.
- Decreasing employee tenure and loyalty.
- Influence of millennials.
- Globalization of the workforce economy.
- Need of employers to always be engaging talent.
- Increased competition for talent.
- HR is under pressure.
- Skills gap in the labor market.
- Talent is one of the last competitive differentiators.
- HR evolves into talent management.

Impact of Digital Technology on the Labor Market

Digital media has forever changed how employers look for workers and how workers look for new opportunities. The notion of either being happy in your job or actively seeking a job has been changed by digital environments. For many in-demand workers, there is an ongoing stream of job opportunities from multiple digital channels such as the web, mobile, and social platforms that come in front of them all the time. Additionally, workers are more connected with one another and have an easier time understanding the real story of what it's like to work in a particular company and what's valued, as well as some of the negatives about a company.

As a result, the Internet and other digital environments have changed the workforce equation and revolutionized the overall talent sourcing and retention process, moving from a print-based to a digital-based effort. Digital technology has also enhanced the word-of-mouth channels through social networks and social hiring channels.

In addition, your employees see an ever-increasing number of recruitment messages from competitors from all directions. Media volume, including recruitment advertising and direct brand building that your employees see and that help form an impression of an employer, has been on the rise for quite some time. In the United States, companies send over 90 billion pieces of direct mail each year trying to influence the behavior of customers.[7] Also, the Radicati Group estimates that nearly 90 trillion e-mails are sent each year,[8] certainly a large percentage of which are helping your employees form an impression about a prospective employer organization. According to Media Dynamics, a media research group, the average American is exposed to a minimum combined total of 560 advertisements each day from radio, print, and television.[9]

At the same time, mobile recruitment usage continues to increase dramatically on a global basis, as does the use of social media and other online content such as blogs or tweets. There are roughly 6.5 billion mobile phone subscriptions worldwide, with some users having service on more than one device.[10] Also, according to the Direct Marketing Association, 36 percent of workers now follow brands on social media platforms.[11]

This new media is taking a lot of the friction out of learning about work opportunities and about choosing an employer. The good news from an analytics perspective is that, with the increase of new media and the multitude of ways to interact online, comes the increase of new data into the recruiting organization and the building blocks of People Analytics. For example, Internet sourcing created an explosion of digital talent data and metrics, and technology has enabled this information to be captured, stored, processed, analyzed, and managed. Every interaction that someone, whether a prospective employee or a current employee, has with your employer brand in an electronic medium such as an Internet search engine, a website, a social media platform, an electronic coupon provider, a blog post, or over a mobile device generates a data trail.

Other interaction points are also growing and generating massive amounts of data in their wake that can potentially be used for People Analytics of your workforce. For example, there are unknown quantities of digital location tracking sensors in shipping crates, electric meters, automobiles, industrial equipment, and various other devices used by employees at many organizations. Additionally, GPS, WiFi, and Bluetooth position tracking by mobile devices is widespread and generates massive streams of location data that companies are beginning to harness in their quest to use analytics to drive workforce optimization.

Given these issues influenced by the rise of digital environments, the world of multichannel talent acquisition and retention requires the effective use of People Analytics to untangle the complex patterns of employer brand and talent perception that arise from being exposed to so many employers from so many channels.

Employee Tenure and Loyalty Are Decreasing

Another trend leading to the greater importance of People Analytics is that worker loyalty is disappearing and workers are not staying with companies for as long as they did in the past. Employees are becoming more fickle, and loyalty for employers is rarer than ever before—so employee turnover is often a substantial business cost. As a result, more and more employees are becoming less engaged, and are planning to look for new work. The decline in employee loyalty is also seen to be affecting the quality of service provided to customers. According to a 2015 study by the American Management Association, employee loyalty has declined sharply over the past five years at North American companies and is thought to harm organizations by causing low morale, high turnover, disengagement, growing distrust, and lack of team spirit.[12]

In recent times, this issue has been laid at the feet of members of the millennial generation, who have a strong reputation for switching jobs frequently. However, the data tell a more complicated story. Certainly, millennials are part of the equation, but job tenure has been declining for at least 50 years, with both older workers and younger workers staying with companies for shorter and shorter periods of time.

For example, the Federal Reserve Bank of Atlanta examined the median job tenure by age group and generation and found that job tenure decline was across the board, not just in millennials. As seen in Figure 1.1, when looking at 20- to 30-year-olds, we can see that the median job tenure was four years among those born in 1953 (baby boomers) when they were between 20 and 30 years old. However, for 20- to 30-year-olds born in 1993 (millennials), median job tenure is only one year.[13] Similar—and some even more dramatic—declines occur across cohorts within each age group. Interestingly, there is also a five-year decline in median job tenure between 41- to 50-year-old "Depression babies" (born starting in 1933) and 41- to 50-year-old Gen Xers (born starting in 1973).

At the same time that worker tenure is decreasing across the board, employee loyalty is decreasing as well. Wharton School management professor Adam Cobb sees the declining loyalty as a symptom of an evolving relationship between organization and employee. Cobb sees employee behavior as being influenced by the major organizational restructuring that began 30 years ago. "Firms have always laid off workers, but in the 1980s, you started to see healthy firms laying off workers, mainly for shareholder value. Firms would say, 'We are doing

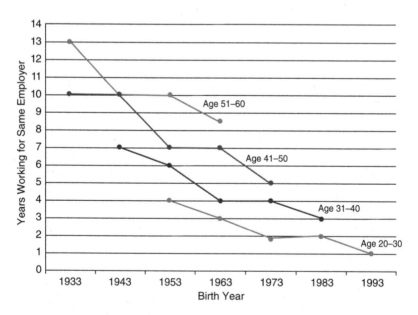

Figure 1.1 Median Job Tenure by Age and Birth Cohort
Source: Current Population Survey, U.S. Bureau of Labor Statistics.

this in the long-term interest of our shareholders,'" Cobb noted. "You would also see cuts in employee benefits—401(k)s instead of defined benefit pensions, and health care costs being pushed on to employees. The trend was toward having the risks be borne by workers instead of firms. If I'm an employee, that's a signal to me that I'm not going to let firms control my career."[14]

The lower levels of employee loyalty and the declining job tenure are both creating a more urgent need for analytics to help understand which employees are engaged and which employees are at risk, as well as how to spot the signs early enough before it's too late. Given all of this, it's extremely critical for businesses to understand employee issues such as what drives attraction to you as an employer, current employee sentiment, and factors associated with a highly engaged and productive workforce. Understanding those issues must be grounded in solid analytics. Doing this without systematic analytics and voice-of-the-employee input is almost impossible.

The Influence of Millennials

Millennials have entered the workforce en masse, and many have different attitudes regarding the employer–employee relationship, what work means, and how they expect to be treated in the workplace. There's a stereotype that millennials are entitled job hoppers; however, the data tell a different story. Younger workers are actually staying in their jobs longer than previous generations did. In the late 1980s, about 50 percent of 20- to 25-year-olds changed jobs each year, but that dropped to 35 percent after the recent recession, according to an analysis by the *Washington Post*.[15] It's not clear if millennials are holding on to those jobs by choice or if they are struggling to find better opportunities.

Regardless, there are some key differences between millennials and other workforce generations that make the importance of People Analytics more evident. For example, the millennial generation expects to be able to give and receive feedback openly and frequently. They expect this at all levels of the organization as well. So, it's not unheard-of for a millennial worker to feel empowered to meet with the CEO and tell her what he thinks about recent happenings in the company. This also influences their expectations for what a manager relationship should look like.

Additionally, millennials have a stronger desire for their job or career to have personal meaning beyond the job task they are tackling. For example, is their company socially responsible, helping others in the community, helping to influence the industry or world, or achieving something great? In other words, buying into the vision and mission of their employer is more critical for this generation compared to previous generations.

As a result, People Analytics is critical to monitor and understand the early at-risk signs for this generation. Concepts like a traditional once-a-year check-in or annual performance review are not going to be enough to make sure you're staying close to and mitigating the turnover risk of your millennial workers.

Globalization of the Workforce Economy

Another driver of the need for People Analytics is the globalization of the world economy. The labor market and competition for talent can no longer be viewed through a domestic lens. There are complex labor market dynamics at play that only analytics can help untangle. For example, Figure 1.2, from Aon Hewitt's annual report *2015 Trends in Global Employee Engagement*, shows the world's largest economies and the world's largest labor pools. Together these countries make up more than 80 percent of the global gross domestic product (GDP) and available labor. These countries also have very different dynamics in economic and population growth/stagnation and wide ranges of average employee engagement levels (from 38 percent in Japan to 78 percent in Mexico). China and the United States are the dominant markets from a GDP and labor perspective, with the U.S. GDP double that of China. Yet China, where 40 percent of the world's workforce resides with almost 1.3 billion available workers, has a labor pool nearly five times that of the United States, whereas India has a very large labor pool but its economy is one-tenth the size of the United States' and China's economies combined.[16]

These data all point to the level of complexity leaders face in driving growth through talent strategies across global markets, all in various

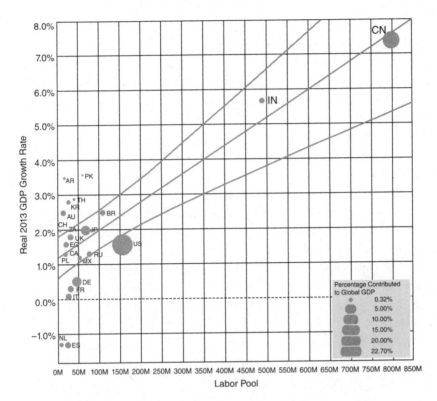

Figure 1.2 Available Labor and GDP Growth for the World's Largest Economies
Source: Ken Oehler, 2015 Trends in Global Employee Engagement: Making Engagement Happen, Aon Hewitt, 2015.

stages of growth and maturity. However, according to Aon Hewitt, there are two very compelling facts about these data. First, there is zero correlation between the size of the economy and growth. However, there is a significantly positive correlation (0.52) between available labor and economic growth. In other words, where there is available talent, there is growth.

Employers Must Always Be Engaging Talent

Another force lending rise to People Analytics is that in the current climate, employers must now always be engaging their employees—current, future, and past. Nowadays, an employer must continually attract, acquire, and advance talent just as brands attract, acquire, and gain loyalty with customers over time. The reflection of this new reality can be seen in the Engagement Cycle framework developed by one of the authors of this book and published previously in *Finding Keepers*.[17]

The Engagement Cycle is a long-term practice combining employer branding, relationship management, and communication. The Engagement Cycle creates strong bonds between employers and potential candidates before, during, and after the brief period we call "recruiting." Its practices ensure that when the economy strengthens—and talent once again becomes scarce—an employer has built a strong bench of talented individuals who are interested, open to discussion, and even grateful for the attention. The Engagement Cycle concept also helps employers take advantage of candidate psychology during a slowdown to attract top talent for the long term.

As companies move from the hiring-as-transaction view to the marketing view, the employer and the candidate follow a clear three-phase cycle in the course of their working relationship. The three phases of the Engagement Cycle determine the level and quality of engagement between employee and employer. Analytics at every phase of the cycle are critical. The three phases are:

1. **Attract**. The Attract phase is a long-term dance between you and the candidate. It includes every activity meant to position the organization as a potential employer in the mind of a candidate. You project a carefully crafted, authentic image as an employer; the candidate becomes aware of your organization's specific attributes. Your employees spread your reputation as an employer; the candidate listens and assesses your company as a potential workplace. It's a similar dance to the way consumers are drawn to brands in the marketplace.

2. **Acquire**. This phase involves all the interactions between you and candidates from the moment they reach out to you. You advertise a position and they apply. You treat their application a certain way, and they react. You find their resume and approach them, and they judge you by your image and your behavior. Your interview process is a series of interactions with different parts of your organization. Both candidate and

employer set expectations throughout this process that will be critical in making a good hire and later in holding onto the best talent. The Acquire stage also includes the honeymoon period right after an employee starts working, in which expectations will be tested against reality. In terms of consumer branding, this is the purchase of a product and its aftermath: Does the product perform as advertised? Is the customer so satisfied that he or she would recommend the product?

3. **Advance**. Keep critical talent moving, not necessarily up, but growing in experience, responsibility, money, or other tangible and intangible ways. Advancing talent in your organization is a key to retaining good people and vital to your company's ability to change as opportunity or necessity require. Retention is the "hold" part of hire and hold; in consumer branding terms, it's the equivalent of customers' becoming loyal to a brand and identifying with the brand's attributes.

Increased Competition for Talent

Part of the increased need for People Analytics is the increased competition for talent. In order to be successful in the war for skilled workers, your company must monitor and stay one step ahead of your primary competition for talent—tracking, analyzing, and integrating everything you know about them into the talent acquisition processes of your own company. For example, do you know the strategies and tactics your competitors use to attract talent, how your employer brand and work environment is perceived compared to theirs, which of your talent segments are more likely to defect to the competition, or whether your talent acquisition costs are higher than your competitors'? Many companies rely, at most, on informal feedback on their competitors and do not have solid analytical systems in place to address these issues.

Given intense business competition, existing companies must continually monitor their employees' behaviors and perceptions, remaining on guard for precursors to employee turnover. Companies are under great pressure to continually and rapidly reinvent themselves and how they offer value to employees and customers. Failing to accurately listen, track, and take action on employee attitudes often results in very high employee turnover costs compared to peer organizations. Take the case of Piper Windows, a UK-based company that started operating in 1980 as a manufacturer of windows for commercial and residential markets with projects ranging in value from £50,000 to £1.5 million. Piper's customers included local government agencies, housing associations, schools, and hospitals, and its annual revenues were about £10.1 million. Although Piper was growing slightly faster than the market, its management believed that the company could gain a bigger market share by being more competitive and by fully using its current capacity. Piper was operating on a single site, split into two units, one for commercial and one for domestic business. The business was buying preformed extruded plastic, and then transforming it into the window/door units. It used two profiles of plastic from two suppliers, with the two units manufacturing one type each.

In 2000, the company was struggling with how to increase plant output while still maintaining quality. Management believed that the ongoing struggle to achieve greater growth was a result of poor productivity and quality control by frontline staff. The UK Department of Trade was enlisted for advice on improving factory output and quality. After some analysis, it was discovered that productivity and quality control were indeed very serious threats, but the cause of those issues was surprising to management. Despite leadership insistence that problems were due to poor use of equipment, bad layout, and quality issues, it was identified that the basic cause was due to the poor levels of employment and high staff turnover.[18]

Apparently, there were a number of deep-seated issues within the operation that were leading to high staff turnover. The company had consistently won a number of regional awards for training and training initiatives, but this was all initial training for new hires, and there was no ongoing training or staff development. It proved hard to convince leadership that turnover was a major threat to the business, as they were convinced that the answer was better performance through better use of their current operations. This may have been true in the long run, but would not be achievable unless leadership acknowledged that high turnover was a threat. Piper failed to do this, and in the long run it hurt the company. The company finally filed for bankruptcy in late 2013.[19]

PROFILE

▼ Interview with Michael Housman, Workforce Scientist in Residence, hiQ Labs, and former Chief Data Analytics Officer, Evolv

JP Isson had the opportunity to speak with Michael Housman to discuss the important topic of People Analytics implementation, and how Big Data is changing human capital and workforce ecosystems.

Isson: Why should a company invest in People Analytics today?

Housman: The timing is right. The most obvious and important decision when it comes to human capital is the hiring decision— essentially, whom to bring into the job. Companies can't afford to make bad decisions. So, I'd say there are two main reasons why a company should make the investment in People Analytics.

1. The United States, in particular, has emerged as a service-based economy. If you look back to 1960, manufacturing used to be the biggest industry; the largest companies were in manufacturing, and that is no longer the case today. In a service-based economy, your human capital is your most valuable strategic asset, and that's why it's important to get the right person in the right job. And this is especially important for customer-facing employees, as you will want to ensure they are reflecting well on your brand.

2. There is more data made available now than ever before. And this is only because of the Internet: Human capital data is being captured through human resources systems, performance management systems, learning and development systems, and applicant tracking

(Continued)

(continued)

> systems. The problem is that all this data is being captured, but not leveraged properly. There is a huge opportunity to use this data intelligently to make better, more informed decisions.

HR, specifically, is an industry that has been guided by gut instinct and intuition. If you think of *Moneyball,* for example, a hiring manager would make the decision based upon a gut feeling. Now, imagine if that same manager injected analytics into that decision-making process; he or she would perform better, hiring employees who would stay longer and perform better. Those hiring managers will, therefore, help their organizations to hit P&L [profit and loss] the right way—by using data to make informed decisions. People Analytics is still pretty nascent; however, to be successful, companies have to get on the wagon and avoid being relegated to the laggards.

Isson: What advice would you give to a company just starting to implement People Analytics? What are the dos and don'ts?

Housman: In terms of "don'ts," I recommend avoiding the "start big and wait" method. Companies that initiate a huge undertaking and then take no further actions as they wait for the complete master data warehouse with all their talent data before they make their next move— this is not a great way to start. I've seen companies with very ambitious project plans. They have tried to get all the master data and fail to start. This is because data is the most difficult element of analytics. It can be easily overwhelming. It has to be cleaned, standardized, aggregated, and integrated. The challenge to resolving this is to fix the data siloes that do not talk to one another. The best way is to start small: Identify a few questions (targets that are low hanging fruit), and pull data together that help answer a specific question.

Additionally, companies should start by leveraging the data that currently exists and is readily available to them. Starting broadly and trying to integrate all that information at once into their systems simply won't work. It could also lead to a data deluge, where the sheer volume of information washes over the company, with no plans for what to do with all those pieces of disparate data. I recommend starting with available data and eventually expanding and adding more data into the mix gradually. The power of Big Data lies in its sheer size; you need a good sample. For smaller organizations, I would recommend they look into partnering with another small business or vendor, and leverage the benefits of a larger sample size. This would help them to separate the signals from the noise, and create more precise and actionable insights.

The best way to get started is by asking one single, interesting question. For example, one company wanted to know what the ROI was for each employee referral. They found that for each referral, they were generating $370 for every $50 invested. You should ask a very specific question aimed at determining a best practice, instead of trying to boil the ocean.

Isson: What are the biggest challenges when implementing People Analytics?

Housman: Data integration and data governance are two of the biggest hurdles. This includes combining data from multiple sources, cleaning, and analyzing it in a consistent way. If there is no playbook, there can be variance in your data governance, which can cause problems and compromise results. Often times, data comes from multiple Excel spreadsheets and from different systems that do not talk to each other, which increases variability. And, in some cases, you may know the data exists, but you can't get access to it.

The second challenge is to change human behavior. Even if we say to hiring managers, "Follow these recommendations, based upon this data," and we can see how those who are using the tool perform much better, we will still see some managers presumably leveraging their own instincts and gut feelings they have developed after 24 years of being a recruiter. You might have the best analytics tool, but if nobody uses it you won't succeed. For some companies, it's difficult to change; people keep on listening to their gut feeling.

HR Is under Pressure

Anyone who works in HR knows there's pressure. The clock is ticking. Business leaders, HR leaders, and boards are recognizing the changing and growing critical business needs related to HR and talent—leadership, organizational change, and talent development are at the top of the list. The time for HR business as usual is over. The CFO is asking to understand the ROI, the CEO is asking for a labor force to carry out a vision, and employees are demanding more benefits—HR is hit from all sides.

At the same time, they're shifting their role from the tactical "where's my paycheck?" function toward being a strategic business partner. HR now has access to huge amounts of computer processing power that makes it possible to take vast quantities of information—so-called Big Data—about the organization and its employees, and analyze it using specialized workforce and predictive analytics tools. These tools interrogate the data and connect different bits in different ways that might never have been thought of before. So they reveal new things, offering insights into what has happened in the past, what is happening at present, and even what is likely to happen in the future.

However, HR is struggling under the pressure. The Sierra-Cedar HR Systems Survey, now in its 17th year, gathers information from organizations across the globe that track the adoption and deployment of HR analytics solutions, gathering data on process maturity as well as the type and amount of data that HR organizations are capturing. According to Sierra's most recent study, only 9 percent of companies use predictive analytics or Big Data to analyze trends related to human capital.[20]

Skills Gap in the Labor Market

Another trend giving rise to People Analytics is the global skills gap in the labor force. And it's going to get worse before it gets better. There are currently millions of unemployed and underemployed workers in the United States as well as millions of job openings. However, many of those workers will remain unemployed and those positions will go unfilled.

In the United States, labor force participation remains histori-cally low, and a jobless economic recovery seems the new normal. Increasingly, jobs are being automated, yet a shortage of skilled work-ers is looming worldwide, even in China, despite its huge labor force. Technology also makes it possible for employers to redesign and parti-tion work, and to reassign routine tasks to lower-skilled employees. In health care, for example, chronic disease management can be assigned to nurse practitioners rather than to physicians.

These and other changes are part of the larger disruptive forces that are reshaping the global economy. In the labor market, some of these shifts are already evident—and the disruption they bring about will only get larger. As a result, People Analytics becomes a critical fac-tor in sourcing, attracting, acquiring, and retaining the skills needed in your workforce.

Talent Is One of the Last Competitive Differentiators

Another phenomenon giving rise to the importance of talent analytics is the increasing value of talent to the bottom line, and the diminishing value of other assets to make a difference.

In the development of new economies, stand-by competitive dif-ferentiators have often faded. For example, capital forms much more freely than in the past, new products are quickly copied, location mat-ters less as workplaces become decentralized, and distribution channel relationships fail to prevent competitors from entering through online channels. These structural changes don't mean these things are no longer important, just that their relative importance is declining.

Talent creates the vast majority of value in the developed world's com-panies, and those who calculate the intangible assets of organizations (e.g., know-how, patents, brand names, ideas, and processes) put the products of brainpower from employees at 80 percent of a company's value.[21]

Globalization plays a part as businesses in more developed econo-mies cede manufacturing and low-end services to emerging econo-mies. Their survival depends on the products of high-end talent, whereas information-rich products and services, business innovation, sophisticated new technologies, better management, and more creative solutions drive the established economies.

This permanent change has increased the value of talent because talent is the last remaining factor that consistently delivers profits. Companies espouse innovation, but it's talent that innovates. A large retailer revolutionizes supply-chain management and then discovers that midlevel store managers are the linchpins that determine whether all the efficiently delivered merchandise gets purchased by the consumer.

This, coupled with the shortage of critical skills in the labor market, means that more than ever, People Analytics is critical in order to give you the advantage over your competition in the talent war.

HR Evolves into Talent Management

Human capital or talent management (TM) is evolving in much the same way as the finance function grew into a decision science, separate from accounting, or the evolution of marketing as a decision science separate from sales. Executives who are focused on talent management must now work side by side with the CEO and other business leaders to identify ways that talent can be used to create new products and services and to inspire new strategies. People Analytics becomes a key enabler of this evolution, helping to understand worker sentiment, predict factors that lead to an engaged and productive workforce, as well as help uncover hidden opportunities for talent-related programs to contribute to the company's bottom line. Figure 1.3 lists some of the ways that HR is evolving from a process-based department into a strategic partner.

Putting It into Practice

To illustrate some of the challenges to People Analytics success, let's take the case of a company we spoke with as part of the background research for this book. Out of respect for the company we won't name it; however, let's just say that it is a fairly well-known media company. This media company expressed some analytical angst to us during our interview. The interviewees said they realized a few years ago that

Traditional Paradigm		Emerging Paradigm
• HR provides support to the business units when asked.	⇒	• TM proactively identifies business oportunities and flags potential human capital risks.
• HR professionals are valued by their responsiveness to inquires.	⇒	• TM professionals are valued for their ability to solve business problems.
• HR deals with the "soft" side of the business.	⇒	• TM uses the same data-driven, fact-based approach as the rest of the organization.
• People problems are the responsibility of the HR department.	⇒	• Managers and TM jointy apply their experience to address employee issues.
• The HR department owns employee development.	⇒	• Employee development is a shared responsibility between managers, employees, and the TM organization.

Figure 1.3 Traditional Paradigm versus Emerging Paradigm

their unstructured data from employee engagement surveys was an untapped resource to help their people strategy as well as their business strategy. So they went searching for someone with the requisite degrees and experience who could lead the work with their data to help them unleash its potential. They searched for seven months (these data analysis people are in demand) and finally found someone with a statistics degree, computer science experience, great references, and a solid track record of helping well-known brands analyze their data. They hired him and put the existing four HR analysts already at the company under his management. They were very optimistic with their new key hire and set him immediately to work on analyzing data from long-tenured employees versus those new to the organization in order to understand how to better target new prospective talent so as to yield long-term employee engagement and a solid return on their recruiting dollar.

They said things started off well at first—the team was optimistic and energized with the new team member. However, problems gradually started to develop. First, the People Analytics team went away for weeks at a time with little data analysis completed, and then when something was delivered it was usually lots of raw data and a graph or two that was difficult for the business's people to understand. Second, the new team occasionally provided statistics that were in conflict with those from other teams in the company or what had been common company wisdom in the past, setting off ill will between departments and spates of dueling data that often took weeks to untangle. Next, it seemed as though the analysts would come out with numbers that were different from the analysis they had provided just a few months earlier, which frustrated the business to no end.

The company attributed these challenges to the difficulty of doing People Analytics and tended to blame the analytics team for these problems. However, as a result of our interview, they gained an expanded view that it was very likely that the overall organizational dynamics within the company may have been the cause of their People Analytics difficulties.

First, we asked what company leadership sponsored the hiring and formation of this People Analytics team. It was explained to us that a long-tenured vice president of human resources commissioned this initiative, and everyone had great faith that she could make the best use of these analytical resources. When we followed up regarding whether the most senior corporate or functional leaders were also in favor of forming this team, we were told that they were not completely sure as nobody beyond the senior vice president to whom the human resources vice president reported was consulted. This illustrates the first internal challenge that People Analytics must overcome: weak executive sponsorship. Unless a senior driving leadership force within the organization is aware of, supports, and believes in the mission of the People Analytics discipline over the long term, then it will likely have difficulties thriving and eventually fail due to shifting corporate priorities, company politics, and lack of corporate accountability.

Second, we asked what process the company had undergone to make sure its corporate business objectives were in line with the objectives of this new analytics team. We uncovered that they didn't really communicate corporate objectives to the new analytics lead or his team, as they thought the team just needed to analyze data, not worry about corporate priorities. This illustrates the second internal challenge that a People Analytics function must overcome: failure to communicate and align People Analytics priorities with corporate priorities.

Third, we noted that surely technology systems and resources were required to help the People Analytics team do their work, so we asked how the analytics team worked with the technology team that supported these analytics initiatives. For example, did the technology resources report into the new analytics team? Was there a direct line of accountability in some other way? We were told that they did not set up any formal arrangement, but relied on the new People Analytics manager to build a bridge and work across the departments. This illustrates the third internal challenge that the practice of People Analytics must overcome: weak alignment and accountability from the technology support function.

Next, we asked whether there was any data quality or governance function within the company to ensure that definitions were standardized and data were accurate. We were told no, that it was the analytics team's responsibility to make sure that whatever data and analysis were distributed were accurate and reliable. This leads us to the fourth internal challenge: lack of formal data governance. It takes dedicated and diligent effort from business and technology to ensure that data being published from various systems are accurate and reliable, and this cannot be just a matter of an afterthought by a few analysts because they happen to be last in the chain of data distribution.

Then we asked how the new People Analytics team's activities were rationalized against other People Analytics–related activities across the enterprise from departments such as finance, strategy, or international business units. We were told that they did not really communicate with one another formally and didn't initially think it was necessary because those teams were working on different analytical tasks. This illustrates the fifth internal challenge: weak alignment of existing People Analytics resources within an organization. We explained that in order to reduce the likelihood of duplication of efforts and dueling data as well as to ensure that the company is leveraging the collective knowledge of the analytical resources most effectively, there must be some type of formal alignment across People Analytics teams throughout the company; whether that is a reporting relationship to a single manager or just a formal communication and management cadence depends on the corporate culture and is open for debate, as we have seen each work well under different circumstances.

There will be many internal challenges on the way. These are just some of the internal challenges a People Analytics function must rise to meet in order to become business-relevant, fast, insightful, and predictive; to have a bias toward action; and to become part of the corporate culture.

Given that economic pressures remain in many parts of the global economy, that the war for talent is more intense than ever, that employee loyalty is all but gone, and that new media and digital technologies are on the rise, it's no surprise that the use of People Analytics is gaining new prominence. These are the challenges for the People Analytics discipline—the challenge to help organizations thrive and prosper. It's clear that effective People Analytics is seen as a way to address these key talent challenges and that People Analytics holds great promise to help organizations understand what their employees want from them, how to acquire new ones, and what will lead to an engaged employee. However, most organizations we speak with are struggling to make sense of what this data can tell them or how they can use it. Therefore, we have designed this book to help businesses think about, organize, and make the most of the people-related analytical assets available to them.

We don't claim this book will solve all of these issues for everyone. However, we know that the best practices, lessons learned, and assessment tools within will go a long way toward helping you to make sure your People Analytics is world-class. Throughout this book, we provide examples of companies that are doing it well, as well as some that are not.

This book is organized in such a way to help you build upon your knowledge as you read from chapter to chapter. We have also attempted to define and organize the chapters so they can stand on their own. For example, if you are primarily interested in learning about using People Analytics effectively for employee onboarding, you can jump to Chapter 7, Onboarding and Culture Fit. However, if you want to learn about how to successfully use People Analytics to leverage talent strategically to meet your business objectives, then we suggest you read the chapters in order and ask yourself the hard questions about whether your company is doing everything it can to leverage People Analytics.

Organizations are in an ongoing war—a war for talent. Everyone working in human capital knows it, business leaders know it, line managers know it, and the most talented employees know it. With some effort (increasingly less and less effort), talented employees can leave you forever. The time and money you spent training them, giving them experience and development opportunities, building key relationships within your organization—they're all gone as soon as your talent walks out the door. So, leverage People Analytics to make sure your talent strategy adds to your organization's bottom line, not just takes from it.

KEY TAKEAWAYS

- The field of People Analytics is evolving and is becoming more common. Companies are struggling with vast amounts of data in different systems, but are starting to see valuable ways People Analytics can be used.

- There are several market dynamics driving the need for People Analytics, including an increased competition for talent, decreased employee loyalty, economic woes, and proliferation of new media.

- The need for HR to move from a tactical partner into a strategic partner can be enabled through People Analytics.

- People Analytics requires many things to succeed, including strong executive leadership support for analytics, effective technology infrastructure and tools, alignment with corporate priorities, and effective communication across departments.

NOTES

1. Josh Bersin, *HR Factbook Study U.S. 2015*, Deloitte Consulting, 2015.

2. *2014 Recruitment Advertising Outlook—The Long, Gray Line*. Borrell Associates, March 2014.

3. *Global Human Capital Trends 2015: Leading in the New World of Work* (Westlake, TX: Deloitte University Press, 2015).

4. "HR Needs Extreme Makeover: Business Leaders," *Inside HR*, March 5, 2015.

5. Joseph Walker, "Meet the New Boss: Big Data," *Wall Street Journal*, September 20, 2012.

6. Janet Yellen, Transcript of Chair Yellen's Federal Open Market Committee Press Conference Opening Statement, June 17, 2015.

7. *DMA 2014 Statistical Fact Book* (New York: Direct Marketing Association, 2014).

8. Radicati Group, April 2010.

9. "Our Rising Ad Dosage," *Media Matters*, February 15, 2007.

10. International Telecommunication Union, November 2011.

11. *DMA 2014 Statistical Fact Book*.

12. *Survey on Employee Loyalty*, American Management Association, 2015.

13. *Falling Job Tenure: It's Not Just about Millennials*, Federal Reserve Bank of Atlanta. June 8, 2015.

14. Doug Horn, "The Reasons Why Workplace Loyalty Is Declining," Recruitifi Blog Post, January 21, 2015, http://blog.recruitifi.com/the-reasons-why-workplace-loyalty-is-declining.

15. Jeff Guo, "Millennials Aren't Changing Jobs as Much," *Washington Post*, September 4, 2014.

16. Ken Oehler, *2015 Trends in Global Employee Engagement: Making Engagement Happen*, Aon Hewitt, 2015.

17. S. Pogorzelski, J. Harriott, and D. Hardy, *Finding Keepers: The Monster Guide to Hiring and Holding the World's Best Employees* (New York: McGraw-Hill, 2008).

18. Gerald L. Barlow, *Putting a Price on Staff Turnover: A Case Study* (Canterbury, UK: Canterbury Business School, 2001).

19. "Jobs Lost as Piper Windows Goes into Administration," *Isle of Thanet Gazette*, August 13, 2013.

20. Sierra-Cedar 2014–2015 HR Systems Survey: *HR Technologies, Deployment Approaches, Integration, Metrics, and Value: 17th Annual Edition*, Sierra-Cedar, 2014.

21. Lev Baruch, "Value of Intangibles Lecture," Stern School of Business, New York University, 2006.

CHAPTER **2**

How to Migrate from Business Analytics to People Analytics

The whole of science is nothing more than a refinement of everyday thinking.

—Albert Einstein

This quote from Einstein highlights the impact of our everyday thoughts and reasoning, and applies perfectly when it comes to translating traditional business analytics into People Analytics. Like many other disciplines, People Analytics, also called Talent Analytics, simply builds on the principles of traditional analytics— something that we have all grappled with at some level, whether it was in negotiating the price when buying a house or evaluating whether to relocate for a job offer. In fact, analytics forms the basis of our logical reasoning process: It helps us weigh our options and take factors such as cost, commute, happiness, and convenience into account.

To ensure that you have everything you need to smoothly migrate from business analytics to People Analytics, in this chapter we will cover:

- The history of analytics adoption.
- The similarities between marketing and human capital management.
- What predictive analytics and big data mean to the human resources (HR) and staffing industries.
- How business analytics corresponds to People Analytics (and how to bridge the two).
- Best practices for building a People Analytics center of excellence.
- Frontline application: Interview with Mark Berry of CGB Enterprises.

A SHORT HISTORY OF ANALYTICS ADOPTION

In order to best navigate today's globally connected, competitive marketplace, which is propelled by an explosion of digital information, companies have been embracing analytics at different paces to help sift through and derive strategic insights.

From an industry perspective, analytics adoption has followed the classic adoption curve: There have been some early adopters who pioneered the adoption of analytics into their business processes; there are those, called the late adopters, who followed the pioneers; and then we have the laggards, a group that trails far behind both. What we've found is that while some businesses are struggling to move beyond basic reporting, the majority of HR managers and human capital leaders do not even know where to start with their analytics journey.

Early Adopters: Insurance and Finance

In *Win with Advanced Business Analytics*,[1] we described how the insurance and financial services industries have been pioneers in collecting, managing, and leveraging predictive analytics to create actionable insights from their data. Given the mandatory reporting environment of these fields, not to mention the direct correlation between accurate data and their revenue, these industries first began using analytics in the 1800s to price life insurance and underwrite marine insurance. They have since continued innovating, undergoing many waves of improvement, including the use of neural networks to optimize premiums; introduction of credit scores to evaluate a customer's financial position; and application of various behavioral, third-party, and social media data sets to supplement their forecasts and future predictions.

Over the years, the success stories have been numerous, and financial institutions that are not using predictive analytics today in product pricing and underwriting would be seen as obsolete and doomed to failure.

Data Analytics Adoption in Human Resources

Even if People Analytics and predictive modeling in HR are fairly nascent, interest in HR metrics started before the current trend of HR and human capital analytics. As a result, 10 major events occurred:

In **1911**, Frederick Taylor, a mechanical engineer who sought to measure the productivity of workers and improve industrial efficiency, pioneered the scientific management of time-and-motion studies. He developed a method for capturing and measuring the effectiveness of an organization's employees' work, and summed up these efficiency techniques and best practices in his book *The Principles of Scientific Management.*[2] Taylor believed in transferring control from worker to management and focused on the distinction between mental labor (planning work) and manual labor (executing work).

To demonstrate these principles in action, Taylor used "The Parable of the Pig Iron," which applied his time-and-motion studies to illustrate the role management plays in determining the correct workload for each employee that keeps him or her the most efficient and happy.[3] Despite a lot of criticism of his work and principles, Taylor spurred a whole movement of analyzing the data behind physical work, which was first implemented in industrial engineering.

Two years later, in **1913**, Hugo Munsterberg, a psychologist and an admirer of Taylor, extended these ideas into applied psychology, including industrial and organizational, legal, medical, educational, and business settings. In his book *Psychology and Industrial Efficiency,*[4] he addressed many topics of industrial psychology and claimed that it is not only the physical strength of a worker but also his or her psychology that defines business productivity. He introduced the industry to the notion of worker selection based on a scientific approach of worker testing and job analysis. This later became known as an assessment center.

Munsterberg also outlined a new science in his book—a blend of modern laboratory psychology and economics. He believed that the question of selecting the best possible person for a particular vocation comes down to making a process very scientific (for instance creating tests that limit subjectivity), and that it comes down to fitting the person with the correct skill set with the correct position to maximize productivity.

During World War I (**1914–1918**), the U.S. Army started large-scale testing called the Army Alpha and Beta Tests of World War I,[5] which were the first mental tests designed for the masses. In developing these tests, psychologists proved that one could be quite intelligent even though illiterate or not proficient in the English language. This led to the creation of two subsequent tests: the Army Alpha for literate groups and the Army Beta for the illiterate, low literate, or non-English-speaking individuals.[6] Both tests were based on the theoretical assumption that intelligence was an inherited trait, and the assumption was made that native intelligence was being assessed. These tests also demonstrated how quantitative analytics could be leveraged for resource selection.

In **1920**, E. L. Thorndike published his psychometric view of social intelligence, dividing intelligence into three facets: abstract intelligence, or one's ability to understand and manage ideas; mechanical intelligence, or one's ability to manipulate concrete objects; and social intelligence. In his classic formulation, Thorndike stated, "By social intelligence is meant the ability to understand and manage men and women, boys and girls—to act wisely in human relations." Similarly, Moss and Hunt (1927) defined social intelligence as the "ability to get along with others."[7]

In **1921** and **1923** in English, Carl Gustave Jung, a renowned Swiss psychiatrist and one of the founding fathers of modern-day psychology, published his book *Psychological Types*,[8] in which he proposed that people are innately different, both in terms of the way they see the world and take in information, and in terms of how they make decisions. In this tract, he expanded the concept of social intelligence into a science of work, and taught that it is not only our individual skills that create productivity, but also our personalities and how we get along with each other.

Jung's work in social psychology spurred a global evolution in personality testing. In **1943**, driven by a desire to help people understand themselves and each other better in a postwar climate, Isabel Myers set about devising a questionnaire that would identify which psychological type a person was. To do this, she enlisted the help of more experienced psychometricians, and her work, which was first implemented in industrial engineering, was later endorsed by professors from the Universities of York, California, Michigan, and Florida. In 1943, she and Katharine Briggs published the first Myers–Briggs Type Indicator questionnaire, which is still in use today as an assessment tool.

While the roots of analytics are firmly planted in the late nineteenth and early twentieth centuries, most of the HR metrics in use today were developed following World War II. With the essential building blocks in place, much progress was made quickly in HR analytics.

In **1978**, Dr. Jac Fitz-enz published the first HR metrics. And in **1984**, he implemented the first benchmark metrics in HR and published his findings in the reference book *How to Measure Human Resources Management*.[9] In it, he created 30 HR metrics that were developed through a joint effort between the Saratoga Institute and the American Society for Personnel Administration that later became the current Society for Human Resource Management (SHRM) in 1989. Some of the original 30 HR metrics identified where predictive analytics can be applied to derive actionable insights are: voluntary separation, involuntary separation, voluntary separation by length of service, time to fill jobs, time to start jobs, revenue per employee, expense per employee, hire as a percentage of total employees, cost of hire, absence rate, human capital return on investment, turnover rate and cost, and vacancy rate. Employee attrition, also called voluntary separation, happens when an employee decides to leave your organization.

One way to apply predictive analytics is to address questions such as: Who are employees at risk of leaving your organization? When will they leave? Why will they leave? To answer those questions People Analytics harnesses all the data available from internal source HRIS (human resource information systems) data to external talent and market data such as publicly available talent data, labor market data, and competition data to anticipate "talent at risk to attrite" and proactive actions to put in place to save them. There is also a body of People Analytics opportunities arising from a combination of 2, 3, or 4 of the 30 HR metrics to better understand some specific workforce challenges you may face.

In **1995**, Rutgers University professor Dr. Mark A. Huselid's work on high-performance systems demonstrated that the systematic management of HR was associated with a significant difference in organization effectiveness. This work provides evidence that the SHRM did, indeed, have a strategic potential. Shortly thereafter, in **1996**, Drs. Robert Kaplan (Harvard Business School) and David Norton introduced the balanced scorecard. And, in **2001**, in their book The *HR Scorecard*, Brian E. Becker, Mark A. Huselid, and Dave Ulrich highlighted how HR scorecards, which demonstrate the alignment of HR activities with corporate strategy and activity, improve organizational outcomes.

In **2005**, the first talent management system (TMS) was created. TMSs are integrated platforms that automate and improve the key major processes of talent management, including recruitment, performance management, learning and development, and compensation management. They are tools that also store a wide variety of employee data, from recruitment data, learning and leadership data, performance and compensation management data, and resume profile data to job postings performance and work data. Today, TMS platforms can also store and manage social media data, as well as other digital footprint and talent behavior data.

It was only around **2010**[10] that predictive analytics began to appear in the HR departments of most leading companies. And, according to Josh Bersin,[11] only 4 percent of Fortune 1000 companies are using predictive analytics and, in doing so, this group's stocks outperformed their peers on the Standard and Poor's 500 by 30 percent.

First adopted and implemented by financial and insurance companies in the 1800s, and then within the HR industry throughout the twentieth century, data analytics has been gradually and meaningfully changing business practices and improving organizations' decision-making abilities.

MARKETING AND HUMAN RESOURCES SIMILARITIES

In many organizations, HR, the so-called intuitive and experience-based group, still shares the same challenges as the marketing department. Oftentimes, the HR department feels misunderstood and is being constantly requested to be more data-driven and become a strategic business function at the C-suite table.

Facing Today's Challenges

Over the past 10 years, we have had the opportunity to speak at conferences across the world and to meet with industry leaders in staffing, talent management, and HR from organizations of all sizes on a regular basis. The most common challenge we consistently hear in People Analytics is that industry leaders are inundated with data from a variety of sources and are hampered by disconnected tools and systems. They are seeking the best analytical practices in order to create innovative talent life cycle management processes and optimize their HR teams.

While some are aware that HR will undergo a seismic change with Big Data analytics, those of us who work in the field believe the odds are high that the analytics revolution, which invaded the marketing industry in the late 1990s (with the beginning of the World Wide Web), is coming in HR. So how do we ready our teams for the future?

Having worked in business analytics for many years, enriched with interviews and research with those leaders, and sharing with them business analytics success stories in other functions of the organization, we have found that one of the best ways to tackle the migration from business analytics to People Analytics is by using the lessons we learned when the marketing industry adopted analytics. Why? This is because HR and marketing have significant common denominators, and they both used to be non-data-driven functions and cost centers for most organizations.

By reviewing how marketing enhanced its role and practice over time, we can then derive best practices for the HR field.

From Business Analytics to People Analytics Following the Marketing Analytic Path

Before 1990 (the beginning of analytics use in marketing), marketing was basically a discipline of creativity, art, "gut feel" judgment calls, and experience. In search of becoming a strategic business partner and more accountable in a growing competitive marketplace, the industry underwent a massive change by integrating analytics into its business practices. Searching to strategically attract, segment, acquire, grow, retain, and reward customers, marketing opened up to analytics in order to fully understand its customer base, target demographics, the 360 degrees of its different customers, and the market, and to optimize the entire customer life cycle management and customer relationship management. Thus, marketing analytics was born.

Marketing analytics ushered in a new era. The old days of "spray and pray" and shooting blindly to acquire and retain customers quickly became obsolete. Top-performing companies gradually began to sunset those old gut-driven practices and started using analytics. For the majority of successful companies, marketing coexists with marketing analytics, and constantly leverages the power of data intelligence, which enables them to become a balance between a disciplined art (experience, judgment, and instinct) and science (the intelligence of data).

Talent management and HR teams can learn a lot from their marketing colleagues, adding or building a People Analytics program in order to proactively embrace the analytics revolution. Similar to traditional marketers, HR professionals are generally not known as "data geeks." The field of HR has traditionally leveraged intuition, judgment calls, instincts, and experience. Although some managers may still rely on isolated metrics from HR dashboards to make major decisions, the field is not historically known for using predictive analytics as a systematic part of the decision-making equation.

Dr. Jac Fitz-enz[12] rightly points out that "HR managers have done a poor job teaching the C-level executive how to achieve a high rate of return on employee investment. On top of that, there is a serious perception issue that the HR function has to fix as well."

In today's globally connected and competitive talent marketplace, HR is facing challenges from multiple fronts, and some HR leaders we have spoken with often say their departments are perceived as:

- Cost centers
- Order takers

- ■ Useless
- ■ Disconnected with the business reality
- ■ Tactical, not strategic
- ■ Useful primarily for regulatory and legal reporting

Let's take a closer look at some of these challenges, so that we can begin to address and rectify them.

- ■ **Perception challenge:** In some organizations, HR is perceived as a cost center, useless, an order taker, and disconnected with the business reality. But why? As Dr. Fitz-enz points out, "We should ask ourselves this major question: Why don't CEOs recognize an investment in people as they do in other initiatives functions?" The answer is twofold:

  1. Often C-level executives can make an investment in a non-human arena, such as sales production and technologies, and feel confident that a reasonable return on investment will ensue. This is not the case with people. Talent management and hiring have high levels of variability, which can make such investments challenging to evaluate without the proper data and analysis.

  2. HR managers have done a poor job of teaching C-level executives how to achieve a high rate of return on employee investment. Analytics can be used to demonstrate the value of these investments and illustrate the important implications for the organization's bottom line—for instance, how a 2 percent turnover would impact sales and profitability.

  There was even an article in *Forbes* claiming that companies should fire their HR departments.[13] In it, a group of economics researchers conducted a study on 2,500 resumes either with or without photos of the applicant and found that being good-looking (in the case of women) did not help an applicant find a job. According to the article, "attractive" women faced an uphill struggle to get a chance at a job, because 93 percent of the HR staff deciding whether to call someone for an interview were female.

- **Strategic challenge:** HR has to become a more strategic business partner, proactively providing recommendations that are directly tied to addressing core business challenges and objectives.

- **Performance challenge:** The challenge is to leverage data analytics in order to master talent life cycle management, bridge the global skills gap, and better attract and retain top talents, as well as to capture the attention of the millennial market in order to ensure succession planning as the baby boomers move toward retirement.

Leaders want to leverage the power of advanced analytics and data intelligence to make more informed decisions. They are seeking to harness the power of Big Data analytics to improve performance in their business practices, and address core business challenges and core talent management questions such as:

- How to attract the best people?
- How to select the best people?
- How to acquire the best people?
- How to engage and develop the right people?
- How to reward the best people?
- How to retain the right people?

These questions are similar to the ones that the marketing industry was able to address by implementing business analytics and predictive modeling into their practices.

At this point, you are probably wondering how HR can piggyback on marketing to undergo its own analytics revolution. To manage human capital for tomorrow, you need HR metrics that are inherently predictive and that will have a high business impact. To move from business analytics to People Analytics, we can simply replace the word *customer* from any marketing analytics strategy with the word *talent* or *employee*. This will provide us with a basic migration of marketing analytics to People Analytics (talent analytics or workforce analytics), as seen in Table 2.1. This is possible because the common denominator

Table 2.1 From Marketing Analytics to People Analytics

Marketing	Human Capital and HR (People Analytics)
Customer life cycle management	**Talent** life cycle management
Customer relationship management	**Talent** relationship management
Customer 360-degree analysis and understanding	**Talent** 360-degree analysis and understanding

between marketing and human capital management is **human behavior**.

Over the past decades, HR has heavily invested in tools and technologies; however, it is time to move beyond simple dashboards, scorecards, and isolated talent metrics and embrace advanced business analytics to derive true value for organizations.

ADVANCED BUSINESS ANALYTICS AND ADVANCED PEOPLE ANALYTICS

The following sections describe how People Analytics can use advanced business analytics paths and mainstream impact to address human capital management challenges.

Advanced Business Analytics Becomes Mainstream

Advanced business analytics starts with a business goal or question, integrates disparate data sources, creates predictions for the future, and leads to strategic actions with measurable results. It is powered by predictive modeling, which has helped marketing teams attract, acquire, engage, grow, retain, and reward their most valuable customers—goals that are very similar to those of HR departments looking to maximize their talent management cycles and that will require HR to think like a marketer.

Depending on their level of analytical maturity and their most pressing business objectives, companies have embraced analytics to create business value at different stages; predictive analytics is becoming a pervasive and competitive differentiator across different industries and business functions:

- **Amazon** uses analytics to recommend what book to buy, and 30 percent of its sales are generated from these recommendations.
- **Netflix** leverages analytics to recommend what movie you are most likely to watch and like. And more than 70 percent of Netflix movie choices arise from its online recommendations.
- Companies are using **sentiment analysis** of Facebook and Twitter posts to determine and predict sales volume and brand equity.
- **Target** predicts when a pregnant woman is due based on products she purchases by simply combining her loyalty card data with social media information, hence detecting and leveraging on changing buying patterns. This allows the company to target pregnant women with promotions for baby-related products. The company also increased revenue 15 to 20 percent by targeting direct mail with product choice models.
- **Google** was able to predict the 2009 flu epidemic two weeks ahead of the Centers for Disease Control, simply by leveraging online search trends (e.g., related to symptoms).
- **Google**'s self-driving car is analyzing a gigantic amount of data from sensors and cameras in real time to stay safe on the road.
- The **GPS** information on our phones is analyzing how fast the device is moving, which is used to provide live traffic updates.
- During the 2012 presidential election, the **Obama campaign team** used analytics to micro-target voters in swing states.
- Also during the 2012 presidential elections, famed statistician Nate Silver used analytics to correctly predict Obama's victory.
- Politicians are using social media analytics to determine where they have to campaign the hardest to win the next election.
- **Pediatric hospitals** are applying data analytics to live streams of a baby's heartbeats to identify patterns, and, based on the analysis, the system can now detect infections 24 hours before the baby would normally begin show any symptoms, which allows early intervention and treatment.

- The **FBI** is combining data from social media, CCTV cameras, phone calls, and texts to track down criminals and predict the next terrorist attack.

- Video analytics and sensor data of **baseball** and **football games** is used to improve performance of players and teams. You can now buy a baseball with more than 200 sensors in it that will give you detailed feedback on how to improve your game.

- Artists such as **Lady Gaga** are using data about our listening preferences and sequences to determine the most popular playlists for her live performances.

It's clear that analytics is being used in nearly every aspect of our lives and across myriad industries. So, how do we apply it in HR to help solve current challenges?

What Is People Analytics?

People Analytics starts with a talent management business question or goal, and then integrates disparate data sources together to create predictions for the future, which can then be used to outline businesses' actions with measurable results. Let's take a closer look at the major components of People Analytics.

Talent Management Business Questions

A good talent management business question or goal will be directly related to workforce planning, talent sourcing, talent acquisition, talent onboarding, talent engagement, talent turnover, talent development, retention, safety, or employee well-being. For instance:

- What skill sets does your organization need to achieve its business objectives?

- What talent should your organization develop, reward, and promote?

- Where should your organization search for the best talent?

- What type of employee to attract?

- Whom to hire?
- Whom to engage?
- Whom to retain?

Integrate Disparate Data Sources

Now that you have a talent management business question in mind, how do you go about integrating disparate data sources? Typically, data sources can be broken down into three categories: talent data, company data, and labor market data.

1. **Talent data** includes things such as overhead, HR department costs, organizational structures, leadership, talent span of control, recruiting costs, quality of hire, employee performance and engagement, compensation and benefits, employee productivity, learning and career development, succession planning, leadership, employee turnover, diversity, historical performance assessment, candidate selection test results, social network footprint (depending on role), workforce well-being, and overall wellness. Also, publicly available data from social media, candidate's social media profile engagement contribution, and content from niche sites provide a complementary set of talent data.

2. **Company data** includes things such as sales performance, associated revenues, customer bases (new, existing, and win-back customers), average order size, wallet share growth, product diversity, loyalty, churn, Net Promoter Score, sales, traffic and conversion, and stock price (for public companies).

3. **Labor market data** includes data from the Bureau of Labor Statistics such as payroll, employment and unemployment rates, gross domestic product, turnover rates, job openings, and layoffs, and wages and salaries. All this data can be broken down by industry, company size, occupation, state, and city.

By identifying these different data streams and linking them to your talent management business question, you will start to see which data points are key to creating an actionable plan.

Create Actionable and Measurable Business Predictions

Creating business predictions that lead to strategic actions and measurable goals for the future requires you to use predictive models to anticipate what will happen with your employee base and to enable you to put proactive plans in place, addressing:

- Whom to attract?
- Whom to hire?
- Whom to develop and promote?
- And whom to retain?

While these questions are critical for any top-performing organization, you need to translate them into measurable actions that can be presented as a business case to your executive team. This means you need to connect this talent data with business data. For instance, consider:

- What impact will proactive retention of top performers have on customer value?
- Who are the best employees to acquire or promote in order to drive customer satisfaction and loyalty?
- How does employee well-being impact productivity, customer lifetime value, and customer up-sell and retention?

The entire process of creating actionable insights with People Analytics is summarized in Figure 2.1, People Analytics Virtuous Process,

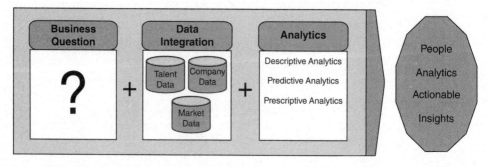

Figure 2.1 People Analytics Virtuous Process

where you start with your talent management business question, and then integrate data and use analytics to gain actionable insights.

What Predictive Analytics Means to the Staffing Industry

Traditionally, predictive analytics has helped companies to address the basic business questions of who, when, and why. However, when applied to the staffing industry, predictive analytics can help to anticipate and optimize:

- **Talent acquisition:** Helps to identify who is the top talent and when they should be contacted. Why is this requisition or job opportunity attractive to this top talent?
- **Talent pipeline planning:** Predictive analytics can optimize a talent pipeline by leveraging macroeconomic and talent data to ascertain key factors that can lead to better resource allocation— for instance, identifying the best locations to invest in recruitment campaigns for certain skill sets.
- **Job-response optimization:** During the recruitment process, predictive analytics helps organizations optimize their job posting responses. Data analysis can provide companies with custom recommendations and tailored best practices to help them achieve better responses to their job postings based on factors such as duration, location, occupation, and industry.
- **Customer acquisition:** A staffing firm's talent database is its proprietary competitive advantage and sales tool. Therefore, with the power of predictive analytics to harness a staffing firm's Big Data and provide valuable insights into the talent on hand, the firm is empowered to drive future sales conversations directly aligned to the talent it has.

What Big Data Intelligence Means to the Staffing Industry

To process, manage, and optimize the exponential growth of resumes and other talent data coming from multiple sources, staffing firms have to leverage Big Data intelligence technology to fully understand

and maximize their recruitment metrics. The benefits of performing this type of deep-dive analysis include:

- **Better awareness of cost per placement:** This can improve recruiter productivity by leveraging the technology horsepower.
- **Analysis of the quality of the candidate:** This can help recruiters to efficiently find a broader range of candidates than they would find using traditional search methods.
- **Improve the time to fill, as well as the fill ratio:** This can reduce search time and provide an accurate candidate ranking that leads to matching the right talent to the right job offering.

Predictive recruitment analytics and Big Data intelligence tools are changing the way organizations view, analyze, and harness their talent data. Leveraged efficiently, predictive analytics allows staffing teams to create economic value from their talent data, helping them become more competitive and, ultimately, more successful.

THE PROMISE OF ANALYTICS AND PEOPLE ANALYTICS BRIDGES

So, by now, you're getting comfortable with the concept of advanced analytics and its associated insights, which include helping with:

- **Information:** Understanding what happened in the past.
- **Knowledge:** Understanding what's happening now and why.
- **Intelligence:** Anticipating what will happen in the future.
- **Actionable insights:** Prescribing what we should do based on our predictions and forecasts.

Armed with this knowledge, we can begin to build connections between our data analytics and our insights through what we call the "actionable insights bridge." One of this book's authors, JP Isson, built and uses this model to illustrate to executive teams how actionable insights can be created using both little data and Big Data (see Figure 2.2).

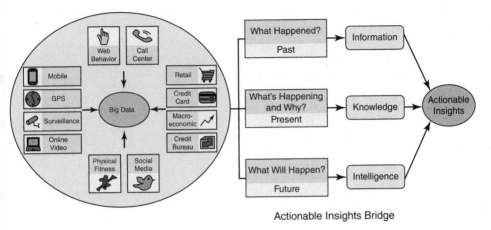

Figure 2.2 Analytics and Actionable Insights Bridge

Business Analytics

Earlier, we discussed that the migration from business analytics to talent analytics happens simply by switching the word *customer* with the word *talent*. With that in mind, Tables 2.2, 2.3, and 2.4 will help us map preliminary reporting analytics to predictive analytics. This begins by translating your business question into a talent analytics question. For instance, a marketing question about proactive customer retention could be translated into proactive talent retention, and can leverage similar analytics techniques.

Table 2.2 Mapping Business Analytics and Talent Analytics for the "What Happened?"

Analytics Question	Business Analytics Solutions	Talent/People Analytics Solutions
What Happened?	Customer dashboards and customer reports	Talent dashboards and talent reports
	Customer scorecard and customer key performance indicators	Talent scorecard and talent key performance indicators
	Cubes	Human capital cubes
	Triggers and alerts	Triggers and alerts

Table 2.3 Mapping Business Analytics and Talent Analytics for the "What's Happening and Why"?

Analytics Questions	Business Analytics Solutions	Talent/People Analytics Solutions
What's Happening and Why?	Customer segmentation	Talent segmentation
	Customer profiling	Talent profile analysis for turnover and retention
	Market research	Market research employment conditions
	Customer satisfaction survey	Employee satisfaction survey
	Voice of customer analysis	Voice of candidate analysis Voice of employee analysis
	Competitive intelligence	Competitive intelligence: Who is hiring? Where and when?
	Social media analytics	Candidate social media analytics
	Text analytics	Text analytics
	Mobile analysis	Candidate mobile analytics
	Social graph analysis	Candidate and employee social graph analytics

Table 2.4 Mapping Business Analytics and Talent Analytics for the "What Will Happen?"

Analytics Questions	Business Analytics Solutions	Talent/People Analytics Solutions
What Will Happen?	**Predictive Models** Customer and prospect predictive models Customer acquisition Customer targeting and selection Customer retention Customer reward and loyalty program Customer upgrade Customer attrition (voluntary churn) Customer involuntary churn (termination due to bad payment)	**Predictive Models** Talent and candidate predictive models Talent acquisition Talent targeting and selection Talent retention Talent reward and incentive program Talent promotion Talent attrition (voluntary churn) Talent involuntary churn (termination due to bad performance)
	Forecasting Forecast market opportunities Forecast number of new customers Forecast number of existing customers Forecast number of lost customers	**Talent Scorecard** Forecast market opportunities Forecast number of new employees Forecast new and existing employees Forecast number of lost employees

Analytics Questions	Business Analytics Solutions	Talent/People Analytics Solutions
	Forecast churn by business function Forecast bottom line	Forecast turnover by business function Forecast bottom line
	Optimization Customer life cycle management Customer relationship management optimization	**Optimization** Talent life cycle management Talent relationship management optimization

BUILDING A PEOPLE ANALYTICS CENTER OF EXCELLENCE

Creating a talent analytics center of excellence requires prudent investments in people, processes, and technology.

People: Creating the Dream Team

The overall data scientist labor shortage prevalent in other industries is even more acute in the talent management and HR field. In a recent *Wall Street Journal* article, Jeanne Harris and her colleagues rightly assert that "It takes a team to solve the data scientist shortage"; one of this book's authors, JP Isson, provided insights to *Wall Street Journal* for his team solution approach at Monster.[14] Similarly, it takes a team to build a People Analytics center of excellence to solve that shortage.

So, how do we do that? In addition to utilizing existing analytics resources, tools, and technologies to minimize your cost, building a multidisciplinary team of people with a variety of backgrounds will enable you to view your data from different perspectives and derive even greater insights from it. Such a skills-diverse team might include:

- **Technical specialists** who will work closely with IT teams to secure the collaboration and support needed to gather data from multiple sources and integrate, standardize, and govern it, so that it can be used to help you understand your talent landscape. This oftentimes can be achieved by using certain reporting features and dashboards.

- **Statisticians, data scientists, and business intelligence specialists** who can help you elevate your talent life cycle knowledge and gain a better understanding of what is happening and why. These professionals offer a different view on the challenges and potential ways to address them, and are hands-on with numerical analyses. Additionally, they can leverage predictive models to anticipate workforce planning needs, such as identifying high-performing employees who are at risk of leaving, candidates who are more likely to be successful once hired, or, say, the number of injuries that might occur in mining and construction industries. These individuals are fact-finding and should help to create actionable insights from your data, and, if you have sufficient funding, you could also include demographers and econometricians for added insights.

- **Business analysts and navigators** who possess storytelling backgrounds and high data visualization acumen. This group will serve as the liaison between the People Analytics team and the rest of the business. After all, it is about using hard data points to paint a picture of how streamlined and cost-effective your organization *could be* that will help win over your C-suite.

Process: Creating a High People Analytics Impact with the IMPACT Cycle

The main goal of every organization, and arguably the reason you are most likely reading this book, is to create a high business impact. In order to do this, you need to ensure you have the right structures in place to properly pull your HR analytics.

Thus, in 2012, Josh Bersin (Bersin by Deloitte), who is one of the leading thinkers in HR analytics, created the HR Analytical Maturity Model to explain the different levels of HR analytics adoption. He defines these stages based on four maturity levels:

- Level 1 is labeled **Reactive-Operational Reporting** and is reflective of companies where HR analytics principally focuses on ad hoc operational reporting. This level is reactive to business demands, is characterized by data isolation, and is difficult to analyze.

- Level 2 is labeled **Proactive Advanced Reporting** and reflects companies where HR analytics focuses on operational reporting for benchmarking multidimensional decision making.
- Level 3 is labeled **Strategic Analytics** and is reflective of companies where HR analytics focuses on statistical analysis development of people models and analytics of dimensions to understand cause and delivery of actionable insights.
- Level 4 is labeled **Predictive Analytics** and is reflective of the development of predictive model scenarios for planning, risk analysis and mitigation, and integration with strategic planning.

With Bersin's HR Analytical Maturity Model in mind, let's explore the IMPACT Cycle that will help you quickly navigate across the aforementioned four stages to create high business impact.

Focusing on the IMPACT

In speaking with industry leaders, experts, and business partners, we realized that the data challenges they were facing could be addressed by leveraging advanced business analytics, and the same approach and methodology used in traditional business could be applied to talent life cycle management. In fact, there are critical success factors that organizations leveraging talent data analytics are using to drive better business outcomes. Companies such as Accenture, Deloitte, CGB Enterprises Inc., ConAgra Foods, Microsoft, Google, Goldcorp, FedEx, Xerox, Hewlett-Packard, SAS Institute, Bloomberg, Bullhorn, Sysco, Shell, CISCO, General Electric, Johnson & Johnson, Dow Chemical, and Harrah's have invested in People Analytics to optimize their human capital and improve business performance, and some have even gained global recognition for being a Best Place to Work.

So, how do these companies do it?

The short answer is that they are focusing on the IMPACT. Coined in our previous book, *Win with Advanced Business Analytics*, IMPACT is a framework for creating actionable insights at every stage of the talent management cycle. While data is a necessary component of every business, it alone is not sufficient to unlock value for your organization—for this, actionable insight is required.

We speak with business leaders on a regular basis about their data assets and challenges, and it never fails—a sentiment we hear consistently is that their organizations are drowning in data but are lacking in understanding and actionable takeaways from that data. Based on our experience leading and building analytics teams from the ground up, as well as taking into account input we received from researching successful analytical organizations, we developed the IMPACT Cycle to help guide analysts through the process of ensuring they are insightful business partners, rather than just purveyors of data. (See Figure 2.3.)

It's not always an easy task to get your analysts to pull their heads up from the data and focus on the business; in fact, it is a bit of both an art and a science. The IMPACT framework is made up of the following steps:

- **Identify the questions:** In a nonintrusive way, help your business partner identify the critical business question(s) he or she needs help in answering. Then set a clear expectation of the time and the work involved to get answers.

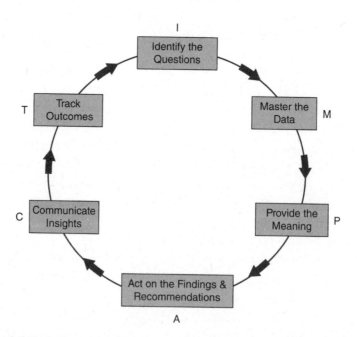

Figure 2.3 The IMPACT Cycle: The Analyst's Guide for Creating High-Impact Analytics

- **Master the data:** This is the analyst's sweet spot—assembling, analyzing, and synthesizing all available information that will help in answering the critical business question. Create simple and clear visual presentations (charts, graphs, tables, interactive data environments, etc.) of that data that are easy to comprehend.

- **Provide the meaning:** Articulate clear and concise interpretations of the data and visuals in the context of the critical business questions that were identified.

- **Act on the findings and recommendations:** Provide thoughtful business recommendations based on your interpretation of the data. Even if they are off base, it's easier to react to a suggestion than to generate one. Where possible, tie a rough dollar figure to any revenue improvements or cost savings associated with your recommendations.

- **Communicate insights:** Focus on a multipronged communication strategy that will get your insights into the organization as far and as wide as possible. Maybe it's in the form of an interactive tool that others can use, a recorded WebEx of your insights, a lunch and learn, or even just a thoughtful executive memo that can be passed around.

- **Track outcomes:** Set up a way to track the impact of your insights. Make sure there is future follow-up with your business partners on the outcomes of any actions. What was done, what was the impact, and what are the new critical questions that need your help as a result?

The IMPACT Cycle can help you guide discussions on some key talent management decisions, including:

- What type of talent to attract and who to select?
- Which employees to engage and develop?
- Which employees to reward and promote, and whom to terminate?
- How to reduce the cost of a bad hire?
- How to best manage people?
- What drives performance and retention?
- How to assist employees with performance improvement?

- How to increase employee engagement, satisfaction, loyalty, and lifetime value?
- How to improve succession planning, leadership, and overall talent life cycle management?

Technology: Talent Management Tools

Over the past four decades, HR has shifted from mainframe computers and manual payroll systems to cloud-based technology, software as a service (SaaS), and client–server solutions. In fact, the emergence of TMSs has enabled companies to capture, store, and manage a variety of employee and HR data, including social media data and talent digital footprints. As we see the amount of data increase, we see the number of HR tech firms who create these solutions also increase. In fact, this industry represents roughly $4.5 billion in business.[15]

But, because this is a journey, it is always best to start small and first master the human capital information at your disposal. As we mentioned, analytics is fairly new in HR, so leveraging experts in the field of traditional analytics technology can help you map out the best approach for your organization.

According to the 2014 HR trends survey conducted by the Information Services Group,[16] there are three major benefits that companies expect to realize from their HR investments:

1. An improved user and candidate experience.
2. Access to ongoing innovation and best practices to support the business.
3. Increased implementation speed to enhance the value of technology to the organization.

When investing in talent management tools and selecting service providers, there are some basic considerations to keep in mind:

- Does it ensure data security and data privacy?
- Does it integrate with existing systems, both HR and your general information technology (IT)?
- Is it customizable (can it align with internal systems and processes)?

- Does it enable reporting and analytics regarding the employee life cycle?
- Is it a cloud-based SaaS solution?
- Is it flexible, with mobile and social platforms that have the ability to handle Big Data?
- Is there a social collaboration tool?
- Does it have an intuitive and user-friendly interface?
- Is it a scalable system?

Before getting started, there are also a baker's dozen best practices to keep in mind for building a successful People Analytics journey.

1. Get buy-in from your senior leadership team.
2. Tie your People Analytics goals, strategy, and activities to the business goals of your organization.
3. Start small, but dream big.
4. Follow a baby-steps approach when implementing People Analytics. It is an approach that needs to be delivered in stages.
5. Don't let the "good" be the enemy of the "best" with your data. Oftentimes, talent data can be very messy and not 100 percent accurate at first. It is challenging to aggregate and integrate because of the quality of the data. Start with what you have and improve as you learn.
6. Have some quick measurable wins to build the momentum and create awareness.
7. Leverage existing tools and resources as far as you can before requesting heavy investment in new tools and software.
8. Start by addressing small questions and pieces of information.
9. Use what you learn, and focus on developing and building capabilities.
10. Don't get lost in the sea of data; let the business question lead your data requirements.
11. Take a collaborative approach with IT, finance, and other departments within your organization. People Analytics should be everyone's business.

12. Proactively prepare by readying for change management, training curriculum, and end-user experience testing to ensure good implementation.

13. Create a People Analytics exchange hub where professionals from various departments in your organization can share best practices and experiences of leveraging analytics. These individuals could become your advocates and help promote adoption by offering fact-based decisions and data-driven approaches across the organization.

PROFILE

Interview with Mark Berry, Vice President, Human Resources (Chief Human Resources Officer), CGB Enterprises, Inc., and former Vice President, People Insights, ConAgra Foods

JP Isson had the opportunity to speak with Mark Berry, HR Trendsetter, 2015 *HR Magazine*, about the implementation of a People Analytics team and HR business challenges dos and don'ts in talent analytics.

Isson: To lead a People Analytics team, do you need to be a guru in mathematics or statistics?

Berry: To lead HR analytics, you don't need to be a PhD in statistics or mathematics. You need three things: (1) a keen understanding of your business—how it makes money, what makes it competitively formidable in the marketplace, and where people can be leveraged to create competitive advantage; (2) a natural curiosity about business challenges and how to align people and processes to optimize outcomes; and (3) resources—talent, consultants, and technology—to make the work easy. The most important thing is the ability to formulate the right business question or challenge: "How does talent affect execution of our business's strategy?" "What capabilities are necessary to help our business succeed?" or a host of others. Analytics acumen has a place, but more important is business acumen—and an understanding of how to leverage people to drive improved outcomes.

Isson: What was your biggest challenge putting People Analytics in place and convincing the CEO?

Berry: Jeff Bezos, the founder of Amazon, has been quoted as saying: "If you are going to innovate, you have to be willing to be misunderstood." The quote can be applied to workforce analytics as well—with one caution: Failing to make your efforts understood can be fatal!

In workforce analytics, many stakeholders don't understand the science behind the capability. In fact, few equate data, analysis, and insights with HR. What analytics leaders must do is help the potential of workforce analytics to become understood—to help stakeholders appreciate the potential of the capability—to improve a business's ability to attract, engage, develop, and retain key talent; to optimize the company's investments in people; and to quantify the impact of HR's programs and practices on the business's outcomes. We can't afford to be misunderstood—most typically, misunderstanding results in defunding and dismantling of analytics initiatives. We must seek to be understood, by explaining and demonstrating the value of analytics to the business in language business leaders understand and will embrace.

Isson: What types of business challenges were you able to address using People Analytics?

Berry: I've been blessed with a pretty wide range of opportunities—the businesses where I've worked have been truly "target rich" environments. There has been no lack of opportunities, but I believe that's the case in most organizations. However, that makes answering your question so difficult—because during a 20-plus-year career in HR, I've used fact-based decision making to address a number of issues.

Here are several examples:

- Calculating the probability of an employee's missing work on days contiguous to a two- or three-day scheduled time off.
- Evaluating the costs of closing a nonprofitable facility versus the investments required to make the facility productive and profitable.
- Defining what prospective and current employees most value in terms of total rewards, how the company measures up relative to those values, and what the organization needs to do to better align its offering to drive improved attraction, engagement, development, and retention of talent.

(Continued)

(*Continued*)

- Determining the degree to which employees affected by a major change initiative are embracing the changes required and defining how to improve change agility.

- Quantifying the total cost of a workforce and optimizing those costs through improved planning, analysis, and forecasting.

In each of the cases, the common components are: (1) focus on people, (2) solving business issues, and (3) using data to drive improved outcomes. The challenges and opportunities are different in every business; our opportunity is to take time to understand the businesses we serve, learn what makes them successful, define what the people "levers" of that success are, and determine how to influence those levers to drive improved outcomes. What is most critical is doing what is meaningful, impactful, and sustainable for your business. Don't get caught in the tendency of many in HR to focus on the "bright, shiny object"—the initiative you heard about at a conference or read about in a book. They might be good, but what's important is what is good for your business.

Isson: What advice would you give to companies starting their People Analytics journey?

Berry: Dream big, start small, and tailor what you do to what your business most needs. Let me break those down:

- Dream big: To be understood, you have to cast a compelling vision: How will the work you do help the business be more successful? How will the work you do change your organization? What is the full scope of the work you want to be able to do—long term—in People Analytics? Vision is critical; it helps stakeholders understand the big picture—where you are going, why you are going there, and what will be different along the way.

- Start small: This may seem contrary to the preceding point, but it's not. Analytics leaders need to cast a big vision but be able to deconstruct that all-encompassing vision into its component parts, breaking it down into small, bite-size projects and initiatives that—over time—will help to bring the greater vision to life. In my world, it's meant starting in places that often are not sexy or exciting from an analytics perspective. An example: "Why are we losing such a high percentage of our college hires?" It's not a question that's exciting for the person looking to do engagement analysis or EVP [employee value proposition] development, but it may be where your business needs your focus. Starting small allows analytics leaders to realize quick wins, building equity for future investments. We must avoid the urge to focus on the bigger and overlook the smaller, more immediate opportunities.

■ Tailor what you do to what your business most needs: I can't emphasize this enough. HR leaders shouldn't delude themselves into believing that they can have a strategy independent of the business's strategy. In my world, my foundational strategy *is* the business strategy.

KEY TAKEAWAYS

■ People Analytics or talent analytics is another type of business analytics that is obtained by simply replacing the word *customer* from business analytics with the word *employee* or *talent*.

■ People Analytics is a journey and not a destination.

■ People Analytics helps organizations to avoid relying solely on gut feelings, instinct, or experience, and instead uses data to address critical business questions such as:

■ What drives performance?

■ What drives turnover?

■ What drives retention?

■ How to best manage people?

■ Whom to hire?

■ Whom to acquire, develop, promote, and retain?

■ To be successful, a People Analytics strategy should start small but have big long-term goals in mind and include quick wins to build momentum and awareness.

- People Analytics requires collaboration of the entire organization to be successful.

- People Analytics requires a talent analytics center of excellence by investing in:
  - People (the analytics resources)
  - Process (the IMPACT Cycle)
  - Technology (to manage, master, analyze, and leverage talent data)

- Similar to the analytics revolution that invaded marketing in the late 1990s, HR will undergo an analytical revolution that will change the way we manage the talent life cycle.

- Human capital decisions will become increasingly a combination of art (human intuition and experience) and science (the intelligence of data analytics).

- People Analytics will become the *Moneyball* of HR/human capital, and companies not embracing People Analytics in the future will be playing catch-up and will be lagging.

NOTES

1. Jean Paul Isson and Jesse S. Harriott, *Win with Advanced Business Analytics* (Hoboken, NJ: John Wiley & Sons, 2012).
2. Frederick Wilson Taylor, *The Principles of Scientific Management* (New York: Harper & Brothers, 1911).
3. Paul L. Govekar, "The Parable of the Pig Iron," www.na-businesspress.com/JHETP/ GovekarPL_Web12_2_.pdf.
4. Hugo Munsterberg, *Psychology and Industrial Efficiency* (Boston: Houghton Mifflin, 1913).
5. Army Alpha and Beta Tests, http://en.copian.ca/library/research/adlitus/page19.htm.
6. Yerkes on "Human Intelligence," www.indiana.edu/~intell/yerkes.shtml.
7. John F. Kihlstrom and Nancy Cantor, "Social Intelligence," http://ist-socrates .berkeley.edu/~kihlstrm/social_intelligence.htm.
8. Carl Gustave Jung, *Psychological Types* (Princeton, NJ: Princeton University Press, 1976).
9. Dr. Jac Fitz-enz, *How to Measure Human Resources Management* (New York: McGraw-Hill, 1984; 3rd ed. 2002). (Fitz-enz also wrote the chapter "Predictive Analytics in HR" in *Win with Advanced Business Analytics*.)
10. Isson and Harriott, *Win with Advanced Business Analytics*, 210.
11. Josh Bersin, "Big Data in Human Resources: A World of Have and Have-Nots," *Forbes*, October 2013, www.forbes.com/sites/joshbersin/2013/10/07/big-data-in-human-resources-a-world-of-haves-and-have-nots/.
12. Isson and Harriott, *Win with Advanced Business Analytics*, 210.

13. Kyle Smith, "It's Time for Companies to Fire Their Human Resources Departments," *Forbes*, April 2013, www.forbes.com/sites/kylesmith/2013/04/04/its-time-for-companies-to-fire-their-human-resource-departments/.

14. Jeanne G. Harris, Nathan Shetterley, Allan E. Alter, and Krista Schnell, "It Takes a Team to Solve the Data Scientist Shortage," http://blogs.wsj.com/cio/2014/02/14/it-takes-teams-to-solve-the-data-scientist-shortage/.

15. Josh Bersin, "The 2013 Talent Management Systems Market: Explosive Growth and Change," Bersin by Deloitte, www.bersin.com/blog/post/The-2013-Talent-Management-Systems-Market-Explosive-Growth-and-Change.aspx.

16. Maribeth Sivak and Debora Card, "Human Resources Delivery Trends 2014," Information Services Group, www.isg-one.com/web/expertise/hr-technology/hr-servicedeliverytrends.pdf.

REFERENCES

Brian E. Becker, Mark A. Huselid, and Dave Ulrich, *The HR Scorecard* (Cambridge, MA: Harvard Business Review Press, 2001).

Josh Bersin, John Houston, and Boy Kester, "Talent Analytics in Practice," Deloitte University Press, March 2014, http://dupress.com/articles/hc-trends-2014-talent-analytics/.

John W. Boudreau and Ravin Jesutham, *Transformative HR* (San Francisco, Josey Bass, 2011).

The Hot HR Technology Trends in 2014: www.forbes.com/sites/meghanbiro/2014/07/20/the-hot-hr-technology-trends-of-2014/.

Information Services Group Study: HR Delivery Trends: www.isg-one.com/web/expertise/hr-technology/hr-servicedeliverytrends.pdf.

Carl Jung: www.ajna.com/great-thinkers/carl-jung/.

Moneyball in HR, *Harvard Business Review*: http://blogs.hbr.org/2010/03/moneyball-geeks-and-the-new-er/.

The Parable of the Pig Iron using Taylor's *Principles of Scientific Management*: www.na-businesspress.com/JHETP/GovekarPL_Web12_2_.pdf.

CHAPTER 3

The Seven Pillars of People Analytics Success

*Give me six hours to chop down a tree and I will spend
the first four hours sharpening the axe.*

—Abraham Lincoln

While no one is chopping down a tree, Lincoln's quote accurately captures the important role that preparation plays in People Analytics. Some leading companies have been applying the same critical assessment and rigorous discipline to workforce management as they do to other aspects of their business—and they're leveraging People Analytics to gain insight and optimize outcomes. Investing the time in performing due diligence with data analytics will not only save organizations time and money, but it will also result in a more satisfied workforce who will drive business performance and help build and maintain a competitive edge.

In this chapter, we'll take a look at the core pillars needed to build a successful People Analytics framework. But first, let's quickly recap how we got here.

In the two previous chapters, we introduced People Analytics. By now, you should have a better understanding of how the Internet has changed the workforce equation and revolutionized the overall talent sourcing process while moving from a print base to a web base. It also enhanced the word-of-mouth aspect of social networks and social hiring channels. Additionally, Internet sourcing enabled the explosion of digital talent data and metrics, changing how this information could be captured, stored, processed, analyzed, and managed. This resulted in a better understanding of specific workforces and improved support through human capital analytics. Having online sourcing also helped to increase the base of potential candidates and perpetuated the talent war.

We also discussed the worldwide workforce status and the global employment conditions. We covered the distribution of global talent and skill sets. You are probably aware of the challenges and opportunities associated with the aging population in Western countries, baby boomers who are poised for massive retirement, the millennials' impact, the labor shortage in some sectors such as science, technology, engineering, and mathematics fields, the global talent and skills gap,[1] the Big Data impact, and the unbalanced supply-and-demand equation challenge.

We also covered how to migrate from business analytics to People Analytics by leveraging the approaches and fundamentals of traditional analytics techniques. We explained how People Analytics, also called talent analytics or workforce analytics, is simply another type of analytics that can be achieved by replacing the word *customer* (from customer analytics) with the word *talent* or *employee*. We discussed how the same analytics principles of understanding past behavior, explaining present behavior, and predicting future behavior could be applied to talent management, leading to what is called workforce analytics, talent analytics, or People Analytics.

A workforce represents both the most invaluable asset and the largest expense line item for any business. Understanding its dynamic and associated trends is paramount for any business poised to lead and succeed. According to some studies, the total human capital cost accounts for 60 to 70 percent of all companies' expenses.[2] This most valuable asset requires a similar approach to that used in traditional business to drive performance. This means organizations should take the guesswork out of their talent management cycle by leveraging analytics, and analytics insights could be applied at every stage of talent life cycle management to optimize outcomes.

Today's explosion of digital information (internal and external), called Big Data, is propelled by the proliferation of tools, software, and infrastructures. It has enabled new possibilities to capture, store, process, analyze, and manage employee data (from a variety of sources, including social media, job boards, offline data, and macroeconomic data from the Bureau of Labor Statistics) to drive business performance leveraging analytics. Similar analytics approaches from customer life cycle management analytics can be applied to the talent life cycle management to drive performance from a company's workforce. Analytics allow the talent management life cycle to be an actionable combination of art (intuition and experience) and science (data intelligence) for human capital management.

Now that we have covered these fundamentals, in this chapter we will discuss the framework that will help your organization to successfully navigate talent life cycle management and the talent data, and quickly put People Analytics to work for your company. We will outline and propose a conceptual framework for successfully implementing talent analytics in any organization so that your talent management initiatives will flourish and bring a positive return on investment. Our ultimate goal in this book is to share practical examples and solutions that have been proven to work for some of the top companies around.

Before we elaborate more on the People Analytics framework, let's provide some background on how we created this framework.

Based on our more than 44 years of combined experience building and implementing business analytics teams and solutions, and enriched by conferences, panel discussions, and keynote speeches and Q&A sessions delivered across the world over the past 10 years, and by listening to people and gathering their most pressing challenges, we realized that there was an opportunity to apply traditional business analytics techniques to workforce and human capital challenges. We then spoke to industry leaders and conducted research with more than 340 industry leaders and experts in talent acquisition and talent retention, talent development, human resources (HR), staffing, and business partners to learn about their most important business priorities and challenges.

Four major challenges emerged from our research and interviews with these leaders and experts:

Challenge 1—Silos and disconnected data and tools: Nearly every individual we've spoken with has wrestled or is wrestling with massive amounts of internal and external siloed data, and different tools that don't talk to each other.

Challenge 2—Lack of optimization: Although the data exists, there is a pressing need to cull the right information in order to optimize the stages of the talent management life cycle.

Challenge 3—Analytics expertise: Beyond reporting, most businesses do not have the qualified resources needed to create and translate the data story into business outcomes.

Challenge 4—Predictive insights: There is a lack of insight, despite the deluge of data, when it comes to determining trends that can anticipate future workforce behavior and organizational needs.

DATA AND TOOLS CHALLENGE

The common business challenge we heard was data: "We have lots of disconnected data and tools." HR leaders are inundated with lots of data residing in multiple silos, and tools and systems that do not talk to each other and that generate countless reports. These teams are not getting enough understanding and insights from that data, and they are looking for actionable analytics from the trove of data so they can optimize their talent life cycle management to drive better business performance. They would like to become more proactive in leveraging predictive analytics to anticipate talent behavior.

They also feel the pressure from the Big Data wave, which has increased the complexity of intelligence they need to distill. The influx of information has caused them to feel confused, perplexed, lost, insecure, unclear, disoriented, and scared. However, they are all convinced that there is an untapped value and intelligence to be captured from that data. They believe that in this new era of a data intelligence revolution the old approach of "spray and pray" or "post and pray" is outdated, and worry that experience plus intuition no longer works. And the majority truly believe that the human resources workforce and the entire human capital management function will undergo a tremendous change thanks to Big Data analytics. They believe that an analytics revolution similar to the one that invaded marketing in the late 1990s[3] is coming into the talent management/human capital world, and they need to be ready to embrace the revolution to avoid being left behind and having to either play catch-up, join the laggards, or simply go out of business—and data intelligence will be a key driver of their talent management cycle optimization.

Talent Life Cycle Optimization Challenge

Industry leaders also shared with us several stages of their talent life cycle management that they would like to optimize by leveraging the power of Big Data analytics and drive business performance. The following are the seven most important talent management stages that the leaders we spoke with consider critical when it comes to creating business value from their talent data:

1. Workforce planning
2. Sourcing
3. Acquisition/hiring
4. Onboarding, culture fit, and engagement
5. Employee churn and retention
6. Performance assessment and development and employee life-time value
7. Employee wellness, health, and safety

Qualified Analytics Resources Challenge

HR teams are not known to be analytics-driven people or data crunchers. The third business challenge they expressed was the lack of resources and skills to harness different sources of data they have. They don't have the skill sets required to create business value from their vast trove of data; they don't have resources to tell the data story and speak the business language. While some lack the analytical resources needed to help them move beyond traditional reporting, others wrestle with capturing the right key performance indicators. They are looking for resources to help them create predictive insights and drive business performance, but they don't know how or where to start.

Predictive Insights Challenge

Experts and industry leaders we spoke with also mentioned that they lacked insights needed to create business value and gain a better understanding of their talent and human capital data. The vast majority of those leaders would like to anticipate their workforce's behavior by leveraging predictive analytics at every stage of the talent life cycle. They all agree that the aforementioned stages are invaluable and are looking for resources and solutions to access the untapped opportunity potential of talent insights to drive business performance.

While some teams don't know where to start, others are still struggling to move beyond ad hoc reports and siloed tools. They want predictive insights and user-friendly tools that could also help them to address workforce questions such as:

- What staff would they need to hire in the next 6, 9, 24, and 60 months?
- Where, when, and how should they source new talent?
- What area(s) of their talent-sourcing pipeline will become weak in the future?
- How should they find candidates: Online only? Offline only? Social media?
- How can they measure the candidate's experience?
- Does the candidate's experience affect her or his loyalty?
- Does the candidate's experience impact performance?
- Does a candidate's interview performance indicate performance at the job?
- Who should they hire by leveraging analytics?
- Who are the high performers at risk of leaving and why?
- How should they engage with their talent?
- How do they measure the quality of a hire?
- What is the impact of employee engagement on turnover?
- What is the impact of employee satisfaction on customer satisfaction and business performance?

- What should be the value of the referral program?

- Should companies hire more millennials? And, if so, what is the best way to attract them?

- What is the breakeven point of a new employee? What is the lifetime value of the talent?

- Should they keep only the high performers on their team?

- How can they keep, protect, and engage high performers?

- What is the dream team to mine talent data?

- What is the right mix of talent to achieve business objectives?

- Did the quality of hire increase or decrease in your organization?

- How to measure new hires' contributions: Have they helped to increase company revenue and profitability?

- Who are the top talent who should be retained?[4]

- How can a company predict and reduce voluntary turnover?

- How is employee lifetime value calculated?

- What is the cost of a bad hire?

- Who are the employees more likely to be injured?

- What is the impact of well-being, health, and safety on talent performance?

- What is the impact of well-being, health, and safety on a company's bottom-line performance?

With those critical human capital business challenges in mind, we gathered research and listened to industry leaders, experts, and business partners, only to realize that the data challenge and the aforementioned talent stages could be addressed by leveraging advanced business analytics. We noticed that the same approach and methodology used in traditional business could be applied to talent life cycle management. And, more important, there are critical success factors between companies that are leveraging talent data analytics and those that are not. Leading companies like Google, CISCO, Johnson & Johnson, Xerox, Hewlett-Packard, Bullhorn, Bloomberg, Microsoft, Deloitte,

Accenture, SAS Institute, Pfizer, Sysco, Dow Chemical, and Harrah's invested in People Analytics to optimize their human capital to create business value and drive performance, and some of them have even been named a Best Place to Work multiple times. Looking at this data, we realized that we could apply predictive analytics to the entire talent life cycle management data to help drive business value for organizations leveraging the IMPACT Cycle.

As discussed in Chapter 2, the IMPACT Cycle provides a powerful guide for creating actionable insights at every stage of the talent management cycle. To review, the IMPACT Cycle is made up of the following steps:

1. **Identify the questions:** In a nonintrusive way, help your business partner identify the critical business question(s) he or she needs help in answering. Then set a clear expectation of the time and the work involved to get answers.

2. **Master the data:** This is the analyst's sweet spot—assembling, analyzing, and synthesizing all available information that will help in answering the critical business question. Create simple and clear visual presentations (charts, graphs, tables, interactive data environments, etc.) of that data that are easy to comprehend.

3. **Provide the meaning:** Articulate clear and concise interpretations of the data and visuals in the context of the critical business questions that were identified.

4. **Actionable recommendations:** Provide thoughtful business recommendations based on your interpretation of the data. Even if they are off base, it's easier to react to a suggestion that to generate one. Where possible, tie a rough dollar figure to any revenue improvements or cost savings associated with your recommendations.

5. **Communicate insights:** Focus on a multipronged communication strategy that will get your insights into the organization as far and as wide as possible. Maybe it's in the form of an interactive tool that others can use, a recorded WebEx of your insights, a lunch and learn, or even just a thoughtful executive memo that can be passed around.

6. **Track outcomes:** Set up a way to track the impact of your insights. Make sure there is future follow-up with your business partners on the outcomes of any actions. What was done, what was the impact, and what are the new critical questions that need your help as a result?

Applying the IMPACT Cycle to the seven stages of the talent life cycle management process to create business value is what we called the "Seven Pillars of People Analytics Success," which is the framework for People Analytics success.

The framework outlined in the following pages can be used to derive actionable insights from data to predict and optimize outcomes. And these pillars will serve as the basic principles discussed throughout the rest of this book.

THE SEVEN PILLARS OF PEOPLE ANALYTICS SUCCESS

The framework (Figure 3.1) is an essential guide to help staffing managers, HR managers, business partners, or human capital managers to be competitive using People Analytics. It could be very helpful to organizations that have expressed an interest in harnessing their talent

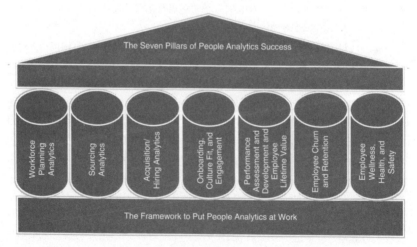

Figure 3.1 The Seven Pillars of People Analytics Success

data leveraging analytics across the entire cycle of talent management to drive better outcomes.

This framework could be the ultimate guide for People Analytics experts/builders and People Analytics end users. It has been built to address key C-suite challenges, offering practical guidance for chief operation officers, chief financial officers, chief health officers, chief people officers, chief human resources officers, chief marketing officers, chief talent officers, and heads of staffing. With People Analytics, companies now have a blueprint to take their talent management to the next level. We hope this framework will inspire creativity in talent analytics as well as spark interesting and constructive debates throughout your companies regarding the talent management cycle.

Armed with the People Analytics framework, HR, staffing leaders, and business partners can definitively link their actions and activities to business outcomes by combining the art of the industry (their experience, expertise, intuition, and storytelling), with science (data intelligence) to address major workforce business questions.

LEVERAGING THE PEOPLE ANALYTICS FRAMEWORK

The ultimate goal of this framework is to focus your organization's attention on those areas that are keys to talent analytics success and will lead to greatest return on investment (ROI). This chapter is an introduction to the elements of the framework. Practical examples are provided throughout the book as well as dedicated chapters to illustrate concepts of the framework.

People Analytics is at a very infant stage, and this framework should be used as a starting point for your organization. Because each company faces unique circumstances, we recommend you adjust it to meet your most pressing goals and priorities, and we welcome any stories and feedback regarding how the framework has helped you to create business value from your talent life cycle data to drive business performance.

There is no specific order to follow with these pillars because the challenges each company faces will differ. For instance, one organization may have a great talent retention strategy but be really weak in talent acquisition. However, you will find that there are natural correlations between pillars within the framework, as well as their underlying analytics. Take the Acquisition/Hiring Analytics pillar, for example. A bad candidate selection could also lead to an increase in turnover rates or high retention costs, represented by the Employee Retention pillar. Depending on the maturity of your company's workforce analytics, each pillar could possibly be addressed separately without following a specific order.

The framework could also be adjusted based on your company's most pressing needs. It should help to master the talent management life cycle, propelling it with the power of analytics that could be:

- **Descriptive:** What happened in the past?
- **Diagnostic:** What is happening now and why?
- **Predictive:** What will happen and why?
- **Prescriptive:** What should you do knowing what will happen?

Analytics used throughout this framework follow an approach similar to customer life cycle management, with the overall idea being a substitution of the word *employee* or *talent* (for People Analytics) for the word *customer* (from business analytics), and similar analytical techniques could be used.

The framework contains seven pillars that are critical to any business eager to successfully implement analytics across its talent management cycle and drive business performance. Optimizing every stage of the employee life cycle management by leveraging analytics is what really matters, as it could influence workforce planning, sourcing, hiring, engagement, termination, retention, promotion, and performance as well as the overall company business objective.

In the next sections, we provide a short introduction to the seven pillars. Throughout the book, we also introduce dedicated chapters, examples, and case studies from companies that are already competing and winning with talent analytics. For each pillar, we will define the pillar, the underlying talent management stage, appropriate analytics, and some business questions that could be addressed using the analytics IMPACT cycle.

The Seven Pillars of People Analytics Success are made up of the seven stages of the talent management cycle where business analytics' impact is created from the talent data.

This is by no means an exhaustive list of the stages of talent life cycle management, but based on our research it represents the most important pillars that industry leaders and experts we spoke with consider critical to successfully creating the best value from your human capital.

WORKFORCE PLANNING ANALYTICS PILLAR

You have probably seen countless definitions of workforce planning, and we will have the opportunity to more thoroughly explore it in the next chapter. However, generally speaking, workforce planning refers to the process that helps identify what talent your organization will require to achieve its business goals and business objectives—from current needs to future needs and succession planning.

Planning should start with a clear definition and understanding of your company mission, and the most pressing business goals and objectives. As with any large undertaking, it is important to be transparent and include all internal stakeholders and executives in the process to ensure full organization-wide support. They should understand from the get-go what their role is, how finding the right talent at the right cost will impact the company's objectives, how HR functions and activities relate to business challenges, and what is the business ROI of the initiative.

The Workforce Planning Analytics pillar is about leveraging analytics to proactively plan for the right number of employees with the right skill sets, at the right place, at the right time, and at the optimal cost. It is one of the most important pillars of the talent management cycle because it is highly connected to the other pillars. For instance, turnover and retention insights will feed the workforce planning analytics pillar. It is influenced by the quality and accuracy of the model used to predict churn or employee turnover, both voluntary and involuntary, as well as talent acquisition and promotion models.

This pillar is useful for gaining insights into:

- The staffing needs your organization had in the past.
- The current staffing requirements.
- What staff will be needed 6, 9, 12, 60, or 120 months from now.

Workforce planning analytics helps organizations to create economic value from their human capital data. When properly executed, this approach enables your organization to reduce labor costs (through acquisition, onboarding, retention, and cost per hire), increase productivity, and drive business performance by providing organizations with the right knowledge and tools to be proactive in managing their most valuable asset: their employees.

In a dedicated chapter later in the book, we will discuss how leading companies like Dow Chemical, Bullhorn, Black Hills, and Société de Tansport de Montréal have leveraged this pillar.

SOURCING ANALYTICS PILLAR

Successfully searching for candidates in today's global competitive talent market requires an approach that leverages the power of analytics to identify and locate candidates, assess their potential, and engage with them. Talent sourcing analytics, or the Sourcing Analytics pillar, is about harnessing all the data and talent information available to optimize your sourcing results, including how to determine staffing resources and what channels will be most effective to engage potential candidates. We define talent sourcing as a talent management process that consists of proactively searching for candidates to fill specific positions (clearly defined from your workforce plan), while leveraging job boards, employee referrals, staffing firms, and headhunters, as well as offline, online, and social media tools and resources.

Once you've completed your workforce planning stage, you will have a solid plan of how you will help your organization achieve its business goals. At this stage, you will also start investigating how you will staff your plan, and what channels you can use to accomplish this.

Talent sourcing analytics is about harnessing all the data and talent information available to optimize your sourcing results: It is the process of applying the IMPACT Cycle to this talent management stage to create business value.

The Sourcing Analytics pillar is also about understanding and capturing both the employer's decision journey data and the candidate's decision journey data to optimize your outcome. It can help a business address questions such as:

- How can a business move a candidate from passive or visitor viewer to a job applicant?
- What is the candidate decision journey?
- What is the competitive employer decision journey?
- What sourcing channels will optimize candidate search results?
- Where are the best places to search for a specific niche of candidates with technical skills such as those in science, technology, engineering, and math fields?
- When and where should an organization increase search activities?
- What sourcing channel delivers the best return on investment?
- How can a business best allocate searching spend and efforts?
- Similar to traditional attribution, should a business assign the highest weight to the first visit or the last click?
- What is the best attribution model when it comes to sourcing?
- What is the impact of employee referrals, social networks, and job boards on sourcing results?
- What is the ideal mix of resources, tools, and processes needed to optimize search efforts?
- What is an organization's dream team for sourcing?
- Does an organization need a Boolean-search black belt expert, a sourcing professional, or an Internet search professional?
- What is the impact of offline sourcing in this era of digitalization?
- How to optimize your talent sourcing by harnessing publicly available talent data?

Organizations should use the Sourcing Analytics pillar to gain insights that can be used to create targeted strategies that effectively use both internal and financial resources to find top candidates from a variety of channels (online, job boards, social media, referrals, and headhunting services) and drive better business performance.

In a dedicated chapter later in the book we will discuss frontline stories from companies such as CISCO, Microsoft, and Bloomberg.

ACQUISITION/HIRING ANALYTICS PILLAR

Whether you have a small company or manage a large organization with thousands of employees, choosing the wrong candidates can have a lethal impact on your business. According to the *Harvard Business Review*, 80 percent of employee turnover is due to bad hiring decisions.[5] Additionally, the Society for Human Resource Management estimates that the cost of bad hiring decisions can add up to as much as five times the annual salary of the hire.[6] So ensuring that your organization makes wise talent investments is critical to both long-term and short-term success.

The Acquisition/Hiring Analytics pillar uses predictive analytics to score all job applicants and select only the best candidates with whom, as a hiring manager, you should meet with. Talent acquisition predictive models help you save resources, time, and money so that you only interview candidates who, if hired, will be loyal and perform well at work. Analytics also help to optimize the interview process, helping to determine the best ways to vet candidates, to set up interview questions, and to create some tests that can be used to analyze the correlation between a candidate's performance during the interview and his or her performance in a particular job function.

Real-World Example

Google's People Analytics team analyzed how many interviews should be conducted before an offer would be made to the candidate. They researched which types of questions helped them gain the best insight into how their applicants approached problem solving, and analytics helped them to adjust their hiring and interview process accordingly. As a result, they ended up removing what they called "useless brainteaser questions" and psychometrical relevancy tests,[7] such as "How many golf balls can fit in an aircraft?" and "How many gas stations are available in New York?"

By applying the IMPACT Cycle to talent data and to the information generated through talent acquisition, advanced analytics can help businesses address talent acquisition questions, including:

- What are the best sets of questions to ask during an interview?
- Should we really still look at resumes today?
- Should we care about the dates on a resume?
- Should the interview be on-site or remote?
- Is there a correlation between interview performance and job performance?
- How many interviews should we conduct before hiring?
- What is the impact of candidate experience and the interview outcome?
- How many resources need to be involved in the candidate selection process?
- When should a business make the final offer?
- When should an organization look to hire a specific skill set?
- Do referred candidates tend to perform better than other candidates?
- Is there a correlation between signing bonus interview questions versus job performance questions?
- What candidates should you hire?

Because of long-ranging consequences of a bad hire[8] and the cost of missing a great candidate, analytics should be used to help employers optimize their practice of making talent acquisition a combination of art and science—a discipline that will help to drive their business value.

In a dedicated chapter later in the book, we will explain how leading companies have been leveraging the Acquisition/Hiring Analytics pillar along with frontline applications.

ONBOARDING, CULTURE FIT, AND ENGAGEMENT PILLAR
Talent Onboarding and Culture Fit

Once the right candidates have been hired, they need to be properly onboarded to ensure they are aligned with the primary business goals and the overall mission of the company. New hires need to have the best first impression of you as a manager and of your company. Depending on the role and position of your new hire, this should be accomplished within the first 6 to 12 months by assisting him or her with a list of resources and tools along with clear guidance on expectations and goals.

We define "talent onboarding" as an ongoing talent management process that consists of introducing, training, mentoring, coaching, and integrating a new hire to the core values, business vision, and overall culture of an organization in order to secure new employee loyalty and productivity. The Onboarding, Culture Fit, and Engagement pillar can be used to enhance a new hire's first impression and create business value from your onboarding activities and efforts.

Taking the time to develop a robust onboarding program will increase employee satisfaction and loyalty, and will accelerate time to productivity through acclimation processes. Similar to the customer welcome program that some companies use to introduce new customers to their business, first impressions really do make a difference, and new hire onboarding is a key component of the talent management process: This is your new employee's introduction to your organization during the period when he or she is still thinking about the decision he or she made to join your company; and, if done properly, this onboarding process can drastically improve ramp-up time.

To accomplish this, however, requires the mastering of data intelligence, which will allow you to optimize the mentoring, learning, and reinforcement needed to drive new hire satisfaction. It will also help your organization address vital talent management questions, including:

- How can a business improve time to performance?
- Does your new employee fit with company culture?

- What are the key drivers of time to performance and productivity?
- What is the impact of talent onboarding on employee commitment, productivity, and enthusiasm?
- What is the impact of talent onboarding on employee satisfaction?
- What is the impact of talent onboarding on an employee referral program?
- What is an appropriate talent onboarding budget?
- What impact does talent onboarding have on employee turnover?
- What is the impact of talent onboarding on employee loyalty?
- How does company culture fit impact new hire satisfaction, engagement, and loyalty?

In this diverse workforce demographic where multiple generations have to work together, cultural fit is critical for the successful integration of your new hire; and employee and company value mismatches are one of the major reasons for early turnover.

With talent retention as a focus, onboarding should be a great experience that provides new hires with all the information they will need for success. Onboarding analytics should help to quickly address the aforementioned questions, generate enthusiasm, and introduce new hires to the materials and resources needed to accelerate and optimize their time to performance, securing overall goodwill, commitment, and loyalty.

Talent Engagement

To stay competitive, it is paramount to keep your employees fully engaged in order to meet and exceed your customers' expectations and achieve your corporate goals. A key component to accomplishing this is monitoring the engagement level of your employee population.

We define an engaged employee as happy, enthusiastic, and motivated, and as an individual who eagerly relishes the challenges of his or her job. Analytics helps to understand the various drivers of employee engagement that deliver happier, more productive workers, and decrease unplanned turnover. It can also help human capital management teams sift through data and talent information to better understand employee engagement and help address some talent management questions such as:

- What are the key drivers of employee engagement?
- How does employee engagement affect productivity and financial bottom lines?
- What are the main drivers of millennials' engagement?
- What are the main drivers of baby boomers' engagement?
- What are the main drivers of echo boomers' engagement?
- What is the impact of hard-to-fill positions or hard-to-find skill sets on employee engagement?
- What is the impact of the Net Promoter Score and Engagement Index?
- How do talent engagement elements, such as relationship with manager and confidence in leadership and company, affect turnover?[9]

Talent engagement analytics can also provide insights on methods for increasing employee engagement via existing channels such as performance appraisals, the voice of the candidate, industry standards, and other metrics that can boost employee satisfaction and assist in paving career pathways. The Onboarding, Culture Fit, and Engagement pillar can also help organizations assess the correlation between engagement scores and employee performance in the past, present, and future—which is important information for reducing and mitigating the cost of bad hires and ultimately optimizing employees' lifetime value.

PERFORMANCE ASSESSMENT AND DEVELOPMENT AND EMPLOYEE LIFETIME VALUE PILLAR

Performance Analytics

Performance analytics can help businesses develop performance and promotion strategies in order to determine how top performers should be rewarded, how to leverage career pathways to better assign resources, and how to optimize promotions that guarantee success.

Performance analytics also help to address talent migration and development questions such as:

- Who are the employees who should be promoted to a senior role?
- Will they be successful if promoted?
- What is the best distribution of merit increases and bonuses?
- Should an organization promote internally or hire externally?
- What is the impact of promotions on performance and employee productivity?
- What is the impact of either internal or external promotion on performance and employee productivity?
- What is the correlation between career pathways and employee network graphs?

It also helps organizations address employee career-transition questions such as:

- What position will an employee want to occupy five years from now?
- What types of companies will employees be interested in working for five years from now?
- What are the next steps an employee should take to get to the next level in his or her career?
- Recent people analytics findings have enabled some leading companies to enhance their traditional annual performance appraisal processes. Companies such as Accenture, General Electric, Starbucks, and Adobe have adopted the new approach that is based on a more frequent review and feedback of employee performance. Sun-setting their old annual performances that used to take place once or twice a year, those companies now track performance and provide employee feedback on a much regular basis. Analytics helped them to replace the cumbersome and lengthy performance paper form with an app that is more user-friendly and appeals much better to a workforce that is more tech savvy.

Employee Lifetime Value Analytics

When we analyze customers in marketing, we usually leverage segmentation in order to derive the customer lifetime value. This is basically the revenue that the customer has generated, offset by the cost of serving that customer over her or his life span or tenure. All of us in business share the same end goal: to provide the best services to our customers and optimize their value, and, ultimately, to prioritize our proactive retention activities in marketing and sales based on the value and profitability of our customers.

To determine employee lifetime value, we can use the customer lifetime value model; we simply need to replace the word *customer* with the word *employee*. Our employees are internal customers, after all, so using the similar lines of thinking and ways of assessing employee value, and categorizing and segmenting employees based on performance can help organizations proactively retain them and create successful internal career pathway activities. By using the IMPACT Cycle, we are able to address management questions such as:

- Who are the most valuable employees?
- Why does one sales rep outperform all of her peers?
- What is the breakeven of a new hire in sales or customer service?
- Who are the employees who will create more value in the next two, three, or five years, and why?
- What are the main drivers of a high-value employee?
- What is the cost of losing a top performer?

EMPLOYEE CHURN AND RETENTION PILLAR

Your ultimate goal with all employees, both new and existing, is to earn their trust, commitment, and engagement, so that they can fully achieve their goals and help your organization be successful. According to the Bureau of National Affairs, U.S. businesses lose approximately $11 billion annually due to employee turnover, "with recruiting costs running approximately 1.5 times annual salary."[10] Additionally, the study noted, "the ability to engage and retain valuable employees has a significant impact on an organization's bottom line."

Some of your employees will be high-value creators and the top performers of your organization, while others may require multiple trials in order to address performance issues, which can have a negative impact on your organization. The separation with your employee, whether voluntary or involuntary, is called churn or turnover. Voluntary churn occurs when an employee decides to leave an organization due to favorable conditions elsewhere, for instance to work for the competition, while involuntary churn, or attrition, refers to the termination of a position. Leveraging employee churn analytics will help to create business value from employee attrition knowledge by analyzing internal and external talent data intelligence, and help your organization address major attrition questions, including:

- Which employees are at risk of leaving?
- Which employees will experience performance issues?
- Who are the top performers who are at high risk of leaving?
- Why would these top performers leave?
- When are they more likely to quit?
- What are the combinations of factors and variables that best explain employee attrition?
- What proactive actions could be done to retain employees?
- What is the cost of losing top performers?

Employee retention is about proactively identifying and understanding which of your employees are at risk of leaving, when and why they would leave. Analytics can help to marry employee data, company data, and market data to predict and interpret top-performing employees' behaviors, giving you competitive insights for your retention strategies.

Using this pillar can provide the key components that any forward-looking organization needs to put in place in order to retain top talent, and in doing so, will help the company to remain competitive and proactively create value with an engaged workforce. Later in this book, we will explore how companies such as Deloitte, Xerox, Pfizer, Google, and HP have been leveraging advanced analytics to retain their top employees and optimize their return on talent investment.

EMPLOYEE WELLNESS, HEALTH, AND SAFETY PILLAR

To be successful, organizations have to create and design an environment and culture that promote the safety, health, and well-being of their employees. This means finances and resources need to be allocated to support these endeavors, which requires a demonstrable linking of investments in employee health, safety, and well-being to company business performance. Best practices include proactive activities such as wellness visits, preventive checkups, and vaccinations to avoid the high cost of urgent reactive procedures.

Leveraged properly, this pillar provides a competitive advantage that can assist organizations in differentiating themselves from their competition, and further showcase the impact of that investment on their bottom lines by addressing questions such as:

- What is the impact of employee satisfaction on the company's business objective?

- What is the impact of employee satisfaction on customer satisfaction?

- What is the overall impact of having physicians on-site, as it relates to employee morale and engagement?

- What is the impact of employee well-being and health on company productivity?

- What is the impact of employee well-being and the company Net Promoter Score?

- What is the impact of employee well-being on companies' American Customer Satisfaction Index?

- What is the impact of employee satisfaction on customer satisfaction?

- What is the impact of employee health and well-being on company retention and acquisition metrics?

By investing in programs that promote the health, well-being, and safety of their workforce, companies can proactively increase the happiness of their employees, boosting engagement and improving the quality of service they provide to the customers they serve—resulting in a healthier company bottom line.

In a dedicated chapter later in the book, we will discuss how leading companies such as SAS Institute, Johnson & Johnson, and Workplace Safety and Insurance Board have been leveraging this pillar to create business value.

Throughout the course of this book, we will be exploring each pillar of the People Analytics framework, providing insights on how to successfully leverage analytics for every pillar, and we will provide frontline stories from companies that have successfully leveraged the framework to improve business outcomes. We will also share best practices and takeaways at the end of each chapter.

CASE STUDY

OPTIMIZING YOUR TALENT ACQUISITION, TALENT RETENTION, AND WORKFORCE PLANNING WITH ADVANCED ANALYTICS

Bloomberg, the world leader of real-time market data, financial calculations, and other financial analytics, has expanded its analytics leadership position to incorporate human capital as well, creating an advanced People Analytics team designed to optimize the way the company sources, acquires, and retains key talent.

JP Isson had the opportunity to interview both Allison Allen, Senior Strategic Organizational and Talent Development Practitioner at Bloomberg, and Durrell Robinson, Data Analyst at Bloomberg, to gain insight on how this leading financial data analytics company is using People Analytics to drive better corporate outcomes.

Bloomberg currently uses People Analytics insights in four major areas of HR management: workforce planning, talent sourcing, talent acquisition, and talent retention.

Talent Sourcing

When it comes to talent sourcing and acquisition processes, Bloomberg quickly understood that the world of work is rapidly changing, and in

(Continued)

(*Continued*)

order to recruit top talent successfully, new approaches were required. The battle for talent has become increasingly fierce, particularly as companies compete to win employees in markets where skills shortage is rampant.

To efficiently source for candidates, the company leverages its People Analytics attribution model to help assess the performance of every source of hire, whether it is the Bloomberg career site, traditional job boards, social media, employee referrals, or university campuses. Armed with this data, the talent management team can anticipate what source should be leveraged for specific positions within the company and can adjust the tactics and hiring budget accordingly. The company is now able to get more nuanced in understanding how much effort goes into acquiring talent and how they perform once hired.

Talent Acquisition

The company has also optimized its talent acquisition process by integrating analytics. Leveraging state-of-the-art location and intelligence models, the HR team is able to identify when and where to source for talent, and determine what the competitive landscape looks like for a specific market. This knowledge helps the team assess the overall talent supply-and-demand balance as it relates to the position, location intelligence gives them data, such as:

- How popular is a specific skill set?
- How popular is a specific skill set within a certain function?
- How popular is a specific skill set with a certain experience level?
- How many companies are looking for similar roles?
- What schools are nearby that teach courses relevant to those roles?

Armed with these types of insights, the company is able to manage its hiring expectations accordingly and use this information to educate decision makers on when and where to hire people.

In the market where "there is a dogfight" for certain skilled talent groups, the biggest benefit of using an advanced analytics model like this is that it has successfully shifted the conversation between managers and People Analytics. The team now can provide data-driven recommendations for workforce planning, such as:

- How many people can we hire?
- What skills are reasonable at a given price point?
- What city or location would have the best supply of talent?

For certain hard-to-fill positions, using a People Analytics model can even recommend that the business hire more people than initially planned. For instance, if the company is looking to hire five data scientists, the HR team uses predictive insights to assess whether five is the right number, assuming the supply/demand balance. Simply leveraging the power of their advanced analytics, they are able to provide a forecast of talent scarcity for data scientists in any given location. This predictive model enables them to have a more data-driven conversation with leadership, helping the business set more realistic hiring goals, as well as speed up the hiring process and set more realistic baseline numbers.

Bloomberg has also built in-house advanced analytics models that help the company forecast the next five years in regard to its durability initiatives, which are designed to stress-test human capital management programs and provide data and analyses that help the company set realistic and reasonable hiring targets.

Talent Retention

Bloomberg considers its talent its most important asset, and talent retention and employee satisfaction are paramount. The company has also leveraged advanced analytics and machine learning to build an in-house employee retention model that helps identify employees who are a "flight risk," as well as those elements that could contribute to their departure. Using this insight, the company can proactively target at-risk employees and ensure they have what they need in order to be happy and

(Continued)

(*Continued*)

productive. Predictive retention models have enabled Bloomberg to retain employees to a much better extent and gain insights such as:

- Understand and address what is working and not working.
- Be more proactive in addressing employee push factors (major reasons that could push them to leave).
- Have better retention. According to Allen, "Every employee we keep is an employee we don't have to go out to the market to find and replace," because it's not about replacing a resource; it's more about finding the right talent with the right skill set, the right experience, and, more important, the best cultural fit in a very highly competitive marketplace. Some talent is extremely difficult to find, and for these hard-to-fill positions where the demand outpaces the supply, if we are looking for 10 qualified candidates and find 15, we do not hesitate to hire 5 extra."
- The talent management team at Bloomberg recognizes that their employees are sought after and have multiple offers. The last thing they want is to unnecessarily lose a good employee. By leveraging their People Analytics insights, they are able to:
  - Use retention rates to provide insights for the leadership team and general management.
  - Provide insights into what programs and initiatives are working and those that are not.
  - Provide insights about the cultural impact across multiple business functions.
  - Provide constant feedback on what is working and what is not working, as well as actionable insights to address these issues (including a feedback loop that helps to look at which intervention is producing great ROI and helps the company improve).
  - Determine what tactics can be used that will encourage employees to stay.
  - Provide strategic insights for retaining talent and maintaining a competitive advantage that empowers them to proactively protect their most important asset: their talent.

When asked to provide three pieces of advice for companies looking to leverage a People Analytics model, Allen and Robinson said:

1. **People Analytics is a journey.** The first thing to do is to master your data and organize it. You need to realize that a lot of articles published are the results of years of data collection. Mastering the data and governing it should be your starting point: Where is the data coming from? Who has access to it? What is the best way to integrate internal and external data? How do you make it available to end users?

2. **Do an assessment of what already exists.** Avoid boiling the ocean, and keep in mind that there is a difference between analytics for academia, analytics for business, and, more important, analytics for people. You don't need to have all the data to start, and you should not expect 100 percent accuracy—this is a building process.

3. **Build a cross-functional team.** This team should include business partners across different departments, sitting around the same table, discussing the same problems. When this team comes to a decision, start small, test, learn from the data, and adjust accordingly.

According to Allen and Robinson, the future of People Analytics is really bright. Both are well versed in the challenges and opportunities of leveraging these models and believe the future will involve a lot more of predictive analytics and forecasting models. People Analytics will be fully integrated with the business and will become a de facto department in any organization poised to succeed.

KEY TAKEAWAYS

■ Companies are inundated with lots of disconnected talent management tools and data but lack predictive insights and analytical resources to speak the business language and create value from the data. Having a People Analytics framework should help to sharpen the axe before cutting the tree.

- Human capital experience and intuition alone are no longer sufficient to optimize talent management. It needs to be supported by actionable analytics to create business value.

- With talent analytics, companies can create high-impact analytical insights by applying the IMPACT Cycle to the seven stages of talent management.

- Operating in today's globally connected competitive arena, the explosion of digital information (Big Data), the proliferation of human resources information and tools, social media, the global talent gaps, skills shortages, and an aging workforce population combined with the unbalanced human capital supply chain have become the principal components of the talent management cycle. As a result, talent management will undergo an analytical revolution that will combine art (experience and intuition) and science (data intelligence and data storytelling).

- To be successful, organizations need to leverage analytics and remove the guesswork from their talent management.

- Similar customer relationship management analytics could be applied to talent management by replacing the word *customer* with the word *employee* or *talent*. Talent analytics is therefore another type of analytics similar to business analytics.

- There are seven pillars critical to building talent analytics capabilities that will help companies flourish and provide the best return on investment. They are: workforce planning, sourcing, acquisition, engagement, promotion and performance, retention, and wellness, health, and safety.

- Every stage of the talent management cycle could be optimized by leveraging analytics, and leading companies are creating competitive advantage with talent analytics. To be successful, talent analytics requires an ongoing alignment with the organization's mission and goal.

NOTES

1. ManpowerGroup, *The Talent Shortage Continues: How the Ever Changing Role of HR Can Bridge the Gap*, 2014, https://www.manpower.de/fileadmin/manpower.de/Download/2014_Talent_Shortage_WP_US2.pdf.

2. Jeff Higgins and Grant Cooperstein, *Managing an Organization's Biggest Cost: The Workforce*, Human Capital Management Institute, www.hcminst.com/files/OrgPlus_Total_Cost_Workforce_.pdf.

3. "The History of Marketing: An Exhaustive Timeline," HubSpot, http://blog.hubspot
.com/blog/tabid/6307/bid/31278/The-History-of-Marketing-An-Exhaustive-Time
.line-INFOGRAPHIC.aspx.

4. Steve Pogorzelski, Jesse Harriott, and Doug Hardy, *Finding Keepers: The Monster Guide to Hiring and Holding the World's Best Employees* (New York: McGraw-Hill Education, 2007).

5. Fred Yager, "The Cost of Bad Hiring Decisions Runs High," Dice, http://resources
.dice.com/report/the-cost-of-bad-hiring-decisions/.

6. David G. Allen, *Retaining Talent: A Guide to Analyzing and Managing Employee Turnover*, Society for Human Resource Management, 2008, www.shrm.org/about/foundation/
research/documents/retaining%20talent-%20final.pdf.

7. Adam Bryan, "In Head Hunting Big Data May Not Be Such a Big Deal," *New York Times*, June 20, 2013, www.nytimes.com/2013/06/20/business/in-head-hunting-
big-data-may-not-be-such-a-big-deal.html?pagewanted=all&_r=0.

8. Ryan Holmes, "The Unexpectedly High Cost of a Bad Hire," HootSuite, November 11, 2013, http://blog.hootsuite.com/high-cost-of-a-bad-hire-rh/.

9. Victor Lipman, "Study Explores Drivers of Employee Engagement," *Forbes*, December 14, 2012, www.forbes.com/sites/victorlipman/2012/12/14/study-explores-
drivers-of-employee-engagement/.

10. BNA Bloomberg Cost of Turnover Study, Bureau of National Affairs, www.forbes
.com/sites/victorlipman/2013/03/18/5-easy-ways-to-motivate-and-demotivate-
employees/.

CHAPTER 4

Workforce Planning Analytics

Knowing is not enough; we must apply. Willing is not enough; we must do.

—Johann Wolfgang von Goethe

Your organization is only as good as its talent, so finding, hiring, and retaining the right people, with the right skills, at the right time is critical for any company's success.

Operating in a globally connected arena, today's talent marketplace is extremely competitive and challenging. The race to hire the best people is heating up, and companies are facing new workforce demographic challenges: The majority of baby boomers who are poised for retirement will be leaving an unprecedented amount of talent gaps in nearly every organization. Millennials, who by 2020 will account for more than 50 percent of the labor force, are not necessarily equipped with the knowledge, education, and expertise to take over in the succession plan. And the skills gap in science, technology, engineering, and mathematics (STEM) fields is becoming more acute and represents a serious hurdle for talent management leaders.

To achieve success in this recovering global economy and challenging workforce ecosystem, companies can't afford to fly blind with their human resources. They must have a comprehensive understanding of their workforce segments and a clear vision of what they will need to achieve their business goals and objectives both now and in the future.

Leading companies are increasingly leveraging sophisticated methods to analyze employee and business data to enhance their competitive edge. They are properly getting a comprehensive understanding of the structure, strengths, and weaknesses of their employee base in order to anticipate their workforce needs. Getting that full-fledged knowledge requires all the building blocks of workforce planning, which also includes addressing some talent management questions, such as:

- How many people will your organization need in the next two to five years?
- How much it will cost to hire those resources?
- Where will those resources be coming from (internal or external full-time employees versus part-time employees, school, industry, location, and region)?
- What will be the expected revenue per employee?
- How much growth will those resources be expected to generate?
- Who are the critical segments of the workforce that will be required to achieve the business goals?
- Which segments of the workforce might not be business critical?
- What technology and processes are needed to achieve new business goals?

Addressing these strategic workforce planning business questions will be the topic covered in this chapter. Workforce Planning Analytics is one of the most important pillars in human capital management as it is defined along with your company's strategic business plan for success. We will explore how companies such as Bullhorn, Dow Chemical, Black Hills, and Societe de Transport de Montreal (STM) have been leveraging analytics to optimize their talent requirements so that they can achieve maximum return.

WHAT IS WORKFORCE PLANNING?

We define workforce planning as the process that enables organizations to identify what talent they will need to achieve their business goals and objectives, from current needs to future demand and succession planning.

Workforce planning should always start with a clear definition of your company mission and your most pressing business challenges and priorities. It should guide your organization into what is required to address its mission-critical challenges. This is a collaborative process that requires all stakeholders such as Finance, Human Resources (HR), Marketing, and Sales to ensure that the acquisition of talent and the retention of top performers are tied to the company's bottom line and represent everyone's business objectives. It also demonstrates the value that proactive assessment and planning of the workforce will have on the bottom line. Getting a comprehensive view of the talent supply-and-demand equation to drive business performance in the future requires the power of analytics to distill actionable insights from the complex workforce data ecosystem.

WORKFORCE PLANNING ANALYTICS

Economic cycles have always been the major drivers of workforce changes throughout the history of employment. During the global recession of 2008, we witnessed with little exception the sharpest downsizing of the workforce in the job market since the 1929 stock market crash and the Great Depression. The majority of companies went from hiring freezes and employment furloughs to massive workforce downsizing, restructuring efforts, and layoffs. Finance and HR teams were at the epicenter of it all, with Finance responsible for communicating budget cuts as well as the underlying workforce reduction that was required, while HR's major focus was about executing the plan and handling the legal purpose of those massive terminations: severance packages.

At some point, most of us probably witnessed a conversation between the Finance and HR departments that sounded something like this:

Finance: We need to cut 30 percent of the workforce.

HR: What levels should we cut? And when should we start?

Finance: Cut 50 percent from level 1, 20 percent from level 2, 20 percent from level 3, and 10 percent from level 4, and start immediately.

In most cases, Finance would hand over the requisition list on which HR was required to execute; however, depending on their size, some organizations did hire consulting firms specialized in reorganization to lead the downsizing efforts. Generally, these companies had little or no knowledge of the organization's day-to-day operations, and the outcome of their intervention was sometime questionable.

After multiple exercises in downsizing, some companies have simply realized they can maintain their minimal operations and service levels by hiring terminated resources as contractors (which can be problematic), and some have even tried to hire these employees back when the economy started to recover. Many had trouble hiring for some hard-to-fill skilled positions of employees who had been laid off, with most wondering why they were let go in the first place.

When talking with talent acquisition and HR leaders, one of their most important requirements for workforce planning was the ability to have a predictive custom model that would help to anticipate the workforce they would need in the future, and a customer model that could factor in internal and external changes, such as economic downturns and political change. They want to know how HR can become a more strategic partner in building acquisition plans during the up cycle of the economy or reduction plans during the down cycle of the economy.

To achieve this level of prediction, traditional workforce planning that only leverages a single set of metrics is not sufficient. Organizations need to effectively utilize advanced analytics and Big Data to build and drive the optimal workforce they need to achieve current and future business goals with the opportunity to dynamically adjust based on internal or external economic or political changes. That means constantly exploring, analyzing, and reviewing all the data available along with the supply-and-demand equation of your organization.

We define workforce planning analytics as the process of injecting advanced analytics into workforce planning in order to optimize outcomes and ensure human capital planning success. It is about leveraging advanced business analytics to address workforce planning challenges and business questions. It helps your company understand the past and the present and to anticipate your future workforce needs. When you leverage analytics, you should start with harnessing the data—Big or little, and from internal and external sources—to create economic value for the business and address human capital business questions.

The Workforce Planning Analytics pillar is strongly connected with other pillars, as well. For instance, a bad candidate triage could lead to an increase in turnover and a decrease in productivity; a lack of a strategic succession planning could affect productivity and retention of top performers, while the lack of well-being, health, and safety policies could undermine engagement, performance, and productivity of the workforce and increase operating costs. Workforce planning analytics offers organizations both short-term and medium-term solutions by identifying current skills challenges, future shortages, or surpluses of critical talent.

WHY SHOULD YOU CARE ABOUT WORKFORCE PLANNING ANALYTICS?

If you don't know how many resources you will need in the future to drive business performance and win against your competition, you are flying blindly and more likely building your path to fail. Workforce planning analytics helps to anticipate what resources your organization would need 6, 12, 36, 60, or 120 months from now to achieve its business goals. It also helps to identify the skill sets and profiles, such as job category, job level, title, education, location, and status, which will be required or no longer needed.

It provides actionable insights in terms of skills gaps with breakdowns by demographics, helping organizations to forecast skills shortage and excesses long before they happen, and enabling them to anticipate acquisitions, retention costs, talent needs, and productivity levels, as well as addressing the following questions:

- How best to leverage and work with millennials who have grown up in a digital and social media world?
- What talent will be required for succession planning?
- Whom to prepare to take over according to succession plans?
- What staff segment will be successful at various and disparate roles?
- Which talent will deliver a high return to warrant the greatest investment?
- What segment and profile of the workforce are essential to achieving business goals?
- What resources would you need if 60 percent of your employee population will retire in four years?
- What staffing needs has your organization had in the past, what needs does it currently have, and what needs will it have in the future to be successful?

Financial Benefits of Workforce Analytics

As per any business analytics main goal, workforce planning analytics enables organizations to create economic value from their business and human capital data, including tangible benefits such as:

- Reduction of workforce costs related to acquisition development and retention of talent.
- Best identification of revenue stream through optimization of the staff needed at the right place, at the right time, and at the right cost.
- Successful execution of the organization's business strategy and design.
- Optimization of learning and development as well as compensation and benefits.

- Anticipation and planning for change to improve business operations and decisions.
- Allocation of talent investment and alignment of HR with the overall corporate strategy.
- Enabling organizations to get the best balance of supply and demand by hiring the needed skill sets and reducing vacant positions and excesses capabilities.
- Decreasing hiring cost and the time to fill while improving the quality of hire.

▼ Interview with Art Papas, CEO, Bullhorn

Bullhorn, Inc., is a global company headquartered in Boston that provides cloud-based software for the staffing and recruiting industry.

JP Isson had the opportunity to interview Art Papas, who was named a 2014 EY Entrepreneur of the Year in New England by Ernst & Young.

Isson: How are you leveraging Big Data analytics when it comes to workforce planning such as planning resources for hard-to-fill roles?

Papas: There is a talent shortage already for some skill sets. By 2030, there will be a labor shortage across the board in almost every skilled labor category. I think about the talent pipeline not from the sourcing perspective, but rather how can I develop processes where we can bring in somebody with no education or experience in that particular field and make them successful. If you want to hire a good software developer, for instance, you will have to wait up to two years, in some cases, to find the right person with the right experience to fill that position. Or, you can hire someone and train them over the course of two years. We choose to do the latter: We hire good and talented people and then train them, optimizing our workforce planning so that we can fill a variety of current and future positions.

In order to successfully execute this strategy, you need to hire someone with the right raw intelligence and personality to fit the job. That's where psychometrics and Big Data analytics come into play. We can give high school students an aptitude test that measures their intelligence, their speed to learn, and personality traits, and map that against other employees' psychometrics that were successful at the same job. We combine our management instinct and experience with advanced analytics models that leverage the Big Data and psychometric factors to help us better optimize our workforce planning; it is not what you know, but what you can learn from it. Companies will increasingly have to take the role of educators in this new challenging labor marketplace in order to remain competitive and optimize their supply and demand equation.

We call the process of training our new employees without traditional education and experience high-potential entry-level (HPEL) hiring. This has dramatically changed our ability to attract and develop our talent. It will definitely play a big role in the future, and has already provided us with strategic insights for our succession planning as well as overall workforce planning.

Isson: Do you apply HPEL for a specific group of your employee population?

Papas: We do it across the board, from sales and finance to customer services—and it is really paying off.

Isson: What is the impact of analytics on the talent management process?

Papas: There's still so much inefficiency in hiring, especially for some roles like customer services reps or sales, where turnover can be as high as 40 percent. There are some companies that hire people and nine months later they are gone.

But you can use analytics to remediate some of this turnover. For instance, if you look at your employees who have been with you long term, you can analyze the profile of the successful and loyal employees, and, from there, identify loyalty and job performance drivers, and create some velocity. Advanced analytics helps to proactively address

(Continued)

(*continued*)

potential challenges and issues, and helps you keep and protect your most valuable asset: your employees. If you put all those triggers in a database, you can build a model that will help you to anticipate who will be loyal and perform well at the job.

JP Isson: You were named Entrepreneur of the Year in 2014. What would be your advice for employers who are looking to make their company a Best Place to Work?

Papas: I have been very fortunate to work with intelligent and great people. I am passionate about many things when it comes to building a successful company, but I will underscore two major things:

1. I am passionate about delivering the best product to our customers and passionate about delivering a great experience to our customers. I want everyone working with our customers to really care about them, so much so that our customers can feel the passion and energy we have for what we do. I want them to know that we believe in what we offer and we are genuinely here to help them.

2. I care a lot about our employees. I want them to be successful. I love seeing them develop their careers, and I strive to create an environment where people like to succeed, where they want to do a great job, where they work harder because they believe in what they do. This is what gets you ahead of the competition, and this will definitely lead to the overall recognition for your company as a great place to work.

KEY COMPONENTS OF WORKFORCE PLANNING ANALYTICS

Being able to successfully anticipate the talent gap in supply and demand of your organization requires a comprehensive assessment of the talent planning matrix and a laserlike focus on its major componentsthatinclude,butarenotlimitedto,people,data,technology, and processes.

People

People refers to resources you need to build and implement your workforce planning strategy. These resources must have the skill sets to build workforce planning models to help your organization transform its data into actionable insights. These insights will help you address your key business questions, optimize your talent requirement analysis, and provide you with a comprehensive picture of your talent supply/demand equation.

Data

Data is the foundation of analytics and represents the backbone of workforce planning analytics. By this we mean taking care of all the data available and building statistical models that will help to assess the current and future human capital needs in order to achieve business goals. There are six major categories of data critical for workforce planning analytics:

1. **Talent data:** Includes data from HR enterprise resource planning (ERP), recruitment data, turnover and retention data, engagement data, training data, performance data, preferences and attitudes data, employee satisfaction data, and succession planning and retirement data.

2. **Market data:** Refers to information such as social media data, competitive intelligence data (getting an understanding of what your competition is doing as far as managing their talent is concerned), and voice-of-candidate data (what candidates are saying about your organization).

3. **Business data:** Includes companies' key performance indicator metrics such as sales, revenue, customers, revenue per

employee, average order size, retention rate, new business, win-back count and rate, payroll data, budget compensation and benefits data, and finance ERP data.

4. **Economic and industry data:** Refers to industry benchmark data and macroeconomic data such as gross domestic product and consumer price index.

5. **Labor statistics data:** Includes labor force data, employment data, job openings, unemployment rates, payroll wages, jobless rate, quits and layoffs, population growth, and forecast.

6. **University graduation data:** Refers to graduation by discipline with a focus on hard-to-fill positions such as those in STEM fields.

Technologies and Tools

Technology plays a critical role in enabling organizations to capture, store, manage, integrate, and analyze data to determine talent shortages and excesses; it is also integral to creating an action plan to balance the right supply-and-demand equation. Analyzing the data described in the previous section requires a statistical or data science skill set that HR and business leaders championing a workforce planning project typically do not possess. Consequently, the companies we spoke with rely on technology solutions, as they provide a great return on investment (ROI) when analyzing massive business and talent data to distill actionable and predictive insights.

There are countless companies that provide workforce planning tools, and it is easy for businesspeople to get lost in all the noise. A common question we hear from talent leaders who are looking to embrace analytics is: "Where do I start?"

In the next main section, we will explore how the IMPACT Cycle introduced in the previous chapters can be used to address these important questions, but first, here is a list compiled by Newman[1] that describes eight groups of technologies to consider in workforce planning:

1. Pure plays for scenarios planning and predictive models
2. Enterprise resource planning for the management of employee data
3. Application tracking system for the management of candidate data
4. Learning management system for the management of the learning process
5. Performance management for the management of the performance process
6. Analytics for the data warehouse
7. Emerging players include entrants into the workforce planning processes
8. In-house solutions for the development of systems to facilitate individual workforce planning needs

Processes

Based on our expertise with building workforce planning models, enriched with input from the industry leaders we spoke with, the process for a scalable and efficient successful workforce planning analytics should include resources planning predictive models and leverage the business analytics IMPACT Cycle discussed in Chapter 2.

Resources Planning Predictive Models

Resources planning predictive models will leverage all the data sets discussed in the previous section and help you to anticipate your workforce behavior and changes and provide actionable insights to your workforce planning questions such as:

- What resources will your organization need in the next 2, 5, or 10 years to succeed and remain competitive?
- How many resources will be leaving your organization in the next 6, 12, 24, or 60 months?
- Who are the top performers who will be leaving for retirement?
- Who are the top performers who will be leaving to the competition?
- How many resources should you prepare for succession plans?
- How many resources will you need during the different upside and downside cycles of the economy?
- Which resources are high potentials who you should promote?
- What resources should you ready for late retirement departure?
- What skills sets should your workforce acquire to compete and win?

Predictive models already discussed in this book help to address some workforce planning questions; however, a comprehensive process for workforce planning analytics implementation is covered throughout the IMPACT Cycle redefined next.

MAKING AN IMPACT WITH WORKFORCE PLANNING ANALYTICS

To put workforce planning analytics to work, we will leverage our IMPACT Cycle. As you may recall from Chapter 2, this framework is made up of six analytics maturity stages:

1. Identify the business challenges to meet goals and objectives of the desired state.

2. Master the data to define your workforce, and conduct supply/demand and gap analyses.

3. Provide the meaning of supply/demand and gap analyses.

4. Act on the findings and recommendations.

5. Communicate the action plan.

6. Track the outcome constantly.

Identify the Business Challenge

By identifying the business challenge, we mean understanding the most pressing business goals your organization aims to achieve in the future. Focusing on these mission-critical priorities will guide the assessment of your workforce needs.

Business goals are usually defined and revisited every year and should be tied to the company's mission, vision, and strategy. For instance, a company's most pressing goals could include:

- Increase market share by 33 percent.
- Increase customer retention by 10 percent.
- Increase average order size by 27 percent.
- Increase profitability of customers by 15 percent.
- Reduce operating costs by 25 percent.
- Become the leader in your industry.

Those goals are obtained from business plan meetings with executives throughout the organization, and these meetings can also help to capture the information needed to build the competency plan, and to socialize the target objectives and desired state.

Outlining major workforce questions and assumptions that must be addressed in order to get to the desired state of human capital and the future changes is a key element to this step. These questions could include:

- What is the target time line for implementing the change?
- Would the desired state require a management change?

- Would the desired state require a new skill set from an external source or simply an internal transfer of resources between groups, locations, or functions?
- Would the desired state require a rationalization and centralization of services? For instance, analytics groups currently existing in silos but focusing on a common goal could lead to the centralization of such groups.
- What are the current employee workload productivity and employee value?
- Would the desired state require an increase or a decrease in full-time employees (FTE) or contractors?
- Would the desired state require changes in head count, qualification, diversity, or work status?
- Would the desired change create a systematic skills shortage?
- Would the desired state require hiring a new specific talent and skill set?
- Would the desired state require terminating or transferring a target function and skill set?

Being able to address these questions by leveraging the power of data analytics will provide insights into your organization's past, present, and future workforce needs. Once armed with this knowledge, you can begin to socialize your plan with the executives across your organization who will be affected by any changes.

Master the Data to Define Your Current Workforce and Perform Supply/Demand and Gap Analyses

Once you have identified the business challenges to address and major underlying business questions to answer, the next step is to gather the available data to accurately describe your current workforce situation and conduct supply/demand and gap analyses.

Pulling together workforce and business data from internal and external sources, human resources information systems (HRIS), legacy systems, and any informal data storage and market data will help you develop a more robust image of your organization's current workforce milieu. Once you have gathered this information, it is important to standardize the data coming from multiple sources in terms of format and definition, with the ultimate goal of gaining a better understanding of the current state of the workforce and establish the needs for the future state.

Describing Your Current Workforce and Building a Competency Plan

Leveraging your existing data, identify and define your current workforce by skills, positions, and functions, and then build up descriptive statistics from your data, including the creation of talent dashboards. An effective competency plan should include workforce characteristics such as:

- Job title
- Job category
- Job level
- Job status (full-time, part-time, or contractor)
- Quantity required
- Quality of hire
- Diversity
- Financial implication, cost per hire, compensation, and benefits

Performing a Supply Analysis

It is important to create a profile of your workforce to assess its state. Statistical models and tools can *and should* be used to create a profile to ensure you are capturing a comprehensive overview of your current workforce. This profile should include the current workload of your employees as well as the scope of work being performed. A robust profile will enable you to estimate which capabilities are needed for the current state, which is called an as-is state. This refers to the estimation of the current workforce supply and future need, and represents the supply side of the supply/demand equation.

To create a target profile (a profile based on job function) of your current workforce, consider each of the following six layers of analytics:

1. Put together a dashboard of each job function, including job category, job level, grade, head count, gender, and job status (FTE versus non-FTE).

2. Profile each job function based on variables such as job title, job level, job category, education, grades, performance rating, qualification, certification, tenure, age, race, gender, job status (FTE versus non-FTE, internal, transition, external hire), benefits and compensation, turnover, top performers, low performers, median, and length of service (LOS).

3. Build up a comprehensive analysis of sick leave, absence, and family leave by job function and then profile by demographic and performance rating data, LOS, job grade, location, and occupation.

4. Factor in environmental considerations such as lateness correlating with lengthy commute times or work by job function.

5. Analyze historical workforce acquisition, turnover, and retention data. Acquisition data should be profiled by the same aforementioned variables and should also include sources of talent acquisition: online and offline social media, headhunting, referral, career fair, or university.

6. Determine strengths and weaknesses, risks, and gaps based on your supply analysis.

Turnover Analysis

There are two types of turnover—voluntary and involuntary.

Voluntary Turnover

The three main types of voluntary employee turnover are retirement turnover, promotion turnover, and employer change turnover. To gain insights into voluntary turnover, data should be profiled based on these categories:

- Understanding the reason for leaving
- Destination
- Correlation between turnover and acquisition channel
- Turnover by grade and performance
- Turnover by demographics for each job function

Based on statistical models, identify your existing employees who are at risk of leaving as well as the likely reason for leaving and the potential date.

Involuntary Turnover
Involuntary turnover should also be analyzed by demographics, company performance, and external factors such as economic upturn and downturn, performance issues, and acquisition channel and cost.

Hard-to-Fill Position Analysis

In this competitive talent market and skills shortage, special attention should be given to understanding hard-to-fill positions and vacancies. This requires a profile for each employee segment that includes demographics, performance rating data, length of service, grade, location, and occupation. An overview of attrition risks is also important to include in the profile. Once you have pulled together this information, set up meetings to validate your estimates and findings with key stakeholders across the organization.

Perform Your Supply/Demand and Gap Analyses and Forecast the Future Supply of Talent

At this stage advanced analytics are used to identify your future workforce demand by building a target profile based on the same variables you used to define your current profile. You can then apply statistical models to analyze historical data and current profiles, and determine future needs and trends. Forecasting the future supply is about calculating the difference between your existing supply (internal workforce) and your estimated demand, which will also help you assess capabilities by job function and determine where there will be a shortage (deficit) or excess (surplus).

Key information to look at for this assessment includes:

- Current workforce profile by head count.
- Turnovers (voluntary, involuntary, retirement, sick leave, family leave, and other).
- Differential (supply and demand).
- Assessment of the as-is state and the to-be state to evaluate the supply/demand balance.

It is important to conduct a gap analysis on the current and future supply/demand workforce needs.

Provide Meaning

Once you have conducted supply/demand and gap analyses leveraging advanced analytics, it is important to provide context, meaning, and business recommendations based on the findings. This includes:

- A clear definition of the workforce scenario for specific key roles that uses statistical models and tools to paint a clear picture for stakeholders.
- Running scenarios against required head counts.
- Building statistical models to analyze and understand workload by target workforce and gain insight into work performed.
- Building supply/demand analysis of workload and current and future states to ascertain demand and supply.
- Identification of strengths, weaknesses, risks, and gaps.
- Determination of whether the analyses result in surpluses or shortages of critical staff who are required to meet business goals and objectives.
- Identification of what skills are needed to accomplish the workload.

Action Plan

After gathering the data and performing the supply/demand and gap analyses, it is important to put together an action plan that enables you to:

- Develop a gap plan from the gap analysis of current and future supply and demand.
- Identify future demand from workload.
- Identify workforce objectives and development strategies leveraging historical trends and data.

This stage is about putting an action plan together to proactively address the outcomes of the supply and demand analysis. The final outcome is that the analysis can flag any potential staffing shortages or redundancies that might require an organization to take action in order to meet its business goals and objectives and maintain a balanced workforce. The ultimate goal of an action plan is to ensure a sustainable supply-and-demand balance that is critical for success.

Staffing Shortages

If your gap analysis reveals insufficient staffing, new acquisitions have to take place. It is important to keep in mind the profile variable for each job function where new talent acquisition is required. That profile will provide ownership and guiding principles to help ensure that the right talent is hired for the right role. These considerations include job category, location, occupation, and grade, and will steer you toward the proper recruitment channels for attracting ideal external candidates.

Excesses

The action plan for a surplus of staff is typically a reduction of the workforce or an organizational restructuring exercise to meet the new demand level for each job function. These actions will ultimately help your company achieve excellence in delivering on mission-critical business goals with optimal resources.

Before proceeding to a workforce reduction, it's important to evaluate alternatives and revisit the following:

- Could surplus employees be redeployed or transferred to other functions or groups?
- Can you leverage early retirements and avoid reducing workforce from an age segment that could deliver long-term growth?
- What is the best timing for the reorganization process to take place—before a holiday, after a holiday, or in the new year to ensure you limit the negative impact on employee morale? The time line should be clear and short to limit uncertainty.
- What promotions or demotions will be taking place?
- What would be the transition plan of the terminated employees?
- With regard to compensation and benefits severances, consider long-term analysis versus short- and medium-term goals.
- How can you ensure continuing optimal service and delivery after workforce reduction?

Communicate the Strategy

When it comes to important decisions about workforce strategy, transparency is best. Good communication from executive leadership teams to employees will map back to the insights derived from planning analytics and will focus on a detailed time line and phased approach that includes:

- Readiness of the organization to implement the change
- Change champions or leaders (for instance, who will champion the process?)
- Training of people
- Change management
- Change experts
- User experience

- Tool and technologies that will be used
- Metrics to track success
- Channels to gather ongoing feedback

Track the Outcome

Measuring the success and monitoring areas of future opportunity in workforce planning require the continual evaluation of the process and profiles and how any changes impact assumptions and results. It is also important that you ensure that any projected changes that will affect the workforce planning assumptions are in line with the top business goals and are fed into the supply/demand findings and recommendations. Without a periodic check-in, the equation could become unbalanced and the data insights inaccurate.

Additionally, any changes made to the action plan should be reflected in the supply/demand plan. It requires constantly capturing feedback and measuring before and after states, as well as the overall ROI in terms of savings in talent acquisition, retention, and development costs. Your tracking should also consist of evaluating the contributions of new staff against the target goal, assessing how far away or close supply/demand action is to impacting the bottom line.

Companies that successfully implement workforce analytics have clear owners to monitor change and keep the larger team apprised with regular meetings to track projections against actuals, ensure they are on track for achieving expected results, and alert stakeholders of any dramatic changes or red flags. Analytics is a dynamic process, and it needs to be monitored consistently in order to detect and track changes that could derail the action plan from the target trajectory.

Many leading companies are using workforce planning analytics to drive positive business outcomes. The following are brief examples of how an organization can leverage data to achieve great results.

DOW CHEMICAL

Dow Chemical is a great example of workforce planning analytics in action. In *Strategy+Business*,[2] Vinay Couto, Frank Ribeiro, and Andrew Tipping wrote an article titled "It Makes Sense to Adjust." The authors describe how Dow Chemical has evolved its workforce over the past decade, mining historical data on its 40,000 employees to anticipate workforce needs throughout the chemical industry's recurrent seven–year cycle of volatility. To account for that volatility with minimal stress on its employee base, Dow needed a workforce planning strategy that was more rigorously quantitative and long-term. The company mined three years of historical data to forecast promotion rates, internal transfers, and overall workforce supply, and then designed a custom modeling tool called the Dow Strategic Staffing Simulator to project workforce needs versus resource availability three years in advance. The tool produces a snapshot of the current workforce segmented by 5 age groups and 10 job levels and then forecasts what the workforce will look like based on historical trends. Based on each business's plan and productivity target, Dow was able to project the head count needed for each business unit.

These detailed predictions were aggregated to yield workforce projections for the entire company. Dow was able to engage in "what if?" scenario planning, altering assumptions based on internal variables such as staff promotions and external variables such as political and legal considerations. As a result, Dow's HR department was better able to plan for various eventualities, including changing head count targets, facility closures, and anticipated volatility in the chemical industry's fortunes.

BLACK HILLS CORPORATION

According to the *Harvard Business Review*,[3] Black Hills Corporation is one of *those* companies. A 130-year-old energy conglomerate, Black Hills doubled its workforce to about 2,000 employees after an acquisition. Like many energy companies, a combination of challenges—an aging workforce, the need for specialized skills, and a lengthy time line for getting employees to full competence—created a significant talent risk. In fact, forecasts showed that within five years, the firm stood to lose 8,063 years of experience from attrition and a retiring workforce.

To prevent a massive turnover catastrophe, the company used workforce analytics to calculate how many employees would retire per year, the types of talent needed to replace them, and where those new hires were most likely to come from. The result was a workforce planning summit that categorized and prioritized 89 action plans designed to address the organization's potential talent shortage.

PROFILE

Interview with Christophe Paris, Human Resources Business Intelligence Manager, Société de Transport de Montréal

Société de Transport de Montréal (STM), or the Montreal Transit Corporation, is a public transport agency that operates transit bus and rapid transit services in Montreal, Canada. STM has more than 9,500 employees with an average daily ridership of 2.5 million passengers.

JP Isson had the opportunity to interview Christophe Paris and his team members Josée Gauvreau and Cedric Lepine to discuss how they have been leveraging data analytics in human resources management, such as workforce planning at STM.

Isson: Why did STM decide to invest in workforce planning analytics?

Paris and team: It all started a few years ago when our CEO came to us with a specific set of business questions, including:

- What is the business value of the human resources department?
- Are we making the right business decisions?
- How many employees we will need in the future to deliver optimal service to our customers?

(Continued)

(Continued)

- What critical roles will we need in the future?
- Can we predict our employees' turnover?

We then realized that we didn't have enough insights to answer his questions. And this was really the overarching point from which our People Analytics journey started. We knew that we absolutely had to look into our databases to find out what talent data or information we had available, and we started analyzing and interpreting our employee data. That was the starting point of our People Analytics.

Isson: What type of analytics did you use, and what were the benefits for your company?

Paris and team: We started to build HR dashboards, HR key performance indicators (KPIs), and HR scorecards. We also started doing some deep-dive analyses of our employees by occupational category, by experience, by profile, and by skill set. The analysis by critical roles was important because there are some critical roles that pertain to really hard-to-fill positions and some that do not. So having that segmentation approach helped us to prioritize based on our company's business goals and the market conditions.

We were able to provide a diagnosis of our employee population and start addressing questions such as:

- Where is our talent mix?
- At what stage is our talent in the overall talent life cycle?
- When will our employees leave for retirement?
- How will our talent behave in the future? (Will they leave? Change jobs? Continue working despite retirement?)
- When will they formally leave?
- How many will leave at the retirement time? How many will formally retire in the next 3, 5, or 10 years?

To answer the aforementioned questions, we were lucky enough to have a lot of employee data and information from the get-go. It was information that we collected and used to report on and communicate for legal purposes and transparency.

We started by looking at some correlations analyses. We were wondering if there was a significant correlation relationship between some of our employee data and our key business challenges. We then explored hundreds of variables and found out that the number of kilometers traveled was highly correlated with the number of resources. And the correlation was pretty high, about 96 percent.

We explored the relationship between the variation in the amount of employee overtime and the number of kilometers traveled by a bus or subway driver, and found that there was a strong correlation. Based on the correlation, we then built a predictive model. This helped us to determine how many people we needed to deliver service and keep our level of productivity and customer satisfaction high. The model helped us to determine how many resources we would need by occupational category, skill set, and experience.

The findings also provided our senior management team with actionable insights for their strategic planning, and were of tremendous value for our overall workforce planning. They also helped us with our recruitment strategies, as we were able to identify how many new employees we needed in the future for each functional group, as well as:

- How many employees we would need to replace due to retirement.
- How many employees we would need to add due to our service expansion (when servicing more territory and more people).
- How many resources we would need due to macroeconomic conditions and company business plan.

The overall correlations and predictive model were driven by the exploration of 10 major factors, such as overall spend, the number of drivers, the number of resources, the number of customers who commute, the overall traffic patterns, and so forth.

We then created a second predictive model called the "retirement predictive model," which we built to help us to anticipate when our employees will leave for retirement. This model helped us to identify which of our employees were candidates for retirement and who exactly will

(Continued)

(Continued)

leave on their retirement date. It also helped us identify employees who are more likely to continue working for an additional three to six years.

In the upcoming year, we will have nearly 2,000 people qualifying for retirement, so as an operational business, it is paramount for us to anticipate which employees will leave and when. With this in mind, we built a model for each category of occupation, from managers and support and maintenance staffs to bus and subway drivers and auto mechanics. The key learning from these models was that there is no single, one-size-fits-all People Analytics model. We needed to go local—by category of occupation, critical roles, and experience.

Additionally, there is about a 20 to 30 percent group of employees who, even if they qualify for retirement, can and will still continue to work three to five years later. To understand this employee segment, we were able to build retirement curves and models to anticipate what is coming and get ready by putting proactive strategies in place to mitigate the risk.

Isson: Did you use any specific tools to build your models?

Paris and team: The beauty of this project was that everything we leveraged was from our internal HRIS [human resources information system] and Microsoft Excel spreadsheet data. So, for a company like STM that is very operational and business driven, having a fast turnaround and leveraging low-cost software was very well received. It also helped us to quickly showcase the value; for instance, our employee retirement predictive model immediately helped us to anticipate and plan for the future.

The power of the models we developed was based on the fact that we could analyze data at a category level, as well as an employee level. This enabled us to develop macro and micro strategies when approaching our employees, and talent acquisition and retention strategies. It also enables us to understand our workforce planning from employee segments to the individual level.

Isson: Were you able to provide employee retirement breakdowns by vertical?

Paris and team: We are now able to provide future employee retirement figures by occupation, by location, and by skill set. We can predict and indicate which employees might leave in the next three, four, or five years. This helps the business to figure out how to best bridge the resource gap and continue delivering high-quality service without impacting operations.

We were able to deliver solid, easy-to-understand data, and we challenged the old adage about HR not being data driven. We are gradually changing that every day with the work we do. We were able to wow our customers, which is great, and we did this by building up our data intelligence and sharing it with senior management, as well as with all our hiring managers to ensure they have all the insights they need to proactively take action. This helped us to anticipate what trends are coming, how many resources we will need to hire, train, and onboard, and, more importantly, to become true strategic business partners within the company.

Isson: What would be your advice to someone new to workforce planning analytics?

Paris and team: It's paramount to understand the top business questions the company aims to address. For our company, it was retirement planning and workforce planning. It is imperative to keep your business question in mind when you build HR scorecards or dashboards so the business value can be easily connected to the data.

From the data perspective, you have to look at what you already have available; for instance, what data is easily accessible, available, and good? Data integrity, data visualization, and storytelling using this information should be front and center, as it will be the way you communicate the findings and success criteria for your analysis. You have to wow your customers, both internal and external. And it's important to remember that you don't have to share all pieces of data you've found. You have to keep it simple, make it easy to understand, and just keep to the most relevant data that helps you to convey the message and key findings. And, most of all, keep in mind that workforce planning analytics is a journey; it takes baby steps and is a matter of testing, learning, and sharing. Your input and insights will provide the business with valuable foresight, helping the organization anticipate talent behavior and help your HR team to become real strategic business partners.

WORKFORCE PLANNING ANALYTICS BEST PRACTICES: DOS AND DON'TS

Based on conversations with leading companies that have successfully put workforce planning analytics into action, the following are key best practices:

- Start small with a focus on a target segment of the workforce to address; the target workforce could be a group of key positions and roles.

- Tie your actions to your business plan with cost-benefit data at the forefront for your discussions with business leaders.

- Link workforce planning and your financial metrics, and align HR strategies with business goals.

- Get buy-in from senior management because their support is paramount to ensure successful building and implementation of the planning across the organization.

- Create a culture of excellence and continually monitor and reevaluate the impact of workforce changes.

- Start by putting together a profile of the target workforce to focus on.

- Keep your focus on critical roles and priorities. Don't get lost in the sea of data and analytics.

- Leverage your findings to create career paths and development plans that will fill future workforce needs organically (internal transition training).

- Be inclusive and collaborative by including all executives across the organization to socialize your plan and avoid missteps. HR should be the key partner to drive this change.

- Be consistent with metrics definition. Standardize metrics definitions used in business planning and workforce planning.

- Put together the right balance of time and resources between planning and implementation to ensure you will have enough resources to implement successfully.

- Start with the low-hanging fruit when hiring. Don't get stalled with hard-to-fill positions.

- Validate every assumption and finding with business partners across the organization as you learn and build up the plan.
- Leverage the IMPACT Cycle to understand the composition of your organization's past, present, and future needs.

KEY TAKEAWAYS

- Workforce planning analytics helps organizations to identify the target segment of employees required to achieve business goals and business objectives.
- To be successful, workforce analytics should be tied to your business plan and strategy, and include all executives of the organization in its buildup phases in order to successfully align the workforce planning cycle with the strategic planning cycle.
- It is critical to interview senior executives and business leaders to gain their buy-in and ensure that they understand the importance and value of the workforce planning exercise.
- Strategic workforce planning helps organizations reduce human capital costs from talent acquisition, talent development, and talent retention expenses.
- Workforce planning is critical for a company's long-term success as it helps to plan for succession and optimize the staff's capabilities by maintaining the best talent balances between excesses and shortages.
- Workforce analytics drives the allocation of talent investment and aligns HR with the overall corporate strategy.
- It enables organizations to get the best balance of supply and demand by hiring the needed skill sets while reducing vacant positions and excess capabilities.

NOTES

1. Madeline Laurano, *The Modern Approach to Workforce Planning: Best Practices in Today's Economy*, Bersin and Associates, 2009, http://fm.sap.com/data/upload/files/the_modern_approach_to_workforce_planning.pdf.
2. Vinay Couto, Frank Ribeiro, and Andrew Tipping, "It Makes Sense to Adjust," http://www.strategy-business.com/article/10213?gko=9e329.
3. *Harvard Business Review*, "Change Your Company with Better HR Analytics," https://hbr.org/2013/12/change-your-company-with-better-hr-analytics/.

CHAPTER 5

Talent Sourcing Analytics

And there is no trade or employment but the young man following it may become a hero.

—Walt Whitman

THE BUSINESS CASE FOR TALENT SOURCING TODAY

Workforce represents the most valuable asset of any organization and defines its ability to drive performance and innovation. To achieve its success in today's marketplace, your organization needs to find the right talent, at the right time, and through the right channel.

We are in the age of technology where the key to an organization's recruiting success lies in its ability to adapt, evolve, innovate, and stay relevant. Today, that means integrating social media, Big Data solutions, mobile cloud services, and marketing tools into the overall sourcing strategy.

Defining Talent Sourcing Today

Talent sourcing is the first stage in the talent acquisition process and is one of the most important phases in talent life cycle management. We define talent sourcing today as the practice of identifying and uncovering job candidates, passive or active, through the use of online and offline recruitment techniques. This can occur through a variety of recruitment channels, which can include (but are not limited to) employee referral programs, social media platforms, talent communities, resume databases, search engine optimization (SEO), agency/third-party recruiters, job boards, niche sites, corporate sites, universities and alumni groups, billboards, and print advertisements (see Figure 5.1).

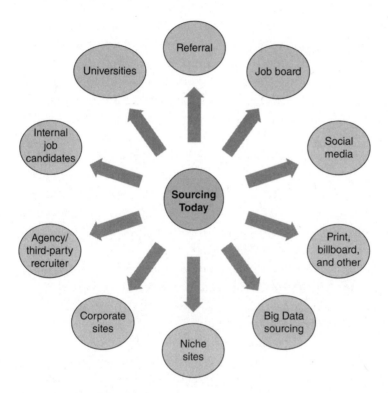

Figure 5.1 Talent Sourcing Today

For most organizations, this initial step of the talent acquisition process is handled by internal recruiters or sourcers, contracted agencies, or a dedicated sourcing resource. The sourcing stage covered here begins with the candidate's discovery and ends when all the information about the potential candidate is obtained by the sourcer.

A Short History of Talent Sourcing

Before we get into the process of talent sourcing, let's take a quick look at its historical roots. Sourcing dates back to the Roman Empire when in 55 B.C. Julius Caesar leveraged a referral program to staff his army, asking his current soldiers to refer their friends in exchange for financial compensation. These types of referral programs were also used throughout ancient Egypt and Greece. Not surprisingly, talent sourcing has evolved since then, and for the scope of this book, we will underscore the five most important changes.

The first major disruption in sourcing occurred in 1800 during Napoleon's reign when the French and the British were using employment services to recruit for their empires. As a result, in 1848 the first search firm was created.[1]

The second major change in sourcing took place during World War I and World War II with the practice of screening candidates for positions in war planning. And, in 1939, the U.S. Employment Services was created with the primary goal of helping unemployed people find jobs during the war. Employment agencies began to advertise for workers who were not obligated to military service in an effort to fill the void in the workplace left by those who were called to duty.

The third major disruption in sourcing took place in the 1990s with the emergence of the World Wide Web, where sending resumes via e-mail become the norm with the birth of online job boards and resume databases available and accessible to candidates and employers worldwide. The resume (as we know it) was actually born nearly a decade earlier in 1980, when recruitment technology was still fairly nascent with sourcing predominantly conducted via word of mouth, referrals, and walk-in applications resulting from printed media. As a result of improved technology, such as the typewriter, WordPerfect, and later the launch of Microsoft Word, resume formats started to become more standardized.

Having a more standardized format enabled an entrepreneur like Bill Warren to found the Online Career Center in 1992. It was the first employment site on the Internet. The idea quickly caught on, and in April 1994, Jeff Taylor created Monster Board, which later became Monster Worldwide. Monster was the first public job board on the Internet, the first public resume database in the world, and the first company to have job search functionalities, job agents, and job alerts. In May 1994, Career Mosaic was founded, which was later acquired by Career Builder.

The fourth major sourcing change occurred during Y2K. The year 2000 marked a revolution for the Internet, with the emergence of online personal branding, weblogs, resume websites, and resume videos. The influx of these different assets changed the landscape of recruitment and technology such as candidate relationship management (CRM) systems and applicant tracking systems (ATSs) entered the marketplace.

Interestingly enough, we are still experiencing **the fifth major disruption** in sourcing. It is one directly born from the emergence of personal branding and is tied to SEO and social media networks, which have become the de facto new standard. As candidates seek to distinguish themselves from the competition through personalized content creation, they are flooding the Internet with information. This has created the need for Big Data and cloud-based solutions that aggregate candidates' digital footprints from wherever they interact on the web. This expands the recruitment universe to include both active and passive candidates leveraging social media platforms, niche sites, user and alumni groups, Google+, Twitter, LinkedIn, and other open-source community forums such as GitHub, Stack Overflow, Dribbble, and Proformative, just to name a few.

In order to successfully source talent in this day and age, a new mantra is required. Jeanne Meister, Founding Partner of Future Workplace, suggests using a different approach in her *Forbes* article "2014: The Year Social HR Matters," in the subsection "Big Data Lets New Jobs Find You Before You Even Know You're Looking": "for this group of talents, social network aggregators, social profile solutions providers such as Entelo, TalentBin by Monster, Gild, thesocialCV, and others could be leveraged to better help recruiters to tap into this pool of talents."[2]

WHY YOU NEED TO CARE ABOUT YOUR TALENT SOURCING TODAY

There are two main reasons that you need to pay special attention to your talent sourcing today:

1. The digital evolution of the workforce
2. The challenges of the new labor market ecosystem

Digital Evolution of the Workforce

Over the past few decades, talent sourcing has undergone two major digital changes. The first was the emergence of the Internet and World Wide Web in the late 1990s, which revolutionized the search for candidates from paper and pencil to online channels such as job boards, as well as internal and external online resume databases used to generate massive amounts of data to uncover the best candidates.

The second major change in candidate sourcing was driven by the consortium of four components: Big Data, the cloud, social media, and mobile solutions. These elements have created the latest disruption in candidate sourcing and have resulted in a digital evolution that has produced an ocean of data to be analyzed.

New Labor Force Ecosystem Challenges

On top of this digital disruption, today's hiring managers, HR staff, recruiters, and staffing managers face new challenges, including:

- **Imbalanced workforce demographics:** This is forcing companies to manage a disparate multigenerational workforce that includes baby boomers, Generation Xers, and millennials—three generations with a wide variance in needs, preferences, and expectations. Millennials, in particular, will make up more than 50 percent of the U.S. workforce by 2020, and require special attention for talent acquisition and retention.[3] After more than 100 years of its traditional annual performance review where the bottom 10 percent of underperformers were let go every year, General Electric (GE), the eighth highest-ranking company in the Fortune 500, is getting rid of annual performance reviews in favor of app-based feedback. GE announced recently that it is replacing the old annual performance review with an app—an app that will provide regular feedback several times a year to adapt to its new workforce demographics that includes a significant population of millennials.

- **Skills shortage:** Companies face increasing competition for highly skilled workers in fields such as science, technology, engineering, and mathematics (STEM). According to the latest

ManpowerGroup study, a skills shortage is the number one challenge for companies.[4]

- **Candidate savviness:** Candidates are more connected and technology savvy; they can learn about your organization and praise or criticize your employer brand without talking to you or your customer service reps, and without stepping foot through your door.

- **A candidate-driven labor market:** The U.S. economy is strengthening, as evidenced by the rapid pace of job additions and the unemployment rate plummeting as low as 2.9 percent for bachelor graduates.[5] The power in recruitment has shifted from employers to the job seekers, as they have several choices and job opportunities. In fact, according to the latest study by MRINetwork, more than 9 in 10 MRINetwork recruiters participating in the semiannual June 2015 survey (MRINetwork Recruiter Sentiment Study) said today's employment market is candidate-driven, a 34-point jump from the 2012 study results.[6] It is clear we are now in a job-seeker-driven market, as opposed to the employer-driven market following the 2008 recession.

These aforementioned changes are challenging organizations to rethink and adjust the way they look for talent, whether it is via employee referral programs, social networking, employment marketing branding, talent communities, or job boards.

The Sourcing Analytics pillar explores the history of talent sourcing and its digital transformation, and provides a comprehensive review of the job seeker's decision journey so that you can best approach the talent supply chain in this new and evolving candidate-driven ecosystem. It outlines how leading companies have leveraged analytics in their sourcing activities in order to optimize outcomes and reduce their acquisition costs in this competitive and challenging recruitment landscape.

This chapter will also provide you with best practices to ensure that your talent sourcing activities, whether they are referrals from mobile, social media platforms, from job boards, or by leveraging Big Data, will flourish and help you create economic value for your organization.

TALENT SOURCING IN THE ERA OF BIG DATA AND ADVANCED TECHNOLOGY

Whether you decide to talent source to fulfill your workforce planning analytics strategy or to fill open requisitions, it is essential to understand the decision journey of your ideal candidates, the ecosystem of sourcing channels you have, and how to leverage the new generation of sourcing in the era of Big Data, mobile and cloud solutions, and social media to be successful in your search for talent.

Job Seeker Decision Journey

During the latest recession, it took only two years to shed 8.5 million jobs, but took 4.5 years to recover those jobs in the United States, with 2014 registering the largest job creation since 1999. As we discussed, the power is now shifting into candidates' hands as the majority of economic outlooks predict that employment in the United States is trending back to full capacity. With unemployment numbers plummeting to the prerecession level, turnovers high, and job openings at their highest, skilled employees have multiple choices and the war for talent is intensifying.

From Figure 5.2, the unemployment rate for those with a bachelor's degree or higher was 2.5 percent in September 2015 while for those with some college or an associate's degree it was 4.3 percent.

In this new labor market ecosystem where skilled candidates are in high demand and can decide for whom they work with a single click, employers need to change their recruiting tools, strategies, and approaches to maximize their interactions with prospective candidates to successfully navigate throughout today's supply-and-demand talent equation.

With multiple options, job candidates will no longer tolerate the shortcomings and bad recruiting practices that they endured during the recession and the recovery period.

To remain successful, companies must understand today's job seekers' needs, preferences, and decision factors. Organizations must perform rigorous competitive intelligence to gain the full scope of what the competition is offering, and use these insights to build

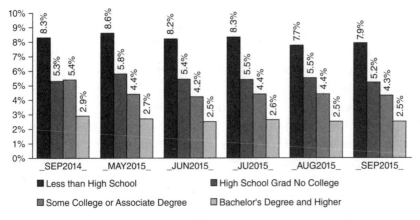

Figure 5.2 Unemployment Rate by Educational Attainment
Data from U.S. Department of Labor, Bureau of Labor Statistics.

a marketing sourcing strategy that will best appeal to job seekers. Once your organization has this information and intelligence, you can begin to approach job seekers in a way that resonates with them, reaching out to them where they are and, more important, finding those with high-demand skills before they even know they are looking for a new job.

Before deciding on the optimal channel for reaching your candidates, it is important to understand the journey your seeker will take when she or he decides to look for new opportunities. This will help you optimize the way you communicate with a candidate.

Before we tackle our Seeker Decision Journey (SDJ), let's discuss the Consumer Marketing Decision Journey, which we will use to derive the principal elements of our SDJ. The management consulting firm McKinsey & Company produced its consumer decision journey as a revision of the traditional consumer buying funnel.[7] The final action for a consumer through the funnel occurs when the person makes the purchase, while for job candidates it will happen when a seeker applies to your job posting or accepts your job offer.

Lessons from McKinsey's Consumer Decision Journey

With today's evolving socioeconomic conditions, advances in digital platforms have changed the way consumers buy products and services.

They research very differently today than before, challenging marketers to rethink the ways they approach them. As mentioned, the traditional marketing buying funnel begins with consumer awareness and ends at the moment of purchase or the postpurchase experience was enhanced by McKinsey & Company.

In 2009, this process was revised by David Court, Dave Elzinga, Susan Mulder, and Ole Jørgen Vetvik in their article that included a dynamic decision-making process called "the consumer decision journey," as described in Figure 5.3.

McKinsey's consumer decision journey is made up of the following stages:[8]

1. Initial consideration
2. Active evaluation (information gathering)

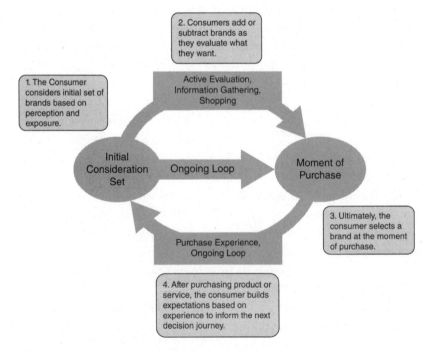

Figure 5.3 Consumer Decision Journey
Source: David Court, Dave Elzinga, Susan Mulder, and Ole Jørgen Vetvik, "The Consumer Decision Journey," McKinsey Quarterly, June 2009, www.mckinsey.com/insights/marketing_sales/the_consumer_decision_journey.

3. Moment of purchase

4. Postpurchase experience (ongoing exposure, loyalty)

As you can imagine, for recruiters the final "postpurchase" stage is critical because if your employees have bought into your value proposition and are bonded with your employer brand, they will be the best advocates: promoting your company values and helping attract new talent by delivering testimonials and firsthand experiences to potential candidates via all your sourcing channels.

The SDJ is based on the same theories we just discussed in McKinsey's consumer decision journey; we will simply replace the word *consumer* with the word *seeker*, and adapt the framework to be relevant to the employment market.

Leveraging the SDJ provides hiring managers and recruiters with a comprehensive map of seeker online and offline behaviors that can be used when interacting with them throughout their journey via the various touch points we discussed earlier. It provides relevant information on how to attract, hire, and retain top talent and ultimately best practices on how to leverage your existing talent as your most important advocates to attract new candidates.

In Figure 5.4, we will leverage the consumer decision journey to derive the SDJ by mapping the seeker's behavior at each stage of the consumer decision journey. It is just about mapping human behavior: whether they click, buy, vote, or respond.

This chart can be used as a guide for better targeting seekers in this new ecosystem. Let's take a closer look at each of these stages and what it will mean for your company.

Stage 1: Why Is a Candidate Looking for a Job?

The Initial Consideration or Evaluation stage is designed to uncover the job-seeking motivation behind your potential candidates. It will provide answers to key elements that should help you optimize your recruitment strategies, tailor your sourcing activities, and seize the right opportunity to connect with a candidate when he or she is beginning to consider a career move.

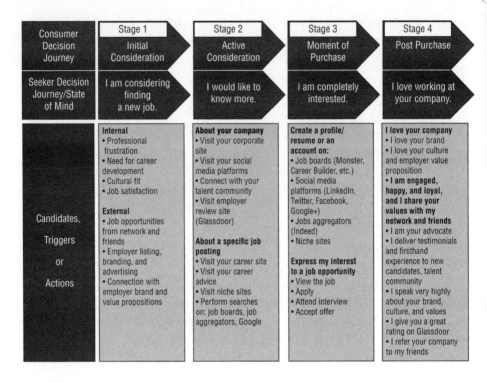

Consumer Decision Journey	Stage 1 Initial Consideration	Stage 2 Active Consideration	Stage 3 Moment of Purchase	Stage 4 Post Purchase
Seeker Decision Journey/State of Mind	I am considering finding a new job.	I would like to know more.	I am completely interested.	I love working at your company.
Candidates, Triggers or Actions	**Internal** • Professional frustration • Need for career development • Cultural fit • Job satisfaction **External** • Job opportunities from network and friends • Employer listing, branding, and advertising • Connection with employer brand and value propositions	**About your company** • Visit your corporate site • Visit your social media platforms • Connect with your talent community • Visit employer review site (Glassdoor) **About a specific job posting** • Visit your career site • Visit your career advice • Visit niche sites • Perform searches on: job boards, job aggregators, Google	**Create a profile/ resume or an account on:** • Job boards (Monster, Career Builder, etc.) • Social media platforms (LinkedIn, Twitter, Facebook, Google+) • Jobs aggregators (Indeed) • Niche sites **Express my interest to a job opportunity** • View the job • Apply • Attend interview • Accept offer	**I love your company** • I love your brand • I love your culture and employer value proposition • **I am engaged, happy, and loyal, and I share your values with my network and friends** • I am your advocate • I deliver testimonials and firsthand experience to new candidates, talent community • I speak very highly about your brand, culture, and values • I give you a great rating on Glassdoor • I refer your company to my friends

Figure 5.4 From Consumer Decision Journey to Seeker Decision Journey

Stage 2: Where Do Candidates Turn When Seeking New Opportunities?

This phase, called the Active Consideration, Evaluation, or Knowledge stage, is when candidates begin to interact with brands and companies that interest them. The key to this stage is finding the right channel in which to interact with them. What are their "watering holes"? What sites do they frequent? From there, focus your approach by listening, connecting, and engaging with them about current and future job opportunities.

Stage 3: How Will a Candidate Respond to Your Recruitment Process?

This stage will force you to consider the process your candidates will go through as they consider, apply, interview, and, one hopes, accept your job offer. It begins with making sure your organization is equipped with the most current tools and technologies that enable a user-friendly job response process for interested candidates.

Stage 4: How Do You Get Your New Hires Engaged and Have Them Become Brand Advocates?

Building a relationship with your current employee base is key to recruiting top talent. This stage is dedicated to connecting with your existing talent so they become your best advocates in attracting and hiring new talent. One way to do this is through employee referral programs and communities.

Once you understand the decision journey of the candidate, it is important to get a clear picture of the sources of hire (SOH)—basically, where your best prospective employees should be coming from. Several researchers provide insights on the sources of hire. Figure 5.5, the annual SOH report compiled by CareerXroads, shows the major sources of hire.

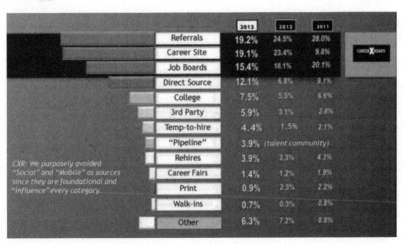

Figure 5.5 Source of Hire Report
Source: Gerry Crispin, www.careerxroads.com/news/2014_SourceOfHire.pdf.

Interview with Gerry Crispin, Principal and Cofounder, CareerXroads

JP Isson had the opportunity to interview Gerry Crispin to discuss talent sourcing, employer branding, employee wellness, and the impact that Big Data and social media have on talent acquisition.

Isson: What are the top three sources of hire that talent acquisition should pay attention to?

Crispin: There hasn't been a lot of change when we talk about the sources of hire, and the following always top the list:

1. Internal recruiting
2. Employer recruiting
3. Job boards

Social media and mobility also play a role, even if I do not categorize them as a pure source of hire. I'd consider them more as a path, not a source. However, they are paramount for any of the aforementioned sources of hire. Today, every candidate being hired is using social media, which means you can't do hiring without taking it into account. They enable affordable sourcing in today's economy—it is digital energy instead of live energy. We are also using some sort of artificial intelligence to interview people. Every person who applies has an interview with a virtual agent that uses artificial intelligence that can ask questions and vet candidates based upon their answers. Technology is redefining the talent acquisition work flow.

Isson: What is the impact of employee wellness on talent sourcing and talent acquisition?

Crispin: Talent acquisition has changed enormously in the last 10 to 20 years and continues to grow in a number of ways. One of them is the importance of corporation branding; in other words, what is employment like at a certain company? In that instance, what we are talking about are companies that have adopted employee wellness as a critical component of their value proposition that helps them to drive results: increased productivity, optimization of talent acquisition, and increased talent retention.

Fundamentally, you want to bring in people who are already predisposed (to the extent possible) to valuing employee wellness, and who see it as a value and fundamental part of their work. Talent acquisition strategy these days can include marketing your wellness program in your job requisition, which ensures interested candidates understand this is a shared value between them and your organization; and those who place very little value on wellness will realize that this is not a place for them.

Employee branding can also help as a selection tool for candidates, demonstrating that employee wellness programs are important. To this end, your wellness program should be well positioned on the company website and can include things such as videos of employees promoting different aspects of the program, and showing wellness as part of the company culture and company values. This type of promotion can be a great way for companies to provide an overview of their organization to potential candidates so before they apply for a job they already have an understanding of how employee wellness could impact their day-to-day activities.

Additionally, there should be a mechanism that enables talent acquisition to provide candidates with the opportunities to ask questions and engage with the company. Transparency is critical, and showing how employee wellness could improve productivity, for instance, can help to engage employees early on, so they are already predisposed to the idea that their company is one that values wellness.

Isson: The economy has been improving in the United States, and the labor market is becoming more and more candidate driven. What do you see as a major challenge for talent acquisition and retention?

Crispin: I think talent acquisition and talent retention is a challenge in a candidate-driven labor market. In most companies, there is a small

(Continued)

(*Continued*)

percentage of jobs that are considered business critical, and for those jobs, there is a shortage of talent. When this talent shortage exists, there is a constant pressure to keep those employees from being drawn away, particularly if they are customer facing or hold extraordinary value for the corporation. Keeping employees is an important strategy, and forward-looking companies are doing everything they can to keep their talent.

Talent acquisition and retention have to do with whether people believe they have the opportunity to fully use their skills and knowledge. They want to come to work and be treated well, live some of their values that they believe in, and this includes things such as contributing to their communities, improving their health and wellness, having flexibility in their work environment, and corporate transparency.

Isson: Do you think Big Data can help to acquire some hard-to-find talent such as for STEM jobs?

Crispin: I think the biggest problem with Big Data right now is much of the data is not available as we would like to believe. I believe accessing some publicly available talent data and content could definitely affect our ability to reach out to passive seekers. There are a number of tools and Big Data solutions that are digging into the conversation—for example, GitHub, Stack Overflow, and many others. I believe accessing that data and aggregating it properly can immensely impact our ability to identify and seek out those potentially hard-to-find candidates and to go after them.

Very few companies are really leveraging that type of data now; we are a couple of years away from getting this data collected and harnessed across most organizations.

However, I think Big Data is not as important as good data. The question we have to ask is: Do we have the data that helps to address the following?

- Would a target candidate accept an offer?
- Would a candidate accept a position?
- Would a candidate be a top performer once hired?

Big Data analytics, applied properly, is helping some leading organizations achieve answers to those types of questions.

In the same way, there is no standard tool available to inform candidates about important information about employers, and that would be useful. Nothing has been done to significantly enhance the decision-making process for candidates. Big Data should help candidates to assess if the hiring manager they want to work for is the one that would help them grow their career, and provide some indication of which managers are developing their employees versus those who are not. We should literally have Big Data decision solutions that are bidirectional: impacting both employers and candidates. These solutions and tools would provide candidates with information that goes beyond the job description and that show whether or not the company really walks its talk. For me, Big Data means answering those questions that have an impact on the important decisions people make around their careers.

There are several sources of hire, as described in the CareerXroads report in Figure 5.5. For the scope of this book, we will simply cover the application of Big Data analytics on some sources of hire, including:

- Employer referral programs and talent communities
- Job boards
- Social media sourcing and Big Data
- Impact of mobile

Building a Successful Employee Referral Program

As we discussed earlier, the concept of an employee referral program (ERP) is one of the oldest candidate-sourcing techniques. While the principle of a referral has not fundamentally changed, the emergence of digital technologies, coupled with the explosion of the Internet and social media, has triggered a sharp evolution in the way candidates approach jobs. This has challenged organizations to adjust and adapt the strategies, techniques, and tools of their ERPs.

A successful ERP requires a satisfied employee base that believes in your brand and organizational mission. By leveraging your existing employees' network to find new talent and financially rewarding your employees with a bonus, you will further incentivize employees to refer someone they know who would be a fit for an open position.

Why Should You Care about Employee Referrals?

According to some studies, between 24 and 50 percent of new hires today are from an ERP.[9] Employee referrals are the best sources of matching candidates, particularly when the referral is from a top-performing employee, as they most likely will recommend similar top performers. Additionally, not only is the probability that a referral will be a good match with your organization much higher, but ERPs also cost less than traditional sourcing methods. This drives confidence and trust in your sourcing and hiring process. In fact, recruiters we've spoken with claim that a great ERP not only helps to identify top prospects who may not be actively searching, but it also serves as an internal vetting process for appropriate skill sets and culture fit. It also helps to promote the company brand as well as job opportunities.

ERPs by the Numbers

A study from Lee Hecht Harrison also found that referrals deliver the best results.[10] According to the findings, referrals were considered the most effective method for sourcing candidates among both HR managers (77 percent) and recruiters (88 percent), and ERPs continue to "offer a cost-effective source for high-quality talent acquisition."

Additionally, research conducted by Dr. John Sullivan, an internationally known HR thought leader who specializes in providing bold, high-business-impact, and strategic talent management solutions to large corporations, found that employee referrals were the most cost-effective and best candidate sourcing method.[11] In those leading organizations, employees play an invaluable role in identifying, assessing, and promoting the employment brand and job offer to their referrals, saving multiple levels of costs and resources.

Making Analytics Work for Your ERP

As we discussed, ERPs are a sound business investment, so the question quickly becomes: How do you leverage analytics to maximize your ERP and gain insights into how referrals will perform by location, job position, role, and projected length of service? It will also help you address the following business questions:

- Are referrals more loyal than hires from other sources?
- Are referrals more productive than other employees?
- Do referrals have a better offer acceptance rate?
- Do they have a better time to productivity and performance?
- Do referrals generate a better quality of hire?
- How much should you reward your employee who refers talent?

According to Oracle's white paper "The Shortest Path to Better Hires: Best Practices for Employee Referral Programs":[12]

- Employee referrals account for between 24 percent to one-third of all hires.
- Employee referral hires perform up to 15 percent better than other types of hires.
- Employee referral candidates accept offers 15 percent more often than nonreferral candidates.

- A study by Ohio State University and Workforce Management found that employee referral hires have a 25 percent higher retention rate than other types of hires.

With these notable benefits in mind, coupled with the scarcity of skilled talent and a competitive talent marketplace, let's take a look at some of the best practices that high-performing companies are using to optimize their ERPs.

ERP Best Practices

From our conversations with executives at some of the most successful companies, we learned that more than 50 percent of their talent is discovered through their ERPs. Here are some best practices that they have shared with us.

- Market your ERP as you would do for a marketing campaign. It is paramount to use your marketing team to design compelling branding that includes a memorable and catchy name, logo, tagline, and message that conveys the purpose of the program and its value for candidates and potential job applicants. And don't forget to provide exciting branded giveaways!
- Develop a CRM capability. Similar to a customer relationship management tool, the CRM will help develop your employees' and candidates' experiences by creating a platform where you can share testimonials of existing employees' success stories and job satisfaction, all targeted at the right pool of talent.
- Provide timely feedback to employees who refer candidates. This demonstrates that you care about their efforts in helping the organization with finding great talent to be their future coworkers.
- Communicate your ERP using a multichannel approach via newsletters, e-mails, videos, blogs, and social media.

- Leverage social media and current social technology to design ERPs that reach multigenerational workforces, such as social network sites, niche sites, and social communities.

- Leverage the latest technology, including mobile channels and robust user-friendly programs that are not time-consuming for your employees to use and that also present fair and accurate information regarding the program with a clear definition of the rules.

- Benchmark your employees' performance, loyalty, time to productivity, cost of hire, quality of hire, days-to-fill ratio, and lifetime value to showcase your ERP's competitive advantage to the business. You can also assess additional metrics such as the click-through rate of the employees who refer candidates, the click-through rate of the referred candidates, the conversion rate of referred candidates (clicks to applicant), the time it takes to reach out to referrals, and the referred time to response. Success is also about having engaged employees, so the key is to make it an easy and rewarding experience for them.

- Reward your engaged employees who refer, and make the entire process user-friendly and empowering.

Another Frontline Story of ERP

Leading companies are leveraging this powerful recruiting source to staff their positions and build out their workforces. Red Hat, a leading open-source technology firm, received more than 50 percent of its new hires from its ERP.[13]

Sourcing via Job Boards

The emergence of the Internet in the 1990s revolutionized the candidate-sourcing ecosystem, shifting it from traditional methods to online recruitment sites and job boards. This, in turn, generated a myriad of clickstream data that could be analyzed; in fact, online channels generate and enable most analytics in sourcing today.

For readers without a sourcing or recruiting background, let's recall the promise of a job board.

A job board is an employment website designed to allow employers to post job requirements for open positions and for job seekers to create or upload their resumes. Think of it as a modern, interactive classified ads section. Job boards also allow seekers to perform job searches and respond to postings. They help employers primarily achieve the following:

- Post a job (advertise a job offer).
- Perform resume searches.
- Provide workforce best practices for employers and for seekers.
- Provide resume writing and interview tips.
- Provide talent management and talent CRM solutions.
- Provide career and job search advice.

With the variety and volume of data generated that include seeker resume data, employers' online job posting descriptions data, seeker profile data, seeker online behavior data when looking for a job and responding to a job opportunity, and data from the matching of employers' needs to seekers' needs, job boards have become the playground of sourcing analytics.

Big Data Analytics on Job Postings

When you post your job opening on a job board, your ultimate goal is to have a talented candidate apply for that job. Traditionally, the job board will provide you with three sets of metrics:

1. Number of candidates who viewed your job opening.
2. Number of candidates who applied.
3. Conversion rate of your job opening (the ratio between the number of views and the number of applies).

With innovation in Big Data and advanced analytics, your organization can be more data-driven and can fully optimize recruitment tactics by implementing analytics and benchmarks into its job performance dashboard. One of this book's authors, JP Isson, has developed and implemented a job posting benchmarking tool called the Job Optimizer. The Job Optimizer provides Monster customer touch points with a benchmark of how a customer's job postings perform against similar postings and what should be done to increase performance when applicable, leveraging predictive analytics.

Let's assume you are looking for a business analyst for your marketing department in Boston. Traditionally, your job board would provide you with a dashboard for this position that includes the number of job views, the number of applies, and the conversion rate. But having these numbers does not really provide you with any insightful feedback about the position you are trying to fill. Advanced analytics creates more value by embedding benchmarks and predictive analytics, which means not only meaningful data about the performance of your specific job posting, but also the associated benchmarks needed to assess the performance of your listing against that of similar jobs (those with the same title, the same occupation, the same location, and the same posting duration that also appear on the site).

Seeing where your job performance ranks against similar jobs paints a much more realistic picture of how your job posting is doing. It also provides you with a status check so that you can assess whether the posting is performing above the benchmark, below the benchmark, or in the average range. With this ranking in mind, you can then adjust your strategy and expectations, and tailor your supply-and-demand activities. For instance, say your Boston-based marketing analyst job receives 300 views per posting (meaning 300 people viewed your job listing) and 27 applies, while postings on the same site for a similar marketing analyst job in Boston average 400 views and 60 applies; in this case you would quickly realize that your job posting is performing below the benchmark, as presented in Figure 5.6.

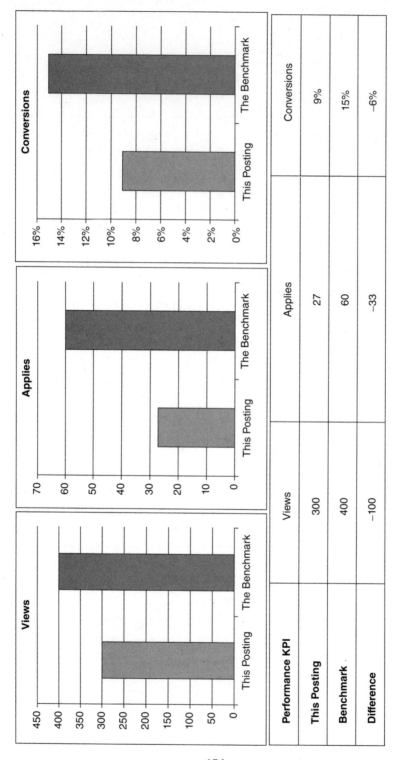

Performance KPI	Views	Applies	Conversions
This Posting	300	27	9%
Benchmark	400	60	15%
Difference	–100	–33	–6%

Figure 5.6 Job Performance Benchmark Views per Posting Expressions of Interest per Posting Conversion

The natural reaction to such a discovery might be to ask yourself, "Why is my job performing below the benchmark?" and "How do I boost its performance?"

The answer lies in advanced analytics. Leveraging this discipline will help you to build a profile of millions of similar job postings by analyzing the title, location, duration on site, job category, occupation, description, number of days posted, and employer branding to paint a robust picture of the employment landscape so that you can diagnose and remedy any issues, and optimize your posting.

Analytics can help you figure out what job attributes would drive better performance among your target job seekers. For instance, jobs with attributes such as Career Ad Network can increase the number of applications to your job ad by posting it on Monster and across hundreds of targeted websites. Helping you to reach passive job seekers, increase your job applications, and maximize your visibility by bolding your ad and including enhanced job branding can offer an uplift of 40 percent in views and 25 percent in applies. Powered by predictive analytics, Big Data analytics helps you anticipate the performance of your posting. You can also leverage analytics to anticipate the job performance by location, occupation, duration on site, job title, and job level. As you might imagine, comparing a vice president position to an entry-level position is not an apples-to-apples comparison in terms of expectations for performance, and this is one of the reasons having a benchmark that takes such factors into account is so important. Think of it this way: Relatively speaking, few people would apply to a vice president position, while a larger number would apply to an entry-level position. Advanced analytics can help anticipate occupation levels, titles, and duration on site, giving you insights into how to best reach your target seekers—for instance, STEM job postings, which are difficult positions to fill.

Advanced analytics helps business leaders better understand their target job applicants, such as when they are mostly actively applying, their motivations for looking for new opportunities, and what sources they use when they do so. This provides actionable insights that allow you to optimize your sourcing strategies and tactics.

Big Data analytics helps to leverage candidate profiles and candidate response behavior, enabling employers to optimize their job performance. Advanced analytics provides understanding of what keywords seekers frequently use on their resumes and what keywords employers use in their job descriptions. The outcome then feeds employers with seekers' most popular keywords and profiles used, and feeds seekers with the most popular terms and concepts employers use in their job descriptions. We move this to the next level by building a predictive model that anticipates the profile of a successful resume for a specific position to determine the most appealing jobs for candidates leveraging text analytics, machine learning, and artificial intelligence. The end goal is to anticipate the supply-and-demand equation.

Some job boards also offer what is called a pay per click (PPC) model. PPC is a service where job boards do not request any fees to post a job, but charge based on the listing's performance in terms of views or applies. Basically, it operates similarly to Google's PPC model. Within the PPC model, advanced analytics helps you to optimize the cost per click (in this case cost per view) and provides you with a full understanding of your postings, as well as insights into your job performance ranking that could be easy to fill or hard to fill, helping you as an employer to adjust your sourcing strategies based on the supply-and-demand outcome and your recruitment budget.

Resume Search and Resume Analytics

The second largest service delivered by job boards is a resume search. The majority of job boards, by their very mission, store millions of resumes in their databases, which they can make available to their customers (employers), assuming some fees. Employers would then have the ability to search the database for resumes. In the era of Big Data, analytics is being utilized to perform powerful resume searches. Just imagine searching a database of 100 million resumes to find applicants. To say that would be cumbersome and take a lot of time would be an understatement. Based on research, recruiters spend approximately 90 seconds to go over a resume, so to review 100,000 resumes could take two and a half years.[14]

Luckily, today Big Data solutions such as Monster Worldwide SeeMore Solutions uses 6Senses Technologies solutions to leverage semantic search, which performs high-speed resume searching from both an internal and an external resume database in mere minutes. Using a Big Data resume search solution can also help address the bandwidth issues that the majority of recruiters face. By using artificial intelligence such as semantic search functionality to optimize resume searches of databases containing hundreds of millions of resumes, you are provided with not only ranked search results based on matching criteria but also business intelligence around the posting itself. And, according to a study sponsored by Monster, 70 percent of recruiters reduced the time it took to search for resumes and sharply improved their searching productivity when using semantic search tools, such as Monster Power Resume Search and SeeMore technology.[15]

Semantic search leverages the power of the Big Data cloud and artificial intelligence to understand the concept and the context of the search. It improves search accuracy by understanding searcher intent and the contextual meaning of search terms in order to provide more relevant results. Semantic search systems consider various points, including context of search, concept, intent, variation of words, and synonyms, and leverages artificial intelligence and machine learnings to provide relevant search results. Semantic search also provides business intelligence around the search results. For instance, when searching for web designer resumes from a resume database, semantic search will gather all relevant resumes and rank them from the best to least relevant that meet the concept, context, and synonyms of web designer that are relevant to you. Big Data solutions for resume search help companies to drive performance, increase efficiency, and reduce costs when searching for the best candidates' resumes.

Social Media Sourcing: Must Have Today

What Is Social Media Sourcing?

Social sourcing or social recruiting is a type of online recruitment where the recruiter, sourcer, or HR manager uses social platforms as talent databases or as advertising channels in order to reach candidates.

This can also include gathering referrals from your employees to fill an open position by leveraging a social network. Popular social media sites for this type of recruiting include Twitter, Facebook, LinkedIn, Viadeo, TalentBin by Monster, Entelo, XING, Google+, and BranchOut.

Why Use Social Media Sourcing?

In today's globally connected talent marketplace, the majority of job candidates use social media sites. In fact, according to the Pew Research Internet Project, overall, 74 percent of online adults use social media network sites, with adoption rates for the 18- to 29-year-old and 30- to 49-year-old age groups at 89 and 82 percent, respectively.[16] Additionally, social media tops the list of channels for millennials who, by the end of 2015, will outnumber baby boomers as the nation's largest living generation, according to the projections from the Bureau of Labor Statistics.[17] And, more important, by 2020, millennials, more than 90 percent of whom now use social networks, will make up 50 percent of the workforce.[18] The adoption of social media is not prevalent only among millennials, however. According to recent data compiled by Callbox-Au, the fastest-growing demographic on Twitter is users in the 55- to 64-year-old age bracket, and for Google+ the 45- to 54-year-old age bracket.[19]

As we have discussed, the recruitment landscape is shifting, and a survey by Spherion Staffing Services found that 47 percent of millennials say a prospective employer's online reputation matters as much as the job the company offers.[20] With that in mind, it becomes critical that companies' sourcing strategies adapt their social channels for sourcing. Most job candidates and prospective hires will have access to a company's employment brand without stepping in the door or speaking to your employees directly. Social media sourcing companies can also leverage their interactions with passive job candidates (even if they're not interested in any current offerings) by keeping them active and engaged, and by making them part of your talent community interested in future job openings. Your sourcing strategy should include a social component that inspires viral job sharing and, more important, taps into passive job candidates who are not always reachable from traditional resume databases and employment sites.

Social media allows employers to go beyond the traditional barriers where work and personal life are strongly separated, and to connect with prospective hires using platforms they access multiple times a day. It also helps to connect with passive job candidates who may choose to interact with your company, and to provide unique insights about potential candidates before they are even involved in the recruitment process. Some additional benefits include:

- Better quality of hire and cultural fit
- Optimized time to hire
- Improved reach of quality candidates
- Help for boosting your brand image
- Connecting with passive candidates
- Providing cost-effective outcomes

Interview with Pete Kazanjy, Founder, TalentBin by Monster

PROFILE

JP Isson had the opportunity to interview Pete Kazanjy to discuss social sourcing.

Isson: How do you describe talent sourcing in the era of Big Data and social media?

Kazanjy: The overarching thing from which everything flows with respect to social sourcing is the notion that work product that was previously known as having a nondigital nature and not publicly available is now becoming digital first, and second, it's becoming more and more available. That's what really drives everything else.

Because if you think about the life cycle of talent availability online, historically resume objects have done a fairly good job of providing proxies of work product. They were the summation and representation of historical work product, kind of correlated with a skills profile.

(Continued)

(*Continued*)

Those resumes would usually make their way into a database, and then make their way online in big databases like Monster and have you there as a prospective job candidate. The furthering of that was LinkedIn's changing the culture with resume proxies. But the fundamental problem with that approach was that the outcome was still a work product proxy, meaning not reflecting the current work activity. Work product is made of two components: a primary document and a secondary document. Resumes are just secondary documents. Historically, resume was proxy for work product. Resumes are secondary work products, as they reflect your actual work but they are not the actual work. Now that you have your actual work activity, that is what matters the most! And the reflection of your actual work activity is the social version of that work product.

With the digitalization of work product, we can capture your actual work activity on the web and social platforms. For instance, if somebody tweets about the fact that they are going to a conference, this leaves a micro work object; and a bigger version of that is, for instance, when people create a presentation on SlideShare, pose or answer questions on Stack Overflow, or put their codes on GitHub. All that comes down to harnessing all those pieces of digital work product information that is available. The new era is about harnessing all that information that is becoming available and making sense of it for the recruiter looking for talents. That's what I mean when I talk about the overarching thing in social sourcing.

Isson: How does TalentBin help recruiters find hard-to-fill skills such as those in STEM fields?

Kazanjy: We are one of the folks who are leveraging work products and, more importantly, helping recruiters take advantage of all the digital artifacts of work product data publicly available by aggregating all those profiles together and making those pieces of digital artifacts of work products correlate to skills profiles, making them behave in a way that is helpful to recruiters, and ultimately have those profiles matched to work products speak to recruiters.

For instance, I can find professionals based upon their professional activities. We started with software engineers because they were having a low unemployment rate, were not receiving a lot of phone calls from recruiters, and were not available in resume databases or on traditional social networks. And, more importantly, software engineers' skills and profiles data were also available and mostly accessible; but now we have expanded into a broader range of occupations such as health care and others.

From the marketing standpoint, the compelling offering as far as sourcing for candidates goes is that social media sourcing also helps to tap into high-end candidates, meaning the highly in-demand skilled candidates for hard-to-fill positions. With social we can find them where they are actively showing their actual work activity.

Isson: What is the overall impact of social media data science in talent acquisition?

Kazanjy: It's all about the work product that was not digitalized or available before that is now becoming more available via social media—the ability to leverage publicly available data to tap into passive seekers and special skilled talent. The digitalization of the work product is the new era. Data science helps to harness digitalized information to reach out to passive seekers and talent groups.

Isson: What are the top pieces of advice that you would give to someone new to social sourcing?

Kazanjy:

1. There are tools out there today to help you speed up your social sourcing. Embrace them, or your competition will do it and take away the top talent you are looking for.

2. Rather than starting something new from scratch, use tools already available to take advantage of them. Don't do it manually. Don't try to have an SEO approach. Rather, leverage all Big Data solutions tools and take advantage of them to quickly find your candidates. The ROI will be much higher than if you try to do it manually.

3. To look for candidates, do not stick with a resume approach only. It's really about connecting with candidates that your competition will not have access to.

(Continued)

(Continued)

Isson: What do you foresee for social sourcing in the future?

Kazanjy: We will start getting deeper and deeper intelligence from publicly available data such as implicit professional activities, tapping into new data such as conference attendees, not for leads generation but rather for consolidation of footprints of professional activities not being leveraged yet.

From a macroeconomic standpoint, more available information will be good for both recruiters and job candidates. People willing to pay new talent more and more for their labors will have easy access to their profiles. We can imagine a world where people would choose artificial intelligence tools or apps to be their personal job agent, asking the app to pay attention to what they are doing and push any relevant opportunities their way.

More and more information will also be harnessed and become available, and people will feel like a social media sourcing tool is becoming their personal job agent that will help to capture their entire digital footprint and showcase their summary profile on the web. They would also request the job app agent to shop for the best job opportunities that would meet their needs and preferences and exceed their expectations. Artificial intelligence should provide talent with an automated intelligent personal work agent that conveys their work activity, their needs, preferences, expectations, and behaviors. It will track your activity and look for what might be helpful to you. I imagine the future where a seeker would say, "Hey, TalentBin by Monster, could you be my personal job agent?" Not just on Twitter, not just on Facebook or GitHub or LinkedIn, but it looks into everything I do and has the jobs find me before I even know I am looking for them.

Empowering Your Social Media Sourcing with Big Data Solutions and Tools

Candidates are leaving a variety of digital footprints on the web throughout social media platforms, niche sites, and alumni groups. While some of them are not necessarily available in any resume databases, those candidates with an IT-related background are heavily active on niche sites and social media networks such as GitHub, Google+, Twitter, and LinkedIn. And those open profiles are usually part of the STEM fields where positions can be hard to fill. However, talent in these fields often will contribute to these social groups, for instance by providing a solution to a programming question from their community. New technology companies such as TalentBin by Monster, Entelo, RemarkableHire, and Gild provide solutions to tap into those traditionally hard-to-reach candidates. These technologies track your entire social footprint to evaluate candidate technical prowess. They then mine a candidate's online footprint and other social information to create a unique profile and actual competency ranking based on the candidate's publicly available social data.

TalentBin, for example, aggregates candidates' profiles from social media platforms such as GitHub, Stack Overflow, Twitter, LinkedIn, Google+, and other niche sites and social media platforms, and then creates a unique identifier profile for each one. These unique identifiers encompass digital footprints, micro work products, and contact and profile information that is publicly available. This is particularly useful for companies with open positions in the hard-to-fill STEM fields. Leveraging advanced analytics in social media sourcing helps organizations tap into a pool of talent that may not typically be reachable via traditional channels, as well as passive seekers. Just as good marketing practices seek audiences where they are, good recruiting will leverage those communities where talent congregates, and invest in tools and technologies that enable you to find them from where they are active: interacting and solving questions from their peers.

MONSTER WORLDWIDE SOCIAL MEDIA RECRUITING

CASE STUDY

Monster Worldwide is a global leader in connecting people to jobs, wherever they are. For more than 20 years, Monster has helped people improve their lives with better jobs, and helped employers find the best talent. Today, the company offers services in more than 40 countries, providing some of the broadest, most sophisticated job seeking, career management, and recruitment and talent management capabilities. Monster continues its pioneering work of transforming the recruiting industry with advanced technology using intelligent digital, social, and

(Continued)

(*Continued*)

mobile solutions, including its flagship website at www.monster.com and a vast array of products and services.

Key Monster Customers' Objectives

The following are the key objectives that Monster customers want to achieve in this globally competitive talent market:

- Target passive candidates such as those for hard-to-fill positions in science, technology, engineering, and mathematics (STEM) and millennials.
- Increase the quality of hire and overall visibility of their jobs on Monster.
- Build out a social recruiting program to engage and connect with candidates.

The Challenge

The challenge is to engage with passive seekers on social media such as Twitter, leveraging a social recruitment solution that is easy to use, efficient, scalable, and cost-effective.

The Solution

Monster provided user-friendly and scalable innovative automated social solutions that helped its customers to increase their candidate reach and overall brand awareness. Its Monster Twitter cards, Monster Social Job Ads, and TalentBin by Monster have helped its customers find, engage, and recruit great talent.

Monster customers who have used Monster's social media recruitment have registered sharp increases in their reach and been able to attract and engage more millennials and hard-to-fill candidates.

Benefits

- Double-digit reduction in time to fill.
- Increase of fill ratio as well as quality of hire.
- Significant reduction of talent acquisition cost.
- Double-digit increase in overall job response and job visibility.

AUTO MANUFACTURER USES TALENT COMMUNITIES TO SOURCE SKILLS

CASE STUDY

As General Motors (GM) sought to ramp up the production of its flagship electric vehicle, the Volt, the company faced a significant talent challenge: a shortage of engineers and scientists with a background in electronics. Drawing talent from Silicon Valley and other technology centers to Detroit proved difficult initially. GM's answer was to enhance its recruiting process by building talent communities and drawing more and more people with the required skills into its network.

To help build these communities, GM enlisted engineers and technical staff to write about their jobs, highlighting the exciting work, the rewarding and socially important job opportunities at the company, the high quality of life and relatively low cost of living in Detroit's suburban neighborhoods, and the many cultural attractions and professional sports teams in the city.

Starting gradually, the company built a growing talent network, amplifying it through social media. New facts and insights about the company were shared among wider circles of talent, creating a positive ripple effect and a more robust talent network. This approach helped GM attract the talent needed to meet deadlines, hiring requirements, and project demands.

From a Deloitte study: http://dupress.com/articles/hc-trends-2014-talent-acquisition/?id=gx:el:dc:dup679:cons:awa:hct14.

TWITTER CARDS

Some online recruitment solutions providers such as Monster Worldwide have become more innovative and are leveraging Twitter by providing features like cards to share their open positions. Contrary to the 140-character limit customary for that channel, Twitter cards enable employers to put out as much content as they want to target their audience via Twitter. They also can use their company logo and Twitter handle to send out related tweets. Findings from Monster demonstrate that clients using Twitter cards have seen their tweeted postings retweeted 30 percent of the time, reaching an impressive potential audience.

Social Media Sourcing Today

Based on our conversations with talent sourcing leading experts, to be successful today your social media sourcing strategy should include eight major steps, as described in Figure 5.7. For your future job candidate search or potential employee, the following checklist will help to optimize your social sourcing strategy:

Listen

Connect

Interact

Engage

Attract

Source/Select

Develop/Promote

Retain

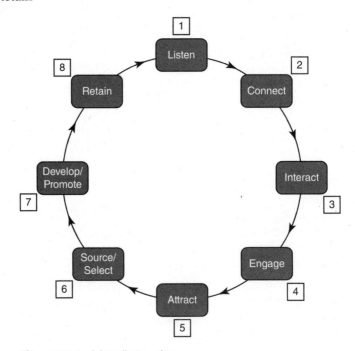

Figure 5.7 Social Media Sourcing

THE MOBILE IMPACT ON TALENT SOURCING

Mobile is one of the key pillars of the talent sourcing strategy in the era of Big Data. It tops the list of tools candidates turn to when they look for new job opportunities, respond to your job opening, or simply gather information about your company.

Getting on the Same Page with Some Vocabulary

To ensure we are looking at topics from the same angle, the following are some useful definitions related to mobile sourcing terminology.

- **Mobile search:** Online search activity that is performed from a mobile device, such as a tablet or a smartphone.
- **Mobile web:** Refers to accessing Internet services from a mobile device, such as a smartphone or a tablet, via a connection to a mobile network or other wireless network.
- **Responsive design website:** A method of developing a site that is completely flexible regardless of device. Rather than detecting a specific browser or device type, the website automatically orientates itself based on the screen size of the device.
- **Mobile optimized:** Refers to a website that will reformat itself for a list of handheld or tablet devices. A mobile-optimized site will generally provide larger navigation buttons, reformatted content, and differently optimized images that appear when the user is on a tablet, an iPhone, a BlackBerry, an Android, or any other mobile device.

Why Mobile Sourcing Matters

Today, more than 80 percent of people have a mobile phone in the United States,[21] and from our conversations with job candidates, mobile is the number one communication platform. In fact, after referrals, no recruiting channel is more important than your company's mobile platform. Your prospective hires and candidates must be able to do everything directly and seamlessly from their phones, whether they are searching your company website, seeing your job offers, applying to an open position, or accepting your offer.

As of December 2014, 44 percent of job searches performed by workers were done via mobile devices.[22] Google reported that 31 percent of searches for jobs on its site were from mobile devices.[23] It also has the highest message response rate, so best practice tells us that all recruiting communications and messaging should be accessible via a mobile site that has a responsive design or is mobile optimized. According to a study conducted by Glassdoor, 43 percent of job candidates researched their prospective employer and read the job description on their mobile device just 15 minutes prior to their interviews.[24]

Mobile devices are literally always on hand and at our fingertips, and this convenience is beneficial to companies looking to reach us, as consumers and as job seekers. Having a mobile-optimized site makes it easier for today's candidates to search for a job whenever they feel like it, so it comes as no surprise that the highest recruitment key performance indicators (KPIs) in terms of jobs viewed and jobs applied occur on these devices. All companies looking for candidates in this hyperconnected labor force battlefield should have a mobile platform that is responsive across all mobile devices and tablets.

Hard Reality: Low Employer Adoption of Mobile-Optimized Sites

As you read this, our guess is that most of you have your smartphones or tablets within arm's reach. So the previous section on the importance of mobile-optimized websites seems obvious. However, according to Jeanne Meister, only 20 percent of Fortune 500 companies have a mobile-optimized career site, and the job listings themselves are still not mobile optimized.[25]

As Meister rightly points out: "Employees are requesting to view new job postings on their tablets, learn and collaborate with peers on their smartphones, and provide feedback on a team member's performance with the click of a button." But they're not able to in most cases.

According to the Glassdoor study "The Rise of Mobile Job Search," more job seekers and employees are using their mobile devices during the job search process, and they're doing it more frequently.[26] Nearly 9 out of 10 (89 percent) of job seekers report they're likely to use a mobile device during their job search in the next 12 months, and some job candidates said they would also search for information regarding a company's culture and values, as well as job openings, on their mobile devices. Consequently, your sourcing strategy should include making job offerings available via a mobile site that is responsive, as this will likely increase your job responses and listing performance.

PUTTING THE IMPACT CYCLE INTO ACTION

In the previous sections we discussed the value of injecting analytics into your talent sourcing strategy to optimize the outcome. In the following section we will recall the main stages of the IMPACT Cycle that drives the analytics part of the talent sourcing pillar.

- **I**dentify the business challenge: business challenges here could include:
  - How to source for hard-to-fill positions in STEM fields
  - Identify the best source of hire (sources that lead to candidates who once hired will become loyal and perform well at his or her job)
  - Identify the quality of hire by the source of hire
- **M**aster the data: Leverage all the data available, including:
  - Source of hire data
  - Seeker resume data
  - Seeker online search behavior data
  - Posting description data
  - Competition data
  - Candidate publicly available data
  - Labor market data for supply/demand
  - Job posting benchmark data
- **P**rovide meaning: Harness the aforementioned data, leveraging advanced business analytics in order to determine:

- Where to source for candidates?
- How to optimize your sources' strategies and costs?
- What are your best-performing postings and why?
- How to leverage social media and predictive models to reach out to hard-to-find candidates
- Where and when to post your job?
- How to target candidates via a tailored channel?
- What candidate profile will more likely respond?
- How to optimize your job description?
- How to optimize your job response?
- **A**ct: Leverage the meaning provided in the preceding section across the entire organization.
- **C**ommunicate the outcomes and sourcing analytics strategies across the entire organization.
- **T**rack the result of the strategy on an ongoing basis to adjust accordingly.

KEY TAKEAWAYS

- Sourcing has been around since the days of the Roman Empire, when emperors and monarchs had to staff large armies in order to conquer new territories and countries. Sourcing has undergone two major digital changes: the emergence of the World Wide Web and the consortium of Big Data, social media, mobile, and the cloud that exploded the volume of data and enabled the use of analytics to optimize sourcing activities and strategies.
- Today's workforce is made up of multigenerational groups. However, with millennials poised to make up more than 50 percent of employee populations by 2020, companies have to rethink and adjust the way they will attract, select, develop, and retain prospective hires and existing employees.
- The global labor shortage for skilled talent is more acute in the STEM fields, and companies need to go beyond traditional sourcing methods and leverage social media, talent communities, and other Big Data solutions and service providers, to reach candidates both passively and actively seeking.

They should speak to job candidates to learn which channels they prefer to use and interact with multiple times a day.

- Referrals are by far the most cost-effective sourcing channel, delivering the best quality of hire and the most loyal and productive employees. Your sourcing strategy should leverage employee referrals as a primary sourcing channel because, when properly implemented, you could staff more than 50 percent of new hires simply by leveraging your employee referral program.

- A great sourcing strategy should include all sourcing channels to maximize the reach and to best optimize the allocation of your sourcing budget, as each sourcing method will deliver and connect with different seeker segments.

- Predictive analytics and Big Data should be used to help you optimize your sourcing outcomes and KPIs, such as your job response and performance benchmark results. Remember to benchmark all your results, whether job performance, volume of resume searches, salary offers, or attribution models, so you can assess your performance. Predictive analytics can be used to gain insights into your posting performances, including what type of seekers will apply and when they will apply. This information can be used to help you to better tailor and target your prospective audience.

- Today, forward-looking job boards offer Big Data solutions, such as semantic search, to parse through hundreds of millions of resumes or candidate profiles. Those features should definitely be a support for recruiters eager to look for talent from large resume databases. In order to be successful, recruiters should leverage today's technologies and solutions and, more important, look at candidates' work product that reflects their current work activities, such as interactions on social media platforms or niche sites, to connect and engage with them for current and future job opportunities.

- In this candidate market where skilled talent has multiple choices, and where positions in STEM fields are very hard to fill, employers will have to leverage Big Data analytics to integrate candidate data from a variety of sources, such as talent CRM systems, ATSs, job boards, social media, and employee referrals, to paint a great picture of talent they are looking for and to augment the talent community and their talent reach. Doing so will make them more successful, as they will be actively listening, connecting, interacting, engaging, attracting, and persuading candidates where candidates congregate.

NOTES

1. Jim Stroud, http://blog.jimstroud.com/.
2. Jeanne Meister, "2014: The Year Social HR Matters," *Forbes*, January 6, 2014, www .forbes.com/sites/jeannemeister/2014/01/06/2014-the-year-social-hr-matters/.
3. Ibid.
4. 2014 U.S Talent Shortage Survey, ManpowerGroup, www.manpowergroup.com/ talent-shortage-explorer/.
5. "The Employment Situation, October 2013," U.S. Bureau of Labor Statistics, www .bls.gov/news.release/empsit.nr0.htm.
6. Nysha King, *Recruiter Sentiment Study: 2014 1st Half,* MRINetwork, http://mrinetwork .com/media/286602/recruiter_sentiment_study_1st_half_2014.pdf.
7. David Court, Dave Elzinga, Susan Mulder, and Ole Jørgen Vetvik, "The Consumer Decision Journey," *McKinsey Quarterly,* June 2009, www.mckinsey.com/insights/ marketing_sales/the_consumer_decision_journey.
8. Ibid.
9. "The Shortest Path to Better Hires: Best Practices for Employee Referral Programs," Oracle, January 2013, www.oracle.com/us/products/applications/shortest-path-to-better-hires-1898145.pdf.
10. Lee Hecht Harrison, "Trends and Best Practices in Sourcing and Hiring Talent," 2013, www.lhh.com/en-US/thought-leadership/Documents/articles/trends-and-best-practices-in-sourcing-and-hiring-talent.pdf.
11. Top 10 Benefits of Employee Referral Program, www.slideshare.net/fullscreen/ drjohnsullivan/people-management-practices-from-google-facebook-and-apple/26.
12. "The Shortest Path to Better Hires."
13. Lisa Barry, Udo Bohdal-Spiegelhoff, Robin Erickson, and Kim Lamoureux, "Talent Acquisition Revisited: Deploy New Approaches for the New Battlefield," Deloitte, March 2014, http://dupress.com/articles/hc-trends-2014-talent-acquisition/.
14. CXP study sponsored by Monster, conducted February 8, 2013, with 574 HR Executives.
15. Monster Worldwide survey with Monster customers: Benefits of Semantic Search.
16. Maeve Duggan, Nicole B. Ellison, Cliff Lampe, Amanda Lenhart, and Mary Madden, "Social Media Update 2014," Pew Research Center, January 9, 2015, www.pewinternet .org/2015/01/09/social-media-update-2014/.
17. "The Employment Situation, October 2013," U.S. Bureau of Labor Statistics.
18. Meister, "2014: The Year Social HR Matters."
19. "Fastest Growing Population on Twitter," data from Callbox-Au, reported by MedNet, www.mednet-tech.com/newsletter/internet-marketing/whats-the-fastest-growing-demographic-on-twitter.
20. "Latest Emerging Workforce Study Discovers New Workplace Realities and Significant Employer/Employee Disconnects." Spherion Staffing Services, January 2013, www.spherion.com/Documents/2013EWSQ1_FINAL.pdf.
21. "Mobile Phone Penetration in the United States from 2010 to 2018," Statista.com, www.statista.com/statistics/222307/forecast-of-mobile-phone-penetration-in-the-us/.

22. ComScore Mobile Metrix Report 2015.

23. Google ad job searches 2015.

24. "The Rise of Mobile Job Search," Glassdoor, May 24, 2013, www.glassdoor.com/blog/infographic-rise-mobile-job-search/.

25. Jeanne Meister, "2014: The Year Social HR Matters," *Forbes*, January 6, 2014, www.forbes.com/sites/jeannemeister/2014/01/06/2014-the-year-social-hr-matters/.

26. "Nine in 10 Job Seekers to Search for Jobs via Mobile," Glassdoor State of Mobile Job Search Survey, May 13, 2014, www.glassdoor.com/blog/9-10-job-seekers-search-jobs-mobile-glassdoor-state-mobile-job-search-survey/.

CHAPTER **6**

Talent Acquisition Analytics

Your dedication should not be confined for your own gain, but should unleash your passion.

—Li Ka-shing

We all know hiring the right employee is critical to an organization's success. Whether the organization is small or large, hiring the wrong person can lower productivity, create a bad working environment for others, and hamper your firm's ability to succeed. Hire the wrong people consistently, and it spells certain disaster for your organization.

Historically, hiring was done by reviewing resumes or applications, in-person interviews, and a gut feeling and intuition regarding how someone would do in a job. You took a chance on an employee because he or she "felt good for the job." To some extent, many organizations still hire this way. However, analytics has been stepping in to take some of the guesswork out of hiring. At a minimum, analytics provides an additional perspective on candidates applying to your job openings. At most, analytics can predict whether someone will be successful in a job, giving you peace of mind and taking some of the uncertainty out of such an important decision.

The hiring pillar in our Seven Pillars of People Analytics Success highlights the importance of using analytics to optimize the interview process and to select job applicants for interviews. It also helps to determine the best ways to vet candidates, how to set up interview questions, and how to create some tests that can be used to analyze the correlation between a candidate's performance during the interview and his or her performance in a particular job function.

WHAT IS TALENT ACQUISITION ANALYTICS?

Talent acquisition is the practice of hiring new resources after the sourcing process is completed. As we discussed earlier, sourcing provides valuable information regarding prospective hires, including information from their social network profiles, resumes, and their work products, both digitalized or offline. In this section, we will focus on four major stages of the talent acquisition process:

1. Application
2. Preselection
3. Interviews
4. Selection

Talent acquisition analytics is a practice of injecting predictive analytics into the new talent hiring process. Analytics could be used to determine which candidates you should meet from a pool of job applicants. It could also be used during the interview or in the final selection stage. And we will look into talent acquisition analytics to evaluate how to understand how analytics works best in each of these stages.

Different elements of analytics can be used during the interview and selection process to determine the best interview approach, including whether it should be in person or via videoconference, as well as:

- Number of participants who should participate in the interview.
- Number of interview rounds before an offer is made.
- Relevancy of a resume (or is the resume even still relevant for today's work world?).
- Number of interview questions to ask.
- Types of questions to ask.
- What work product is still relevant (primary and secondary).
- What candidate profile is most relevant to the job opening.
- The interview performance versus the candidate's resume.

Predictive talent acquisition analytics can also help to assess key performance metrics, such as:

- The correlation between interview and job performance.
- Type and number of questions asked during interview and job performance.
- Quality of the resume and the interview performance.
- Number of questions properly answered versus job performance.
- Academic background versus job performance.
- Resume highlights versus performance at work.
- Work product versus interview performance.
- Work product versus performance at work.

Analytics can also anticipate job performance versus the quality of a resume or the candidate's interview performance. Similar to customer acquisition, predictive behavior models should be used by your company to identify the best candidate, whom we define as someone:

- Who is a great cultural fit.
- Who enjoys your company's culture, employment brand, and value proposition.
- Who is engaged and motivated to relish challenges.
- Who will be a top performer, productive, loyal, and a strong advocate.
- Who will stay with your organization.

HOW GOOGLE HIRES

CASE STUDY

"Hiring is the most important thing you do."

—*Eric Schmidt, former CEO of Google*

By leveraging its People Analytics team's findings and recommendations, Google has reduced the number of interview questions, as well as the number of interviews—no more than four—before an offer is made. After analyzing the data through its People Analytics Project,[1] and after crunching dozens of numbers and analyzing thousands of interview variables, Google decided to get rid of problem-solving questions such as "How many golf balls would fit in an aircraft?"

They also found that educational background and degrees from big-name schools do not guarantee an employee's performance quality at work. In fact, according to a *New York Times* interview with Laszlo Bock, Google's Head of People Operations,[2] grades don't predict anything about who is going to be a successful employee: "One of the things we've seen from all our data crunching is that GPA's are worthless as criteria for hiring, and test scores are worthless—no correlation at all except for brand-new college grads, where there's a slight correlation." He continues: "Google famously used to ask everyone for a transcript and GPA's and test scores, but we don't anymore, unless you're just a few years out of school. We found that they don't predict anything. What's interesting is the proportion of people without any college education at Google that has increased over time as well. So we have teams where you have 14 percent of the team made up of people who've never gone to college."

WHY SHOULD YOU CARE ABOUT ACQUISITION ANALYTICS?

The employment world is changing and the war for skilled talent is far from over. Companies now operate in a global, competitive talent marketplace that is propelled by Big Data, social media, an intergenerational workforce, and a myriad of publicly available data. All this digital information, when properly mined, can help organizations to compete on talent analytics and, ultimately, win the war of talent acquisition and retention.

Today, talent is in high demand and the competition to acquire skilled employees is increasing, particularly as we are seeing tremendous improvement and unprecedented growth in the U.S. job market, which is changing the supply-and-demand equation. The labor market is becoming candidate driven, and job seekers now have multiple choices. Consequently, acquiring the right talent is becoming one of the most important priorities for a lot of employers.

This new work ecosystem is challenging companies to change the way they source and acquire talent. A Deloitte study found that 67 percent of companies surveyed have updated their talent acquisition strategy to adapt to the new world of work.[3] Predictive analytics is one of the ways they are ensuring they reach their target audience, select the best candidates, and avoid the costs of bad hires.

Trying to navigate your way through the Internet revolution that has digitalized talent information and sharply increased the volume of the publicly available talent footprints requires new tactics to acquire new talent. Forward-looking companies are leveraging the power of predictive analytics to adapt and enhance the way they do this. This approach is helping them to succeed when competing on talent analytics and, more important, ensures they are making the right hires for their organization, avoiding early turnover and the associated negative financial impact. With this approach, they focus on the right job applicants, and analytics helps them hire the right people.

Your Employees Are the Most Important Asset of Your Organization

People are the most important asset of any organization, and the quality of people you hire is the backbone of your workforce. Wisely investing in this resource defines the ability of your organization to perform, innovate, compete, succeed, and lead. To reach that success and high performance, organizations must hire the best people: the right employees with the right skills and who are a good cultural fit.

Traditional talent acquisition approaches that are solely based upon resumes and interviews are no longer sufficient in proactively identifying the best applicants. This methodology also fails to identify which candidates will be successful at the job once hired.

There is also the very real issue of recruitment bandwidth. Depending on the popularity of the open job requisition, hiring managers can quickly become inundated with myriad resumes and job applicant profiles that they are required to sift through in order to uncover the best candidate matches. To succeed, employers must act quickly, precisely, and cost-effectively. This requires the use of advanced analytics tools and solutions when looking to fill these types of roles.

With talent scarcity and an extremely competitive labor market, propelled by Big Data and the availability of candidates' publicly available digital footprints, companies failing to leverage predictive analytics in the hiring process will take two major bottom-line hits: the cost of acquisition to replace the turnover, and the overall cost of the bad hire.

Doing the Math: The Basic Cost of Talent Acquisition

On average, the cost of acquisition for an entry-level role is estimated to be $3,000.[4] Therefore, if an organization with 2,500 customer service representatives has a turnover rate of 40 percent, it will have to replace 1,000 employees each year, and that translates to $3 million in basic acquisition costs. Restarting the acquisition process usually requires beginning from the first step in talent acquisition and, more important, offsetting the cost of making a bad hire.

The Cost of a Bad Hire

Hiring the wrong person for a job can undermine your company's success and interfere with its ability to compete and lead in the market. According to Ryan Holmes, CEO of Hootsuite, "One subpar employee can throw an entire department into disarray. Team members end up investing their own time into training someone who has no future with the company."[5]

Tony Hsieh, the CEO of Zappos (now an Amazon-owned company), estimated that his own bad hires have cost the company well over $100 million.[6] That's part of the reason he now offers new hires a $2,000 bonus to quit after their first week on the job. And most recently Jeff Bezos, the CEO of Amazon, the behemoth online retail company, was offering up to $5,000 to employees who were not engaged to quit their jobs.[7]

The U.S. Department of Labor currently estimates that the average cost of a bad hiring decision can equal 30 percent of the employee's first-year potential earnings.[8] This means a single bad hire who has an annual income of $50,000 can cost an employer a potential $15,000. Others say it could be even higher than that. According to a study by the Society for Human Resource Management, it could cost up to five times a bad hire's annual salary.[9]

Not all impacts are financial, however. A bad hire also impacts productivity and team morale. Some studies point out that as much as 80 percent of employee turnover is due to bad hiring decisions.[10]

Playing the "What If?" Game

- But what if you could leverage predictive analytics to have your hiring manager or recruiter meet *only* with potential candidates who are best suited for the job and are likely to be successful at your organization?

- What if you could reduce your new employee turnover by selecting the right job applicants to interview, and focusing your HR team's efforts on only meeting with those who would be the best fit for the position?

- What if you could avoid all the costs of hiring the wrong candidate from the get-go?

- What if you could use analytics to anticipate which candidate will be the right employee for the job?

- What if you could use analytics to assess the impact of resumes of applicants who went to schools with well-known names on candidate performance at work?

These questions are components of a talent acquisition analytics business case, and predictive analytics is designed to help recruiters and HR managers to focus on the best potential talent—those who will be successful at the job.

Your organization's turnover and performance are linked to the people you hire, and traditional hiring methodologies are no longer efficient or accurate. The world of work is changing and requires a combination of art (intuition and experience) and science (data analytics) to the get the speed, precision, and cost efficiency your organization needs during its talent acquisition process.

 PROFILE

Interview with Dawn Klinghoffer, Senior Director of HR Business Insights, Microsoft

JP Isson had the opportunity to discuss the impact of People Analytics in talent acquisition with Dawn Klinghoffer of Microsoft, a multinational technology company with more than 118,000 employees worldwide.

Isson: The majority of organizations I've spoken with have told me they are being inundated with data and reports, and do not have enough understanding of what that talent data and those reports mean. Would you agree, and, if so, how is your organization working to leverage its talent data in a way that leads to better understanding and insight (such as acquiring, developing, or retaining talent)?

Klinghoffer: I completely agree—we have more data and reports than you could imagine—but we can't expect anyone to take the time to go through all of them on a regular basis. *It is really important to understand the problem you are trying to solve before you start diving into the data,* and then it is easier to make sure you are looking at analytics that helps you take action. We actually teach our HR professionals that in a course we lead internally called "Using HR Data to Drive Decisions." Another way we are helping the organization to leverage data is to provide reports in a visual format—we have been fortunate to leverage our PowerBI tools to enable more data visualization when it comes to looking at attrition and/or hiring trends.

Isson: Can you give me examples of workforce/ human capital challenges your company has addressed with analytics in the past? What solutions did you leverage, and what were the benefits of your investment?

Klinghoffer: One of the challenges that we have addressed with analytics is around hiring. There was a feeling that we should only recruit from certain schools that would yield the highest-quality candidates, but that was not something that we actually measured—it was more of a feeling that we had, that certain schools produced highly qualified candidates. We created a Quality of Hire measure, where we looked at this deeply, and it really ended up changing some of our hiring strategies once we were able to analyze the results.

Isson: What is the number one benefit or top reason to invest in People Analytics? What is the biggest hurdle you will face when implementing?

Klinghoffer: People Analytics can really give you the insights on how to attract and retain the best employees. The biggest hurdle is often getting your data in a state in which it is easy to analyze.

(Continued)

(Continued)

Isson: In this Big Data era, what advice would you give to a company trying to get the most out of its People Analytics capabilities? What are the dos and don'ts of this undertaking? What strategies are important to make the project successful?

Klinghoffer:

- People Analytics is a journey; and it is important to bring your clients along on this journey.

- Make sure they understand the value that looking at data can bring—it is not the answer to all questions, but it is a valuable input when making decisions. It is critical that you work with your clients to understand the problems they are trying to solve; don't just provide an answer to the question, but ask questions back to really understand the context.

- Make sure your data is clean; if you are trying to make decisions on data that is not accurate, you may end up making the wrong decisions.

- Start small—prove the impact you can have with data.

- And finally, hire the right people. Hire people that are passionate about analytics, but that are just as passionate about people.

Isson: How do you see People Analytics being used now and in the future? What do you foresee as the single biggest impact that People Analytics will have on businesses?

Klinghoffer: Being able to be proactive about your talent decisions and not reactive will save time and money.

Lessons Learned from Marketing Customer Acquisition Processes

Although it's been nearly 17 years, one of this book's authors, JP Isson, still remembers his days in telecommunications, where he was working as a customer behavior modeling manager, helping the marketing team to address their new business and customer attrition challenges, called "churn" in industry jargon. Back then, the company had an aggressive customer acquisition team known as "hunter ninjas." The hunter ninjas were solely focused on converting new prospects to customers. These aggressive acquisition techniques were propelled and rewarded with generous commissions based on the volume of monthly new business and new customers the hunter ninjas brought into the pipeline. The retention team was then responsible for welcoming these new customers, and was tasked with relationship development strategies to get them to become profitable and loyal customers.

The challenge with this approach was the sharp ongoing new business attrition. In fact, the company's new business attrition skyrocketed. The majority of these newly acquired customers were not loyal; they were leaving after just three or four months after generating a mediocre revenue per user (RPU) that was 30 percent less than the average existing customer's RPU. It was a flawed model.

It was only a matter of time before the finance team began questioning these acquisition results, comparing key performance indicators (KPIs) such as RPU, churn, and retention rates, and requested answers from the marketing team. Under pressure, the marketing team decided to review their approach, and sought to first understand the profile of new business, asking for insights that would enable them to anticipate new customers' behavior—all by leveraging predictive analytics and customer lifetime value. The ultimate expectation of using analytics was to select new, high-potential customers from the source.

It was JP's role to help build an understanding of these customer profiles needed for new business acquisition and create predictive models for identifying what type of prospects the company should acquire, when, and why. The way he accomplished this was by crossing the best prospects against their potential value in order to ensure that the acquisition team was focusing its efforts on converting the most valuable prospects who had a probability of becoming loyal. After completing these analyses, predictive model scores were used to prioritize the ninja hunter team's activities.

A Hunter Ninja's Guide to Acquiring New High-Value Customers

The first step in implementing actionable strategies based on our predictive model scores was to understand the profile of new business attrition and analyze these customers against the nonchurners. After looking at a variety of variables, we analyzed target versus control groups to assess the quality and the performance of the model versus acquisition activities. After completing our predictive analytics, we realized the importance of five variables:

1. ZIP code
2. Credit score
3. Product diversity
4. Type of handset upgrade
5. Sphere of influence

These variables were the most important drivers of new business attrition, providing a profile of the customers who were more likely to leave after just three months of tenure. The acquisition team was mandated to use predictive model scores to prioritize their activities, which meant they targeted only high-scored prospects.

To measure the return on investment (ROI) of injecting analytics into this new methodology, target versus control group KPIs were analyzed, and the target group recorded a 37 percent increase in retention. With a difference of $30 RPU compared to $42 RPU, the new model clearly demonstrated it was assisting the acquisition team with early churn, and reducing new business churn by 37 percent. The early churn (one to four months) recorded a sharp drop from 50 percent to 30 percent. This decrease in new business attrition helped the company to improve new customer loyalty and recover its acquisition costs by building better, longer, and more profitable relationships with new customers.

This was a story with a happy ending for sure, particularly if you keep in mind that 17 years ago, the cost of customer acquisition in the telecommunications industry was between $350 and $600. This meant that in order for the company to break even, a new customer needed to stay at least 12 months if she or he had an RPU of $30. Having the vast majority of newly acquired customers leaving after their third or fourth months was costing the company a lot of money despite those high acquisition numbers.

The injection of predictive analytics into customer acquisition practices demonstrated great results because it helped both the acquisition and marketing teams to focus on the most valuable and loyal customers who would create strong margins for the company and drive profitability.

Those lessons learned can be extrapolated to talent acquisition practices, and by following a similar framework of using the power of predictive analytics, your organization can acquire the best talent and build a workforce that is engaged, motivated, productive, and loyal, and that will become keepers and advocates for the company employment brand and value proposition.

Interview with Ian Bailie, Director of Talent Acquisition Operations, CISCO

PROFILE

JP Isson had the opportunity to speak with Ian Bailie of CISCO, the worldwide leader in Internet services, to discuss the impact of data analytics in talent acquisition.

Isson: Why did CISCO decide to invest in People Analytics?

Bailie: At CISCO, talent analytics helps us to determine where we should be hiring, where to find that talent, and how we can best plan for shortages in specific occupations and given regions. And that can only happen by leveraging People Analytics.

The CISCO leadership team also wants to have strategic conversations with HR when addressing company business challenges. They are involved with helping hiring managers to find the best talent. You cannot achieve workforce planning, talent acquisition, or talent retention goals without data analytics, and our leadership team understands that. Talent analytics helps us to become more strategic as a company.

(Continued)

(*Continued*)

The great thing about recruitment is that it is a measurable process and it directly impacts the business. Tying metrics [to business objectives] and telling a strategic story filled with data about quality of hire, time to fill, best employees, best performance, and the ROI of the investment are tangible across all stages of the talent management cycle.

This is helping us to provide better understanding of how to bring in the best persons we can find to fill our open requisitions. When you leverage data to do that, then you are more likely to reduce your talent acquisition costs, retention costs, and onboarding costs, and drive the overall business performance.

Isson: What was your next challenge after mastering all your talent data, and how did that impact the business?

Bailie: Once you've got a good handle on your data, your next goal is to address the question of how to make sure everybody has what they need in the report and present it in a format that is easy to use, accessible, and visually appealing and empowers the recruiters with salient information. This is where you can stop being reactive and start to become more predictive, using the data insights to make future decisions.

It's really about changing the conversation and providing recruiting teams with insights to drive their conversations with their business lines, as opposed to just talking about how many requisitions they need to fill for the organization. It's about providing guidance and relevant metrics about the quality of hire, the satisfaction level of the employees, products, services, and the overall performance.

Data analytics also helped us to educate recruiters to look beyond the recruitment aspect and focus on the business angle—for instance, by considering the impact of these recruitment decisions on the rest of the company, and tying data and reports to key business objectives.

Isson: What did the strategic reporting and insights help you to achieve?

Bailie: Strategic reporting helps us to understand several things, including:

- Defining our strategies for attracting and acquiring talent for specific hard-to-fill roles.
- Determining how to best leverage data (and have the appropriate resources in place to mine the data) to best assess sources of hire.
- Identifying the best time to source for talent.
- Determining where to find those talents and how best to connect with them.

The data now provides us with answers to all those questions. We are using analytics to be more efficient, and can now address complex questions, such as "Should we use a job board, referral program, or social media to find specific talent in a given region?" We are becoming more efficient and successful, and it is helping us to have a more strategic conversation with management and compete on talent analytics.

Isson: How do you look outside of the recruitment space?

Bailie: Typically, the way we use performance measurement for some roles is a great model for how one can look outside of recruitment.

Take sales, for instance: We hold our sales teams to a target, and we look at how they are doing against that target. We need to change the conversation to be more about what the business needs to get in order to be successful, and how in HR we can use data to help the business hire the best employees who will stay long term and perform well at work. It's about improving the overall quality of hire for the organization. This will also help to reduce sourcing and talent acquisition costs, and reduce the time to productivity, because you will be hiring the best talent.

Changing the conversation is paramount: Recruiter conversations should be about what the business needs in order to be successful. And they will be successful if we get them the best candidates, but we need to be good to get them the right talent. If it usually takes 90 days to fill a given role and we can get the candidate in in 60 days, that is a huge

(*Continued*)

(Continued)

gain for the business. We play an integral role in helping the business meet its goals by supplying them with the ideal candidate they need to drive performance.

For recruiters, these business conversations should cover:

- The quality of hire.
- The impact of new talent on the bottom line.
- Talent band rate/cost of talent.
- Showcasing the incremental retention value of acquiring great talent who fit the role.

It's about hiring the best talent and creating the best pipeline. At CISCO, we are able to tie talent acquisition metrics and insights to business metrics to create an actionable strategic business story. This has enabled us to help our company to leverage data to make more informed decisions.

HOW TALENT ACQUISITION WORKS

The hiring process varies from organization to organization. At some places, talent selection is a chaotic and disorganized process that is different for each department. Yet, in others, hiring is a long, arduous, and bureaucratic process that is painful for candidates and employers alike. However, generally, the selection process involves four stages:

1. Application
2. Preselection
3. Interviews
4. Selection

Whatever your selection process is, injecting analytics throughout it will make for more engaged workers and happier hiring managers.

When thinking about talent acquisition and hiring, most HR departments focus on process-related outcomes such as the number of qualified candidates sent to the hiring manager, time to hire/fill, cost per hire, time to productivity, and 90-day retention rate. These are important metrics to monitor, but not what impactful acquisition analytics aims to accomplish. Effective acquisition analytics attempts to understand the candidate criteria and inputs that lead to a business outcome—in other words, something the hiring executive, CFO, or CEO would care about. Therefore, the first step in creating a high-impact selection analytics program is to identify and gain buy-in on what success looks like for hiring in a particular role. What's the critical business outcome of having that role in your organization? For example, the following is a list with job roles and example business outcomes they may drive.

Role	Business Outcome
Salesperson	Quarterly sales
Customer service rep	Call resolution rate
Engineer	Bug fixes; code released
Media buyer	Marketing cost per new lead
Financial analyst	Time to accounting close
Internal tech support	Case resolution rate

These are the outcome measures that you ultimately want to leverage analytics to model and successfully predict the right talent before they even join the organization.

APPLICATION PHASE

Applications for any given job vary greatly from organization to organization. Even within a company, one department may have a form that it prefers candidate information come in, whereas a different department may require a longer form. The federal government is notorious for requiring a very long and complicated application form for any candidate being considered for a position. In terms of effective application analytics, you should encourage your organization to move to standardized data collection as much as is possible.

Despite the use of application forms for employee selection, illegal (or inappropriate) application items are still somewhat common. Laws vary from country to country; however, questionable items are generally those that request personal information such as gender, race, national origin, education dates, and disabilities. The most commonly found inappropriate questions involve past salary levels, age, driver's license information, citizenship information, and Social Security numbers. Although the majority of applications do not explicitly ask about age, many include inquiries about an applicant's education dates (year of high school graduation), which can be used to infer an applicant's age. Adhering to good practices is especially important if you intend to engage in extensive selection analytics. You want it to be clear that your information collection practices are consistent with the hiring laws for your country and that you're not directly or indirectly engaging in illegal hiring practices. You'll need to rely on your HR Equal Employment Opportunity Commission expert to make sure your data collection and analytics programs are consistent with the hiring laws for your area.

Most large organizations use an applicant tracking system (ATS) that requires the online submission of an application or resume. These ATSs can scan applications and resumes for keywords, thereby minimizing the time spent by HR in reviewing documents. Obviously, this saves time in the HR department, but employers using automated tracking systems must be cautious. Applicants are becoming more sophisticated in the process and stuffing their applications and resumes with keywords even when they are not truly qualified for the open position. Regardless of the methods used, it's typical to get hundreds of applications for an open position. Wading through them can be very time-consuming. This is where analytics can help.

DATA SCIENCE APPLIED TO CANDIDATE SELECTION

We asked Matt Gough, CEO of Echovate, what talent data points are really important for a data-driven candidate selection:

Gough: We throw around a lot of terms in traditional HR to sound exciting and edgy: terms like *Big Data, data analytics, people intelligence, workforce analytics, predictive talent selection, engagement, retention*, and on and on. It all comes down to one real thing we have lost track of: It's all about people. People build companies, people service customers, and people live the vision. People have families, hopes, and dreams. Companies live or die by their people. How do we get at the very heart of a person? How do we understand people's individuality and where they will thrive in an organization? How do we empower them to reach their greatest success in life?

We need to turn to two key areas to truly understand people's uniqueness:

1. **A person's behavioral fingerprint.** This is the core of their being, their personality that was locked in by first grade or the age of 7. These attributes tell a story about their future performance in an organization and how they will collaborate with others. When you look at these stories in unison, a blurry picture comes into view. This is not rocket science; it is behavioral science with nearly 100 years' worth of psychology at work digested into five or six fundamental groups. This science is used by the world's best organizations with a high degree of success.

2. **A person's digital footprint.** This is the trail they leave when moving around from web property to web property or from company to company. We are not suggesting Big Brother monitoring of people. For example, if they have always worked doing social good at companies with fewer than 200 employees, they may struggle to excel on Wall Street at a 10,000-person firm. This might especially be true if you layer in their international travel to remote areas and their excitement for new experiences and unstructured environments.

This falls into the category of People Analytics, a mash-up of people and data to make more insightful decisions in real time. The impact is extraordinary and directly correlates to success, defined differently in each organization and by

(Continued)

(*Continued*)

each person. Sometimes it is very tangible like reducing turnover, increasing a Net Promoter Score, or increasing sales. Other times it is less tangible like improving team collaboration, building greater trust, and improving overall morale.

The most exciting opportunities are when small-to-medium businesses (SMBs) leverage People Analytics to solve high-impact business problems. This will level the playing field with their larger competitors, significantly reduce failure rates, and build a stronger employment outlook as a result. These SMBs will further accelerate their growth by aggregating and making anonymous the data on their people and performance, and sharing it across industries or job categories. For the first time they will have a data set that has been unavailable due to the very nature of their relatively small size. With this data set, they will drive their businesses forward in ways they have never before been able to do.

The pendulum is shifting. For years we used technology to move large amounts of people through a process. Now we are leveraging technology to discover a person's uniqueness, his or her individuality, and how the "power of one" can impact an entire organization, creating microcultures along the way.

PREINTERVIEW ASSESSMENT ANALYTICS

After you have used analytics to narrow your applicant pool, you still are probably left with dozens of people whose resumes look good and who appear on paper like they could be successful. There's still a ton of work left to do in your selection process. Fortunately, analytics can help in narrowing down the pool of candidates even further:

- Which candidates are most likely to succeed in the role?
- Which candidates should we interview?
- Which candidates are the best cultural fit for my organization?
- Which candidates have the skills they claim?
- What type of candidates typically succeed in my organization

There are a number of methods organizations use to determine if an applicant has the potential to be successful on the job. Selection tests are used to identify applicants' skills that cannot be easily determined in an interview process. Using a variety of testing methods, applicants can be rated on aptitude, personality, abilities, honesty, and motivation. Properly designed selection tests are standardized, reliable, and valid in predicting an applicant's success on the job.

To objectively compare applicants, the processes used for testing those applicants must be as identical as possible. The content of the test, the instructions, and the time allowed must be the same for all candidates. Also, you should ask yourself whether the test is reliable. In other words, does it provide consistent results each time an applicant takes it? A test's reliability should be questioned if it does not generate consistent results each time it is used. Last, you should consider test validity. In other words, does the test measure what it claims to measure? For example, do higher test scores consistently predict higher success on the job?

You can also use analytics to get a perspective on so-called soft skills among prospective candidates. These skills primarily refer to interpersonal and general analytic abilities like teamwork, empathy, leadership, negotiation, adaptability, and problem-solving ability.

However, soft skills can be subjective and are very difficult to assess, especially before one can evaluate a candidate on the job. Can a candidate think innovatively? Collaborate with other team members? Assimilate feedback and coaching? Will the candidate be adaptable to new environments and successfully integrate with teams? It is very difficult to reduce these questions to discrete qualifications and quantifiable metrics in the same way we assess recognized degrees and numerical grades.

Certainly some valid approaches exist. For example, businesses have used type-based personality tests for decades in an attempt to measure the soft skills of prospective candidates, assuming that certain personality types correlate with high performance. One example is the Jung Typology Profiler for Workplace®, which purports to measure qualities such as *power* (leadership potential), *assurance, visionary, rationality*, and so forth.

For developing existing teams, there is also evidence that type-based personality tests can help managers better develop and deploy the talent they have already hired. For example, Gallup's StrengthsFinder

2.0 is a tool that helps individuals understand and describe their own talents, and is commonly used by managers to understand and capitalize on the strengths of those they hire.

For example, Facebook uses StrengthsFinder in a clever way to deploy talent efficiently.[11] Regardless of the job openings it has available, Facebook simply hires the smartest people it can find, and then uses StrengthsFinder results to understand their talents and create a job tailored to each new hire.

INTERVIEWS: SEPARATING THE WHEAT FROM THE CHAFF

Preselection testing and analytics will trim your pool of candidates, but you'll likely need to narrow the list even further to a reasonable number for in-depth interviews. Therefore, many organizations prefer to do a screening interview of those applicants who appear qualified based on all of the information obtained so far in the process. The interviewer asks a few straightforward questions, usually via phone, to determine the candidate's job qualifications and appropriateness for the open position.

If it is determined that the applicant is not appropriate for the position, the interviewer may refer the candidate to another open position within the organization if there is something available that matches the applicant's skills. If there is nothing else available and the candidate is obviously unqualified for the position, the process ends there, saving both the candidate and the organization the time and expense of going further into the selection process.

The nature of the job and how much time you can afford to allot to the interview process will determine how many applicants you choose to interview. Three or four may be plenty, but choosing more may be important for you to get a good feel for the candidates' qualifications. The interview is really a verbal test for the candidate. However, there is no clear right or wrong answer in many cases. The results are subject to interpretation by the interviewer and thus can have a huge potential for error, depending on the questions asked, the answers given, and the interviewer's own personal bias.

A 1998 meta-analysis by Schmidt and Hunter evaluated which employee selection methods were predictive of job success. The short answer is that nothing was perfect. However, unstructured interviews stood out as especially ineffective and were almost equivalent to hiring randomly.[12] That doesn't mean the interview has no purpose. Their analysis showed that work sample measures combined with a structured interview had high predictive power of performance in job training programs, as well as performance on the job.

The structured interview is a widely used interview technique and can be leveraged through analytics to see which answers are predictive of future job success in your organization. In a structured or patterned interview, the interviewer follows a preset list of questions asked of all candidates. This allows for consistency in the process, ensures that important questions are not left out, and helps guarantee that all candidates will be assessed by the same standards. The more you can standardize your interview questions, the more analytics can help you understand which responses (if any) are predictive of future success in the role and the business outcome you desire for the role.

Leading companies are using analytics to make the interview process more effective. Take Google as an example. Laszlo Bock, Google's senior vice president of people operations, did a study to determine whether anyone at Google is particularly good at hiring. Bock's team looked at tens of thousands of interviews, at everyone who had done the interviews and how they scored the candidate, and how that person ultimately performed in the job. Bock found zero relationship, saying that "it was a complete random mess, except for one guy who was highly predictive because he only interviewed people for a very specialized area, where he happened to be the world's leading expert."[13]

However, there were positive findings in other areas. For example, they were able to figure out how many job candidates they should be interviewing for each position, which team members were better interviewers than others, and what kind of attributes tend to predict success at Google. They also found that brainteasers are ineffective. Questions such as "How many Ping-Pong balls can you fit into an airplane?" or "How many gallons of paint does it take to cover a skyscraper?" do not predict anything about people applying to work for Google.

Instead, what works well for Google are structured behavioral interviews, where there is consistency in how people are assessed, rather than having each interviewer just ask questions differently.

Behavioral interviewing is where you don't give someone a hypothetical, but you start with a question like "Give me an example of a time when you solved an analytically difficult problem." Behavioral interviewing provides an opportunity not only to understand the literal answer given, but to get an example of how the candidate interacted in a real-world situation as well as a sense of what the person considers to be difficult.

Examples of Google interview questions that were found to be predictive of job performance include:[14]

- Tell me about a time when your behavior had a positive impact on your team. (Follow-ups: What was your primary goal and why? How did your teammates respond? Moving forward, what's your plan?)

- Tell me about a time when you effectively managed your team to achieve a goal. What did your approach look like? (Follow-ups: What were your targets, and how did you meet them as an individual and as a team? How did you adapt your leadership approach to different individuals? What was the key takeaway from this specific situation?)

- Tell me about a time when you had difficulty working with someone (can be a coworker, classmate, or client). What made this person difficult to work with for you? (Follow-ups: What steps did you take to resolve the problem? What was the outcome? What could you have done differently?)

Also, after years of forcing job candidates to endure endless rounds of interviews and tests, Google used data to discover that, for them, after a candidate has gone through four different interviewers, every interview after that is largely a waste of time.

PUTTING IT ALL TOGETHER: PREDICTIVE ANALYTICS FOR SELECTION

Predictive talent acquisition models leverage Big Data and statistical models to anticipate which candidates you should select, why you should select them, and the best time for hiring them. This approach generally relies on predictive behavioral assessment models that assign a predictive score to every prospective hire or job applicant after they answer a set of assessment questions that can include topics addressing happiness/fulfillment, performance, cultural fit, and job requirements. This primary score allows hiring managers and recruiters to evaluate all prospective hires and group them into high, medium, and low buckets, and focus their attention and efforts on the high segment, or those who are more likely to be successful at work if hired. This group will include candidates the manager should meet with for a soft skills assessment to further evaluate them based on their experience, instinct, personality, and cultural fit. Predictive analytics helps HR teams to select the right candidates from the best-scored candidates, as described in the Talent Acquisition Analytics Funnel (Figure 6.1).

So, what are the stages of the Talent Acquisition Analytics Funnel?

1. Job applicants from sourcer fill out the predictive model assessment questionnaire.
2. Predictive models are run to produce a score tied to success at the job for every job candidate based on their questionnaire inputs.
3. Every candidate is assigned a score and categorized into high, medium, or low segments based on their scores.
4. The hiring manager then meets only with high-scoring applicants and selects the best candidates. The final selection combines the art of recruitment (the hiring manager's instinct and experience) and the science of recruitment (though the predictive analytics score model).
5. The best candidate is then selected and hired.

Additionally, to be successful, this overall talent acquisition analytics requires the right people, processes, and technology:

■ **People:** Assembling the team:
1. Sourcer to provide initial list of candidate profiles
2. Hiring manager to interview and select candidates
3. Data scientist to provide actionable insights to help hiring manager to make the best candidate selection

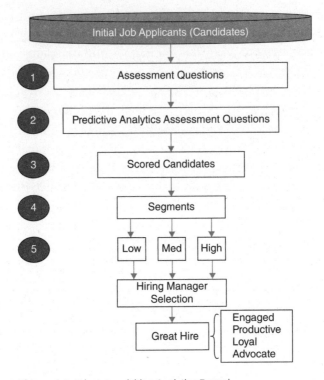

Figure 6.1 Talent Acquisition Analytics Funnel

- ■ **Process:** The Talent Acquisition Analytics Funnel, as described previously
- ■ **Tools and technologies:** Data science and workforce analytics providers/third-party vendors: Talent Analytics, Corp., Evolv (now acquired by CornerStone OnDemand), hiQLabs, Hogan Assessment, and others)

Hiring the Best Salesperson

Josh Bersin is the founder of Bersin by Deloitte, a leading provider of research-based membership programs in HR, talent, and learning. One of his clients, a large financial services company, operated under a belief system that employees who earned good grades at highly ranked colleges would be good performers. So the company's recruitment, selection, and promotion process was based on these academic drivers.

Several years ago some of its analysts performed a statistical analysis of sales productivity and turnover. They looked at sales performance over the first two years of a new employee and correlated total performance and retention rates against a variety of demographic factors. What they found was astounding. The results were as follows:[15]

What did drive sales performance:

■ An accurate, grammatically correct resume.

■ Having completed some education from beginning to end.

■ Having successful sales experience in high-priced items.

■ Having demonstrated success in some prior job.

■ Ability to work under unstructured conditions.

What did *not* matter:

■ Where candidates went to school.

■ What GPAs they had.

■ The quality of their references.

Within six months of implementing a new screening process, revenues increased $4 million.

XEROX: LESSON FROM THE FRONTLINES

CASE STUDY

Xerox, one of the leviathans of technology and business solutions, had a huge attrition problem; however, with Evolv's help it managed to leverage predictive analytics to reduce churn and employee turnover by 20 percent. Using predictive analytics, they also discovered that the experience of the service representative does not necessarily guarantee his or her performance at work. They also found that personality and social media activity (defined as being active on at least one but not more than four social channels or networks) is a good indicator of successful performance as a customer service representative.

In a written case study of Xerox's success, experts described Xerox's approach as follows:

San Francisco analytics start-up Evolv helped Xerox reduce call center turnover by gathering and studying data on the

(Continued)

(*Continued*)

characteristics and job performance of front-line employees, and then applying what it learned to the hiring process. Evolv found that employees without call center experience were just as successful as those who had it, allowing Xerox to broaden its candidate pool. Creative personalities stayed longer than those with inquisitive personalities, as did candidates who belonged to at least one but not more than four social networks. Armed with such detailed information on what made a successful hire, Xerox was able to reduce attrition by 20 percent. Given that it costs Xerox $5,000 to train a call center employee, that reduction had a real financial impact. And therein lies the attraction of predictive analytics: It offers a myriad of opportunities for cost savings and efficiencies related to a company's recruiting and talent management efforts. As other areas of the enterprise increasingly use analytics in their work, more pressure is being brought to bear on HR to develop the same capabilities.[16]

By integrating analytics into their acquisition processes and leveraging predictive models, companies are seeing clear and measurable benefits, as they possess insights into where and when they should invest time and resources on the right job applicants. They are also empowering their hiring managers and complementing their skills, experience, and intuition by helping them hone in on the best candidates for the interview process. Because the world of work is changing and the job market is increasingly more competitive, finding skilled talent is challenging employers to rethink and adapt the way they approach their talent acquisition strategy.

Faced with the scarcity of skilled talent and operating in a candidate-driven labor market in the United States, leading companies have turned to Big Data analytics solutions to optimize their talent acquisition efforts. This approach is helping them avoid the significant costs associated with bad hires and, more important, enable them to hire the best people for their organization: employees who will help innovate, drive performance, lead, and succeed. This is why today's best companies are competing on talent analytics.

KEY TAKEAWAYS

- The benefits of predictive analytics models that are used in marketing customer acquisition strategies can also be applied to workforce talent acquisition.

- In today's candidate-driven market, companies should leverage predictive analytics in their hiring process to remove guesswork, using the Talent Acquisition Analytics Funnel as the preliminary job applicant selection criterion.

- As quoted by Eric Schmidt, former executive chairman of Google, earlier in the chapter, hiring is the most important thing you do and requires the same rigor as you would have in engineering, sales, marketing, or customer acquisition to get valuable, loyal, and profitable talent.

- For some positions, resumes may be a secondary work product, and may not always be reflective of the candidate's performance abilities. Insight can also be obtained through their social media activity, as it exhibits how candidates are engaging with others and being recognized by peers on professional sites such as GitHub, Google+, Stack Overflow, and Twitter.

- Analytics helps to harness all the available data needed to streamline the number of resources and minimize the costs associated with interviews and the candidate selection process.

- Leveraging analytics allows organizations to reduce new employee turnover and the cost of a bad hire that can undermine your company's success.

- Today's state-of-the-art tools and technologies can empower your HR and acquisition teams, enabling them to be more productive when sourcing, connecting, and engaging with job candidates via social media and your career site.

- Acquiring talent today should be a combination of art (hiring manager instinct, intuition, and experience) and science (the power of predictive modeling) to deliver the best prospective hires.

NOTES

1. Adam Bryant, "In Head-Hunting, Big Data May Not Be Such a Big Deal," *New York Times*, June 20, 2013, www.nytimes.com/2013/06/20/business/in-head-hunting-big-data-may-not-be-such-a-big-deal.html.

2. Thomas L Friedman, "How to Get a Job at Google," *New York Times*, February 24, 2014,www.nytimes.com/2014/02/23/opinion/sunday/friedman-how-to-get-a-job-at-google.html?_r=0.

3. Lisa Barry, Udo Bohdal-Spiegelhoff, Robin Erickson, and Kim Lamoureux, "Talent Acquisition Revisited: Deploy New Approaches for the New Battlefield," Deloitte, March 2014, http://dupress.com/articles/hc-trends-2014-talent-acquisition/.

4. Karen O'Leonard, *Talent Acquisition Fact Book 2011*, Bersin and Associates, November 2011, http://marketing.bersin.com/rs/bersin/images/111111_ES_TAFB-Exec-Summ_KOL.pdf; Rachel Emma Silverman and Nikki Waller, "The Algorithm That Tells the Boss Who Might Quit," *Wall Street Journal*, March 13, 2015, www.wsj.com/articles/the-algorithm-that-tells-the-boss-who-might-quit-1426287935.

5. Ryan Holmes, "The Unexpectedly High Cost of a Bad Hire," Hootsuite, https://www.linkedin.com/pulse/20130716151946-2967511-the-high-costs-of-a-bad-hire-and-how-to-avoid-them.

6. Ibid.

7. Martha C. White, "Amazon Will Pay You $5,000 to Quit Your Job," *Time*, April 11, 2014, http://time.com/58305/amazon-will-pay-you-5000-to-quit-your-job/.

8. Rebekah Cardenas, "What's the Real Cost of a Bad Hire?" Human Resources IQ, April 3, 2014, www.humanresourcesiq.com/recruitment-retention/articles/what-s-the-real-cost-of-a-bad-hire/; Bureau of Labor Statistics, www.bls.gov/; Aoife Gorey, "Who Are You Really Hiring? 10 Shocking HR Stats," HR.com, March 2012, www.hr.com/en/app/blog/2012/03/who-are-you-really-hiring-10-shocking-hr-statistic_h09y2ol0.html.

9. Ava Collins, "The Cost of a Bad Hire and How to Avoid One," *Digitalist Magazine*, January 27, 2015, http://blogs.sap.com/innovation/human-resources/the-cost-of-a-bad-hire-and-how-to-avoid-one-02110549.

10. Fred Yager, "The Cost of Bad Hiring Decisions Runs High," Dice, http://resources.dice.com/report/the-cost-of-bad-hiring-decisions/.

11. Nicholas Carlson, "How Facebook Managed 3,000 Twenty-Somethings into a $100 Billion Company," *Business Insider*, March 28, 2012, www.businessinsider.com/facebooks-100-billion-management-secrets-2012-3.

12. Frank L. Schmidt and John E. Hunter, "The Validity and Utility of Selection Methods in Personnel Psychology," *Psychological Bulletin* 124, no. 2 (1998): 262–274, http://mavweb.mnsu.edu/howard/Schmidt%20and%20Hunter%201998%20Validity%20and%20Utility%20Psychological%20Bulletin.pdf.

13. Bryant, "In Head-Hunting, Big Data May Not Be Such a Big Deal."

14. Lazlo Bock, "Here's Google's Secret to Hiring the Best People," *Wired*, April 7, 2015, www.wired.com/2015/04/hire-like-google/.

15. Josh Bersin, "Big Data in Human Resources: Talent Analytics (People Analytics) Comes of Age," *Forbes*, February 17, 2013, www.forbes.com/sites/joshbersin/2013/02/17/bigdata-in-human-resources-talent-analytics-comes-of-age/.

16. Mark Feffer, "HR Moves toward Wider Use of Predictive Analytics," Society for Human Resource Management, October 6, 2014, www.shrm.org/hrdisciplines/technology/articles/pages/more-hr-pros-using-predictive-analytics.aspx#sthash.4ognwOdz.dpuf.

CHAPTER 7

Onboarding and Culture Fit

A great person attracts great people and knows how to hold them together.

—Johann Wolfgang von Goethe

ll employees create a personal curve of achievement. Some get off to a fast start and then falter, whereas others get up to speed at a good pace and still have the resources to build momentum. Employees engage the organization in a virtuous cycle of productivity and personal growth. Getting off to the right start, as opposed to just a fast start, can make the difference.

Sirota Consulting has been conducting employee research on behalf of companies for the past 40 years, and has discovered some surprising facts when it comes to new hires.[1] The good news is that approximately 90 percent of employees are engaged and motivated when they start a new job. But track employee engagement over time, and a different story emerges. New employee engagement levels often drop dramatically—as much as 20 percentage points—during the first six months on the job. Sirota found that just 10 percent of companies are able to successfully maintain engagement levels over the course of the first year. That means that in most companies, much of the positive energy and enthusiasm that employees arrived with on day one has dissipated six months later. In order to help guard against this erosion of engagement during the first year, analytics must play a key role in ensuring that the new hire experience is successful and leads to positive outcomes for the employee and the organization.

ORGANIZATIONAL CULTURE

Every organization has a unique workplace culture and values. Some companies are more aware of what makes their culture unique, but each workplace has something about it that feels distinct. It might be the passion of employees around a common cause, an intellectual curiosity that's embedded in everything the organization does, the efficiency by which things are accomplished, or the close bond of employees in the company.

Take a company like Constant Contact where the culture is uniquely open, friendly, and collaborative among employees. People are willing to help one another with almost anything, collaboration is valued, and there's a belief that life is too short to work with difficult people. In order to maintain these values, hiring becomes a critical enabler of this culture. If people who are hired are difficult to work with, don't enjoy collaboration, and aren't very willing to help, the entire culture will break down. As a result, successful onboarding becomes a must as new employees learn what's important to the company, how to navigate its resources, and how to become a productive member of the team.

Regardless of your unique culture, one of the keys to successful onboarding is to ensure that each new employee understands and is aligned to the mission and values of your organization so he or she can be effective and get things get done within your four walls. Analytics can play a role in ensuring that you onboard effectively and efficiently.

ONBOARDING PROCESS

Once the right candidates have been hired, they need proper onboarding to ensure they are aligned with the primary business goals and the overall mission of the company, as well as your organization's culture. New hires need to have the best first impression of you as a manager and of your overall organization. Depending on the role and position of your new hire, full onboarding should be accomplished within the first 3 to 12 months, assisting him or her with resources, tools, and clear guidance.

We define talent onboarding as an ongoing talent management process that consists of introducing, training, mentoring, coaching, and integrating a new hire to the core values, business vision, and overall culture of an organization in order to secure new employee loyalty and productivity. And research shows that when organizations have effective onboarding programs, the three-year retention rate of employees jumps by 58 percent.[2]

The Onboarding, Culture Fit, and Engagement pillar can be used to enhance a new hire's first impression and create business value from your onboarding activities and efforts. Taking the time to develop a robust onboarding program will enhance employee satisfaction, increase loyalty, and accelerate time to productivity through an acclimation process. Similar to the customer welcome program that some companies use to introduce new customers to their business, first impressions really do make a difference, and new hire onboarding is a key component of the talent management process: This is her introduction to your organization during the period when she is still thinking about the decision she made to join your company, and, if done properly, it can improve ramp-up time.

This requires mastering data intelligence to optimize the mentoring, learning, and reinforcement to drive the satisfaction your new hires need and to help your organization address vital talent management questions, including:

- How can a business improve time to performance?
- What are the key drivers of time to performance and productivity?
- What is the impact of talent onboarding on employee commitment, productivity, and enthusiasm?
- What is the impact of talent onboarding on employee satisfaction?
- What is the impact of talent onboarding on an employee referral program?
- What is an appropriate talent onboarding budget?
- What impact does talent onboarding have on employee turnover?
- What is the impact of talent onboarding on employee loyalty?

With talent retention as a focus, onboarding should be a great experience that provides new hires with all the information they will need for success. Onboarding analytics should help to quickly address the aforementioned questions, generate enthusiasm, and introduce new hires to the materials and resources needed to accelerate and optimize their time to performance, securing overall goodwill, commitment, and loyalty.

STAGES OF ONBOARDING

Over 75 percent of top-performing companies put new hires through a formal onboarding process.[3] The process can take many forms—classes, activities with departmental and cross-company colleagues, online and written information, and more—and is experiential. People learn their jobs largely by doing, and they learn the best ways to be effective in a company largely by doing as well. A formal process, moreover, assumes that consistent information spreads through the organization. For this reason, getting current employees engaged in the onboarding process for new hires reinforces your employer brand with existing staff.

During onboarding, you're still trying to acquire the hearts and minds of your new employees. You've worked hard to land a talented employee, and that person is with your organization, but not fully of your organization. Engagement is the goal during onboarding. Fortunately, in the early days, a new employee is immersed in all the reasons he took the job—and good onboarding experience reinforces those reasons.

Monster and Benchmark Partners created a five-step outline for a strong onboarding experience, one that engages the new employee closely with the organization, monitors progress, and helps form the bonds of trust that are the cornerstone of retention. Analytics can be an enabler to building an effective onboarding program on this foundation.

Stage 1: First Week, First Impressions

Most employees decide in the first three weeks on the job if they are a fit for the organization. Therefore, the first days and weeks are critical, and you need to put your organization's best foot forward. For example, have a workstation ready with the tools needed to do the job (it's amazing how often this doesn't happen). Get the paperwork out of the way. Introduce the new employee to the team, tour the facilities, and review procedures. Reinforce the job interview and decision process by reviewing short- and long-term goals of the job. Educate new hires on the organization's mission, values, and history. Have a senior leader talk about strategy and market factors like the competitive environment. Assign a buddy in the department and a mentor outside the department—that person's job is to answer questions quickly and in confidence. This is also the best time to get feedback on the recruiting process. Ask "What convinced you to come here?" and "What would you change about the hiring process?"

Stage 2: Getting Acquainted and Avoiding Buyer's Regret (the First 30 Days)

In the first month, new hires should learn their roles and responsibilities in the context of real projects, problems, and activities (as opposed to the job interview). They need to spend time with a manager as well as contacts and leaders of other groups with whom they work. This is the best time to learn the important procedures (such as filing expenses) and work-related technologies.

It is also a good time to create a habit of "walking around"—networking informally across the company to understand the big picture. An assigned mentor can introduce the new employee to other groups. Contact with senior leaders one-on-one or in group settings can form a stronger bond to the bigger vision. Strong bonding to a single manager is great but risky in terms of retention if that manager leaves. The mentor should also ask these questions at the two-week mark:

- Was there a desk, computer, and phone for you (or keys to the loading dock, or gas in the hedge trimmer, or whatever else you needed)?
- Could you be effective on day one?
- Does your boss communicate with you?
- Is this the job for which you thought you signed up?
- What concerns do you have?
- Are there any obvious gaps in your knowledge?

Stage 3: Settling In (90 Days)

Orientation is over. This is now a time to log a few concrete achievements, and onboarding shifts focus from giving information to giving feedback. How effectively is the new employee working? What's the relationship with the manager? (Both the manager and the mentor should ask this question.) If the new employee is a leader, has he or she established credibility with other leaders?

Stage 4: Adjusting (Six Months)

Although the sense of newness recedes, the new employee is still developing cross-functional relationships and should by this time be a full-fledged member of the group. The employee and manager should be able to describe their relationship in similar terms, and describe similar goals and expectations. The employee should have received regular performance feedback and begun a development/growth plan. It is an excellent time to check engagement and commitment to company goals, values, and strategy.

Stage 5: Fully Engaged (One Year)

At the one-year mark, you should be measuring the new hire's level of achievement and/or engagement with leadership, culture, work–life balance, work satisfaction, work relationships, personal growth, and the values expressed in your employer brand. Dissatisfaction with one or more of these factors puts an employee at risk of leaving.

Onboarding people in a leadership role follows much the same pattern as the five stages outlined, with the important differences being that leaders are often winning the engagement of others. Leaders need a few early wins, and a lot of listening to judge the cultural, informational, political, and market forces that will determine their success. To retain leaders at the highest levels is a measure of their success at achieving stated goals, but they aren't all-powerful or all-seeing, and their onboarding requires an active and trustworthy feedback mechanism. Losing a leader, like losing a talented employee at any level, indicates a failure of the system that attracts, acquires, and engages talented individuals.

Getting off to the right start will not guarantee long tenure, but getting off to the wrong start is a waste of time, money, and talent.

EARLY EMPLOYEE NEEDS

Based on research and working with clients for more than 40 years, Sirota Consulting has found that the key to successful onboarding is making sure your employees are having the right experience at the right time during the different stages of onboarding. Sirota found that employees have four unique needs during the course of their first year.[4] Figure 7.1 illustrates each need unique to the early tenured employee.

First, new employees need to feel welcomed. New hires want a few basic things. They need information, introductions, and a place to call their own—a desk or workspace with tools and resources. If you don't meet these needs in the first few days or weeks, new hires often become anxious and feel overlooked.

Second, new hires need to feel they are getting the support and training they need to do their job. If these needs are not being met

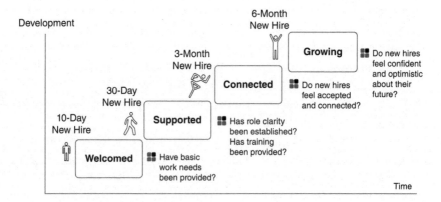

Figure 7.1 Critical New Hire Needs during First Six Months

during the first month on the job, your new hires may start to feel disoriented and overloaded.

Third, new hires need to feel connected to their boss, their team, and their colleagues. This can take time, but if your new hires are not feeling a sense of connection to the company by the three-month mark, they may start to reconsider their decision to join.

Finally, new hires need to feel like they are competent, capable, and growing. Few things are more engaging for today's employees than a sense of growth and development. If your employees are not starting to experience a sense of personal development, mastery, and growth by the six-month mark, they will likely start to feel frustrated and demoralized.

When these critical needs are met, new employees are not only more engaged, but they are also likely to perform better.

OPEN ANALYTICAL FRAMEWORK FOR EFFECTIVE ONBOARDING

An effective and consistent onboarding program must be grounded in solid analytics. Let the data inform you as to which approach works best at each onboarding stage and the elements that are critical for your onboarding program. The intelligent use of analytics can also help you understand how each new employee is progressing through your onboarding process as well as predict which aspects of your program predict future employee success. Through the use of our OPEN onboarding analytics principles (**o**rient, **p**rovide, **e**ngage, and **n**ext), you can make sure to measure each step of the onboarding process.

Let's take a look at each area of the OPEN analytical framework.

Orient

This aspect of the framework relates to how successfully you're able to orient your new hire to the organization, both to literal places and the things the new hire needs as well as to your culture and processes. The data to capture as part of this area is mostly qualitative and derived from simple checklists of whether new hires did or did not accomplish a task. Some examples of the data that's relevant to whether you've oriented your new hires effectively include:

- Frequent check-ins with your new hire—informally and formally.
- Gathering early employee questions—over time, they can drive onboarding improvements.
- Mentor and buddy interviews.
- First-week survey of early impressions.
- Have they taken care of administrative tasks/milestones?
- Assessments (e.g., do they understand the company mission, departmental mission, company values, etc.?).
- Did they view training modules?
- How are they feeling?

Provide

This aspect of the framework relates to how successfully you're providing resources and training on key processes, skills, or technology that will be required for the job. The data to capture as part of this area shifts more to the quantitative, using things like assessment tests and completion of tasks. Some examples of the data that's relevant to whether you've oriented your new hires effectively include:

- Early assessment of skill/knowledge.
- Employee rating of job resources available.
- Training modules attended.
- Review of training and sessions attended.
- Ask them what they need more of.
- New hire experience survey.

Engage

This area of the OPEN framework relates to how engaged your early employees are becoming. For this area, there are some simple quantitative measures you can use, as well as some softer qualitative indicators.

- Meetings attended within the first 90 days.
- E-mails sent and received within the first 90 days.
- Projects engaged in.
- First 90-day new employee observations.
- Early supervisor assessment.
- Absenteeism.
- Tardiness.
- Social events attended.

Next

This area relates to whether you've prepared your new hires for full integration into the organization. The data to track here is outcomes focused—how effective the person is in his or her role, as well as cultural fit and perceptions of success.

- Early employee success measures (see Table 7.1).
- A 360-degree new hire assessment.
- Mentor/buddy interview.
- Employee survey.
- New employee in-depth one-on-one with HR business partner.

Table 7.1 Connect Onboarding to Employee Performance .

Role	Performance Measure Example
Sales	Time to first sale; sales within the first 90 days; talk time; connect rate
Customer service	First call resolution rate after three months; customer satisfaction
Engineering	Code error rate; production rate; average time to fix product issue
Business development	Time to first deal; deals closed in first six months
Accounting	Average first three-month report production; report error rate
Manufacturing	Percentage of output that passes certification; first 90-day productivity rate
Clerical/administrative	Internal customer satisfaction; number of meetings scheduled; percentage of calls answered within two rings

TIME TO PRODUCTIVITY AND OTHER OUTCOME MEASURES

Besides measuring the perception and activities of new hires during the onboarding process, you need to analytically tie your onboarding programs to outcomes. In other words, a successful onboarding process should predict, in part, whether a new employee will be successful over the long term with your organization. Outcome measures will be different depending on your organization and the roles for which you are hiring. Additionally, these measures must be tied to critical business outcomes that specific departments or roles are trying to achieve. For example, salespeople have an outcome of sales revenue, engineers may be tied to quality output, and customer service reps may be tied to customer resolution rate. These are some examples of outcome measures to model against onboarding programs for specific roles. Table 7.1 provides a sample of possible outcome measures for different types of roles.

A type of role that's especially important to tie onboarding to outcome is your sales staff. Refining the onboarding and training process for sales staff may be one of the most difficult challenges onboarding managers face. Although the onboarding process may be relatively short compared to the overall time workers spend with the company, the knowledge, skills, and experience new workers gain during onboarding will impact their professional development in the future.

To help make crafting the onboarding and training process smoother, you need to invest in sales analytics that will enable effective measurement of the success of your onboarding program. You must tie your onboarding program to the metrics that give managers insight into their sales representatives, such as sales conversion rate, prospect connect rate, total talk time, meetings per month, and so on. These are some metrics that can help companies determine whether their current onboarding and sales training generate the results they are looking for when molding workers into star performers.

CREATE AN ONBOARDING PREDICTIVE MODEL

After you have gathered your early employee performance metrics for the business-critical roles in your organization, use a predictive analytics expert (internal or external) to help you create a statistical model that helps explore whether aspects of your onboarding process can predict critical early employee performance outcomes such as those in Table 7.1. Some examples of onboarding process measurement inputs can be found in Table 7.2.

Working with your predictive analytics expert, you can use statistical modeling to see which onboarding combination of activities is most predictive of getting a top performer up to speed. You're likely to find that it may differ depending on the type of role, the career level of the employee, and the department in which he or she is working. Regardless, armed with this data-driven, predictive model approach, you'll be able to evolve your onboarding program to make sure it meets the needs of each employee type.

TYING IT ALL TOGETHER

Let's bring to light how analytics can help the onboarding process with a day-in-the-life story of people leveraging analytics to make better decisions when it comes to onboarding new hires.

Table 7.2 Onboarding Data Inputs to Explore in an Employee Performance Model

Onboarding Program Measures That May Predict Employee Performance
Onboarding compliance
Onboarding modules attended
Resources for employee available
Early employee satisfaction/sentiment
Early employee knowledge attainment scores
Number of e-mails sent or received within the first 90 days
Number of different employees connected to in the first 90 days
Optional training sessions attended
Onboarding social events attended
Time with mentor/new hire buddy

Imagine the company headquarters of a medical supply company, Health4U, which has become a major medical supply player in just a few years. That kind of rapid growth has been great for shareholders, but has left some shortcomings in the company's approach to talent development that it has been working to address.

The first character in our story is Adam. He was put into the role of onboarding program manager six months ago due to high turnover that was being seen in the first 90 days.

During that time, Adam has been steadily building and improving the new hire program. It includes a Day 1 Welcome Experience where each new employee is assigned an onboarding buddy for the first six months. Adam has moved away from the standard curriculum that all new hires go through and toward a tailored approached to training both to roles and to experience. This is supported by a virtual community of new hires and a role-specific simulated project or challenge that all new hires go through.

When Adam came into the role, there was really no data on the effectiveness and impact of the former onboarding program. Adam had always believed that you can't manage what you don't measure, so, as a first step, he worked to establish the right set of key performance indicators to focus on. These fell into four categories:

1. Onboarding program effectiveness
2. Speed to performance
3. New hire engagement
4. Business performance

He uses the data to monitor progress and also communicate the value and impact of the changes he has been making. These have been positive across the board, but Adam knows there's opportunity for further improvements.

One of the beneficiaries of Adam's work is Steve, who has just been hired as a new product manager at Health4U. Steve was recruited from one of Health4U's competitors—he has high expectations that the culture and environment of Health4U will be a step up from that of his former employer. The onboarding program can make or break that impression.

The morning of the first day includes a highly motivational event about the future of Health4U and how Steve can contribute to it. After going to lunch with his new coworkers, Steve takes a handful of tests that assess his level of knowledge coming into the role.

After each test, he's able to see how he did. He's coming into the job with quite a bit of relevant knowledge and experience. Results from the tests are automatically fed to Health4U's learning management system, which automatically passes him out of some of the required new hire training.

Adam is able to look at pretest scores of new hires by individual and in the aggregate. This is one measure of quality of hire that he passes back to the talent acquisition function.

As Steve goes through his new hire training, he completes periodic evaluations. Adam has it set up so that Steve does not need to complete an evaluation after every single session; rather, he'll complete one evaluation per week that covers the range of sessions and modalities over that week.

Adam receives automated reports that inform him that there are still improvements to be made in the quality of classroom instruction and in providing better context and examples of how the new hires will be using what they have learned on the job.

He reviews the low instructor scores with the delivery manager and works with the course developers to add more role-based examples to the content.

After 30 days, Steve is asked to complete a New Hire Onboarding Survey, which asks him about his experience with the company and the training he has received thus far. Steve will get similar checkpoints at 60 and 90 days. To ensure that these are deployed consistently and to minimize administrative effort, a simple data feed from the human resources information system is imported into the survey software, which includes:

- The start dates of new employees.
- Their contact information.
- Key demographics, such as job type, department, and tenure in the industry.
- Their manager's contact information.

Natalie is Steve's manager. She's the director of product strategy. And when it comes to onboarding, her primary need is for new hires like Steve to ramp up faster.

An onboarding feedback report is generated for Natalie (and all other managers with new hires going through onboarding).

Natalie is able to compare feedback from Steve and her other new hires to feedback received by other Health4U managers. She sees that her new hires are looking for her to be more involved in the onboarding process. They want more recognition, constructive feedback, and coaching. Before this report, Natalie wasn't aware of this disconnect, so she immediately sets up recurring weekly meetings with each of the new hires in which they will discuss their progress and set expectations.

When Steve and the other new hires fill out the 60- and 90-day checkpoint surveys, Natalie is already seeing her scores improve.

Adam is able to see the feedback across departments and notes that manager support is a critical need during onboarding throughout much of Health4U. As a result, Adam provides a training session for managers to help them understand the difference they can make. He also institutes regular checkpoints with the managers as a part of the onboarding program.

After Steve has spent three months on the job, he, Natalie, and Steve's peers complete a 360-degree multirater assessment, providing feedback on the competencies that Steve has demonstrated.

Steve and Natalie receive a report with the 360-degree feedback. It shows that Steve demonstrates great initiative and has useful new ideas, but he could work on collaborating better with others and adapting to change with a more positive attitude. They agree to focus on developing these competencies over the upcoming months.

Adam is able to look across the 360-degree feedback for all new hires. He uses this data for a couple of different purposes:

- Determine common competency deficiencies across the organization that could be addressed as part of the onboarding program curriculum.

- Use manager feedback to inform measures for both speed to competency and quality of hire (which is then fed back to the talent acquisition function).

Adam has established a quarterly process in which he presents an executive report on the effectiveness and outcomes of the onboarding program. The purpose of this is not simply to justify that it's making a difference. Instead, Adam aims to show that he's a good steward of the investment by measuring and continually improving results. Additionally, he uses it as an opportunity to discuss areas in which collaboration with the business units would substantially improve results.

The accountability that he has demonstrated and his focus on aligning with business needs has led to Adam's having a great partnership with leadership in the talent function and the business.

In our example, each of our three people at Health4U has benefited from the use of onboarding analytics. Adam has a scalable approach to tracking important metrics, gathering feedback from new hires, and reporting for himself, managers, and executives. The learning helps enable him to improve and optimize the onboarding program on an ongoing basis. Steve thought it was great to be able to skip training that he was already comfortable with. The 360-degree feedback will be instrumental in his success in his role. Natalie was able to become a better manager by receiving timely information on the perceptions of new hires. By seeing how she compared to other managers in the company, she was able to prioritize the areas she needed to focus on to improve the experience of new hires.

KEY TAKEAWAYS

- Employee onboarding is a critical and sensitive time for the new employee and the organization.
- Employee onboarding strategies should be authentic and grounded in what makes your company unique.
- The onboarding process has several stages and lasts for many months after an employee starts.

- Use the OPEN analytical framework to make sure you're measuring the critical aspects of your onboarding process.

- Measuring new employee performance is critical to assessing the impact of your onboarding process.

- Use predictive modeling techniques to identify which parts of your onboarding process are leading to early employee success.

NOTES

1. "A Brief Introduction to Springboard: Sirota's Onboarding Assessment Program," Sirota Consulting, 2014, https://training.sirota.com/Springboard_introduction/.

2. Jeff Grisenthwaite, "Metrics That Matter, Onboarding Edition," Knowledge Advisors, December 11, 2013, www.slideshare.net/JeffGrisenthwaite/onboarding-analytics-metrics-that-matter-onboarding-edition.

3. Society for Human Resource Management, SHRM Survey Findings: Onboarding Practices. April 13, 2011.

4. "Onboarding New Hires: Current Practices & New Directions," SirotaScience Webinar, November 15, 2012.

CHAPTER 8

Talent Engagement Analytics

Your dedication should not be confined for your own gain, but should unleash your passion.

—Li Ka-shing

To stay competitive, it is paramount to keep your employees fully engaged in order to meet and exceed your customers' expectations and achieve your corporate goals. A key component to this is to understand the engagement level of your employees.

We define an engaged employee as a happy, enthusiastic, and motivated individual who eagerly relishes the challenges of his or her job. Analytics can help to understand the various drivers of employee engagement that deliver happier, more productive workers and decrease unplanned turnover. Analytics can also help human capital management teams sift through data and talent information to better understand employee engagement and help address some talent management questions, such as:

- What are the key drivers of employee engagement?
- How does employee engagement affect productivity and financial bottom lines?
- What are the main drivers of millennials' engagement?
- What are the main drivers of baby boomers' engagement?
- What is the impact of hard-to-fill positions or hard-to-find skill sets on employee engagement?
- What is the impact of the Net Promoter Score and Engagement Index?
- How do talent engagement elements, such as relationship with manager and confidence in leadership and company, impact business performance?

Talent engagement analytics can also provide insights on methods for increasing employee engagement through existing channels such as performance appraisals, the voice of the candidate, industry standards, and other metrics that can boost employee satisfaction and assist in paving career pathways.

This pillar of employee engagement analytics can also help organizations assess the correlation between engagement scores and employee performance in the past, present, and future—important information for reducing and mitigating the cost of bad hires and ultimately optimizing employees' lifetime value.

IMPORTANCE OF EMPLOYEE ENGAGEMENT

There's a wide range of views regarding what engagement really is. They range from engagement being as qualitative as something you can sense when entering a room to a highly sophisticated analysis of attitudinal and behavioral data. Regardless, it now commands serious attention from the human resources (HR) and leadership communities.

Employee engagement is a workplace approach designed to ensure that employees are committed to their organization's goals and values, motivated to contribute to organizational success, and able at the same time to enhance their own sense of well-being.

There are differences between attitude, behavior, and outcome in terms of engagement. An employee might feel pride and loyalty (attitude), and be a great advocate of the company to clients or go the extra mile to finish a piece of work (behavior). Outcomes may include lower accident rates, higher productivity, fewer conflicts, more innovation, lower numbers leaving, and reduced sickness rates. But we believe all three—attitudes, behaviors, and outcomes—are part of the engagement story. There is a virtuous circle when the preconditions of engagement are met as these three aspects of engagement trigger and reinforce one another.

Engaged organizations have strong and authentic values, with clear evidence of trust and fairness based on mutual respect, where two-way promises and commitments between employers and staff are understood and are fulfilled.

Although improved performance and productivity are at the heart of engagement, they cannot be achieved by a mechanistic approach to extract discretionary effort by manipulating employees' commitment and emotions. Employees see through such attempts very quickly; they lead instead to cynicism and disillusionment. By contrast, engaged employees freely and willingly give discretionary effort, not as an add-on, but as an integral part of their daily activity at work.

Researchers use the term *discretionary effort* to describe the behaviors that accompany engagement. We see employee engagement as both an attachment to the work at hand and a drive for growth, achievement, and going beyond reasonable goals based on an inner psychological reward. We see it in the team that stays up all night to solve a problem, the boss who postpones an important meeting to be with an employee facing a personal crisis, and the entry-level worker who stays late studying to increase her skills not because she's being paid but just because she loves the work.

Engagement is also profitable. In a survey of 664,000 worldwide employees, the research firm Industry Standard Research found large gaps between companies with highly engaged employees and those with low engagement scores:

- On operating income: engaged = 19.2 percent gain; nonengaged = 32.7 percent decline.
- On net income growth: engaged = 13.2 percent gain; nonengaged = 3.8 percent decline.
- On earnings per share: engaged = 27.8 percent gain; nonengaged = 11.2 percent decline.[1]

An engaged workforce also clearly contributes to the bottom line, and managers build the road to engagement one employee at a time. For example, data from PricewaterhouseCoopers (PwC) has shown that:[2]

- The rate of voluntary attrition of the most highly engaged employees was less than half of that of the least engaged employees at a 15,000-person professional services organization.
- Up-selling and cross-selling performance rose as engagement rose among workers at a customer care call center of about 500 employees over a six-month period.

In their *Harvard Business Review* article "Competing on Talent Analytics," Thomas Davenport, Jeanne Harris, and Jeremy Shapiro found that almost every company they've studied says it values employee engagement, but some—including Starbucks, Limited Brands, and Best Buy—were precisely able to identify the value of a 0.1% increase in engagement among employees at a particular store. At Best Buy, for example, that value is equivalent to more than $100,000 in the store's annual operating income.[3]

Engagement really comes down to transcending the typical supervisor–employee relationship with authenticity and a full set of retention-focused practices grounded in what makes your company unique. Great companies get this, and they tailor engagement to their core values. For example, Google—after hiring creative, smart people—encourages virtual teams to form around new products someone just dreamed up. Additionally, Wegmans—after hiring employees who are customer-focused—encourages people to find new ways to delight customers.

EMPLOYEE ENGAGEMENT SURVEYS

Employee engagement analytics for most companies involves a periodic survey to employees, asking them about the degree to which they agree with statements like:

- My immediate manager inspires me.
- I feel proud to tell people where I work.
- I have the tools I need to do my job effectively.
- I have enough opportunities to contribute to decisions that affect me.
- I understand how my role contributes to achieving business outcomes.
- I trust the information I receive from my immediate manager.
- My manager values the work I do.

Engagement surveys are sometimes nothing more than a way for employees to vent frustrations about their boss or the food in the company cafeteria. However, company action is critical if these programs are to be successful.

"If you are going to ask for opinions, it is incumbent upon you as a leadership team to act upon the results," PwC manager Chris Ippolito said during a webcast about how to the get the most from your engagement surveys.

Engagement surveys can drive change that leads to business improvement, PwC director Chris Dustin said during the webcast:

- When employees see that their suggestions are acted upon, their engagement increases, Dustin said.
- Increased engagement leads to better performance and decreased turnover, according to PwC research.
- Organizations that keep engagement data can combine it with other data to create predictive analytics that can lead to sophisticated workforce planning and preemptive interventions.

But many organizations are missing out on those opportunities. Eighty-six percent of respondents in PwC's 2013–2014 human capital effectiveness survey report said their organizations measure employee engagement. But just 40 percent said directors and managers are required to develop an action plan for engagement of employees who report to them.[4] Dustin said organizations often make the mistake of failing to act on surveys, or treating them as human resources initiatives with little relevance to the rest of the organization.

While HR may administer the surveys, it's important for managers and the leadership team to use them to put together a global action plan. According to Dustin and Ippolito, action plans generated by employee engagement surveys should:

- **Take feedback seriously.** Engagement can suffer among employees who believe their suggestions are being ignored.
- **Implement changes where possible.** This increases engagement by showing employees that management is listening to them.

- **Be transparent.** The company should describe what changes are being made based on the survey. If changes are not feasible or practical, explain why employees' feedback won't result in action.

- **Be accountable.** Tying engagement to performance metrics and including it on organizational dashboards will help ensure that engagement gets serious treatment throughout the organization.

MAKING EMPLOYEE ENGAGEMENT SURVEYS PREDICTIVE

To make employee engagement surveys predictive means moving away from a reliance on the simple survey measurement of "engagement." Instead, it means moving to viewing the employment relationship as a dynamic social and economic exchange between employer and employee that can predict business results. To know that your engagement score has risen by two points may be interesting, but it's seldom actionable. The key is to understand the components of engagement that are predictive of business results.

Organizations that do act on employee engagement results typically dedicate 90 percent of their engagement effort to postsurvey activity to inspire people to do great work and match their efforts with business needs. Only 10 percent is attributed to closing the loop on engagement activities to understand what worked and what did not.

As you have seen mentioned throughout this book, effective People Analytics is grounded in business outcomes. The goal of People Analytics initiatives, including measuring employee engagement, should not be to measure a process or thing just for the sake of understanding it. Rather, it should be part of an analytical program that seeks to understand the drivers of business outcomes and predict the influence of those drivers.

In the case of an employee engagement survey, typically the focus is just on understanding whether employees are engaged and why or why not. However, practitioners should seek to predict how programs to improve or sustain employee engagement lead to favorable business outcomes.

The first step is to determine the two or three most critical business outcomes you expect from high employee engagement. For example, outcomes such as productivity, turnover, and customer loyalty are commonly desired outcomes—but there are others. Financial indicators such as revenue per employee as well as cost and safety-related data are all outcomes that could potentially be impacted by employee engagement.

Employee engagement/satisfaction/commitment is not a business outcome, but it can be a driver of business outcomes. People Analytics will allow you to link the survey data that you collect to important business results and then focus your initiatives on those key areas that drive results.

As surveys accumulate over the years, there is an opportunity to aggregate them and consider them in combination with other data to create predictive analytics. Engagement survey data can be combined with onboarding and exit survey data, recruiting data, other HR data, learning and management data, customer survey data, and macroeconomic or industry data to put together an analytic data set. Analytics can then be used to predict performance, turnover, quality of hire, and other outputs based on the data.

One financial services company gathered 93 data files collected over 10 years that contained a lot of trended employee opinion data. The subsequent analysis of the data resulted in predictive analytics that can drive business improvements in the future.

"You don't just approach your employee survey from the perspective of a feel-good exercise or a check-box exercise," according to PwC's Ippolito. "When you do gather those employee opinion data, and you have them at hand, especially over a few years' time, you have a powerful element of a predictive model already in hand, and those employee opinion data can really raise the efficacy and the accuracy of the predictions."

As mentioned before in this book, getting buy-in from internal stakeholders regarding the most important outcomes of employee engagement is critical. This will help ensure success as you make your engagement analytics more predictive. However, there are other important steps to consider.

According to Strategic Management Decisions (SMD), a talent management and analytics company, in order to develop the most effective employee engagement predictive analytics, you should ask the following six questions:[5]

1. On what outcomes/metrics are the senior leaders in this organization most focused?

2. Who owns the specific data/metrics that senior leaders are focused on? How do I connect with those individuals to obtain the data?

3. Are the important business data/metrics collected at the appropriate level for me to make apples-to-apples comparisons (i.e., department level or district level)?

4. Do I have the statistical capabilities in-house, or do I need to look at a university or consulting firm to help me analyze the data?

5. Based on the linkage analysis, what is the highest-priority or highest–return on investment project that I should execute first?

6. How do I assess the change that has occurred and make adjustments to maximize effectiveness?

SMD had the opportunity to help Baptist Health Care analyze its employee survey data to make it more business-focused and predictive. Due to the health care reform law, a patient survey known as the Hospital Consumer Assessment of Health Providers and Systems (HCAHPS) survey has become a critical business outcome with important financial implications for the organization. The organization typically viewed its employee survey as a way to gauge employees' level of engagement, something the organization believed can drive high HCAHPS patient scores. However, it needed new tools to improve HCAHPS scores, and viewed its people as an opportunity to influence the scores.

SMD took the survey data at the manager level and directly linked it to HCAHPS scores at the manager level using a statistical technique called structural equations modeling. The analysts calculated survey results for each manager and then aligned their year-to-date HCAHPS scores. They then used the Amos program in SPSS statistical software to analyze the data using structural equations modeling.

What they discovered was that quality and safety were the two survey categories that significantly drove HCAHPS at Baptist Health Care. More specifically for safety, it was that employees at Baptist felt safe at work, both in the building and walking to their cars. This meant that feeling safe at work was directly related to employees's treating patients more effectively. This result makes sense, as it is difficult to focus on making patients feel cared for if you are looking over your shoulder or you feel uncomfortable in your surroundings. Furthermore, the hospital had recently experienced a significant safety incident in the emergency department—so safety was certainly top of mind for employees.

As a result of the linkage analysis, Baptist Health Care raised the sense of urgency around safety even more. Survey results that were not high on the to-do list now had the full support of the entire senior team, including the CFO, because of the demonstrated impact on financial outcomes. In this case, having the facts and data from SMD to support the improvement of a critical business outcome (HCAHPS), and the ability to show the level of impact and specifically on what needed work, created an impact opportunity for HR at Baptist.

MOVING BEYOND THE SURVEY: EMPLOYEE ENGAGEMENT MEASURES

As we have discussed, the typical approach to measuring engagement is an annual engagement survey where employees are asked to rate their own level of engagement. When combined with predictive analytics, this approach can provide good input into the impact of employee attitude on engagement (for example, how engaged they perceive themselves to be) and business outcomes, but may not provide objective data on just how engaged employees actually are. While knowing what employees think certainly is important, this data suffers from the same challenges of any other survey-based effort: There may be response bias if not all employees respond, results become dated quickly, employees are likely thinking of more recent events, and people may potentially tell you what they think you want to hear rather than what they really think.

At the same time, most companies are now inundated with a large volume and velocity of data from multiple locations and sources: business-to-business data, business-to-consumer data, traffic data, transactional data, third-party vendor data, macroeconomic data, and so on. On top of the more traditional data sources, web data, social media data, mobile data, and new third-party sources have added another layer of complexity to the Big Data puzzle that companies now have available to them.

Although not yet commonplace across corporate environments, the field of People Analytics is uncovering measures of employee engagement that attempt to document engagement quantitatively without burdening the employee to complete a survey. While some don't even know where to start in dealing with these direct measures of engagement, others are still struggling to move beyond the basic engagement survey. A company might begin examining direct measures of engagement by analyzing the following:

- The amount of work that occurs outside of normal working hours (e.g., evenings and weekends).
- Work e-mail volume and timing.
- The number of network connections and time spent with people outside of the immediate team.
- The percentage of participation in ad hoc meetings and initiatives versus recurring meetings.
- Time spent collaborating directly with customers or employees outside of the normal scope of work.
- Sematic analysis of e-mail content, call center transcripts, or sales calls for changes in percentage of negative tone.
- Time spent viewing nonwork content online.
- Recruitment site activity (e.g., Monster, Career Builder, LinkedIn, Indeed, or other career resources).

- Productivity measures relevant to the job such as units produced, talk time, calls answered, and so on.
- Participation levels in work social events.

For any of these direct measures, it's important to remember that everyone is different and roles at organizations are different; therefore, absolute benchmarks for these direct measures are often impractical. For example, a software engineer may spend several half-hour blocks each day walking around the office talking to others because this is a necessary break from such intense work, whereas a telephone sales rep talking all day may spend time reading personal Internet content in order to get some down time. In order to be most impactful, these data must be evaluated in a time series for how they change over days, weeks, or months for a particular job function, department, or person. Additionally, these data must be tied to critical business outcomes that specific departments or roles are trying to obtain.

Companies like Seattle-based VoloMetrix are stepping in to make it easier for organizations to directly measure engagement. VoloMetrix's service allows businesses to better understand how their employees are spending their time at work. For example, it can allow companies to look at how much time their employees in a sales team spend with customers, or how different teams work together (or not). All of this data is collected right from the corporate communications system and then anonymized.

While VoloMetrix aims to give deeper insights into how a company functions, it does not focus on the individual employee. Instead, the idea is to use this data from e-mails and calendar events to create analytics that help businesses streamline their operations. Some of the company's customers include Genentech, Seagate, and Symantec, as well as a number of other Fortune 100 companies.

Used properly, engagement analytics can play a big part in creating effective employee programs that drive business results and keep workers happy. A lot of the analytics discussed in this chapter can be foundational in creating a propensity to quit model, as will be described in Chapter 11.

Interview with Kathy Andreasen, Chief People Officer, Endurance International Group

Harriott: As a senior HR leader for over 20 years, can you tell me how you became involved in talent analytics?

Andreasen: I became interested in HR metrics early in my career when recruiting in the hottest tech market ever known during the first dot. com boom in the late '90s. Acquiring and keeping good tech workers was very difficult, and although compensation was escalating at a fast rate, it was important to attract and keep talent. It was engagement that was the predictor and lever that drove retention. I quickly learned that measuring and understanding your employee's engagement was the crystal ball into the future. It was the one measurement you could create an equation around—where an increase in engagement would predict an increase in effort/productivity, which translated into an increase in the business's performance.

As a result, I was an early proponent of HR analytics for decision making. When I was at Cendant Corporation over 10 years ago, I was on the corporate leadership council of the corporate executive board. This was their first analytics council, and I had access to different analytics tools when they first came out. Also, while I was the CHRO at AOL we had Tableau and a great HR team and data—so we were able to look at retention by performance, engagement, and other great metrics.

Harriott: What advice would you give to smaller companies that want to put a greater emphasis on using analytics for talent management?

Andreasen: Having spent 25 years as CHRO in fast-growing tech companies, where talent is the largest expense for the company, I believe that we all need to do a better job at using data to ensure that our investments in talent, both monetary and precious management "bandwidth," are well targeted and delivering the desired results. Well-intentioned "textbook" ideas and programs that are not rooted in data to support their value have no place in modern HR practices. I sometimes use the example of turnover. You often hear about companies concerned about an increase in turnover and their efforts to reduce it. I ask them how they know if they are losing their best performers or their worst. A strong culture of performance can drive up turnover of low performers— in which case you may not want to drive it down. If your best performers are leaving, then you need to jump on it and change your culture. A

(Continued)

(*Continued*)

company that wants to take advantage of talent analytics needs to align those analytics to the key business challenges they are facing.

I believe that the next frontier for analytics is talent acquisition—not just for big companies with the resources to build that capability—but for all companies depending on talent for their success. We know big companies do it, and the top RPO companies do it, and the smaller companies need to find a way to use data in their efforts or risk being at the bottom of the food chain for talent."

KEY TAKEAWAYS

- Employee engagement is related to business performance.
- Employee engagement strategies should be authentic and grounded in what makes your company unique.
- Employee engagement surveys are necessary but not sufficient in your quest to understand what drives engaged employees.
- Employee engagement surveys should be predictive of business outcomes.
- Aggressively search for the business outcome metrics related to engagement.
- Employee engagement analytics require leadership alignment on desired business outcomes in order to be effective.
- Direct (e.g., nonsurvey) measures of employee engagement are gaining traction and hold promise for early warning signs of employee risk.

NOTES

1. "Engaged Employees Help Boost the Bottom Line," cited by HR.com, June 29, 2006, www.hr.com.
2. "Dealing with Disruption: Adapting to Survive and Thrive," 16th Annual Global CEO Survey, PricewaterhouseCoopers white paper, 2013.
3. Thomas H. Davenport, Jeanne Harris, and Jeremy Shapiro, "Competing on Talent Analytics," *Harvard Business Review*, October 2010, https://hbr.org.
4. "State of the Workforce: Results from PwC Saratoga's 2013/2014 US Human Capital Effectiveness Report," PricewaterhouseCoopers, 2013, www.pwc.com.
5. S. Mondore, S. Douthitt, and M. Carson, "Maximizing the Impact and Effectiveness of HR Analytics to Drive Business Outcomes," *People & Strategy* 34, no. 2 (2011): 20–27.

CHAPTER 9

Analytical Performance Management

It is not enough to do your best; you must know what to do, and then do your best.

—W. Edwards Deming

WHY YOU SHOULD CARE ABOUT PERFORMANCE MANAGEMENT ANALYTICS

Top performing organizations believe people are their most important asset. Among leadership, there is a strong belief that leaders, managers, and frontline contributors are all critically important to achieving long-term growth and sustainability. However, most companies have not figured out how to best manage the performance of their people, on which growth and sustainability so critically depend.

People are the sole source of innovation. Their passion strengthens organizations and creates competitive advantages. To realize any of this value, organizations need to proactively align the individual goals, strengths, and passions of their workforce with the organization's short- and long-term objectives. *Performance management* is the process of continuously aligning people and organizational objectives to realize the value of each individual and team.

Most organizations take a very traditional approach to performance management. This includes individual planning, check-ins, and periodic evaluation of progress, all feeding into compensation and promotion decisions. For most, performance metrics are established in collaboration with a manager and, if well designed, they are actionable and benefit the overall effectiveness of a work group. At most organizations, performance management has evolved through iteration and does a very good job of capturing the strengths and weaknesses of each employee. The challenges are linking this information to the business on an ongoing basis and constantly adapting the overall performance management process to your workforce

238

needs and preferences such as frequent feedback and performance management via an app.

LINKING INDIVIDUAL OBJECTIVES TO COMPANY OBJECTIVES

Individual objectives are typically tracked and subsequently used for evaluation (e.g., complete, partial, incomplete) through the performance review cycle.

Examples of individual objectives include:

- Create a basic disaster recovery plan by July 1, 2016.
- Assume leadership for reconciling e-reports for unit.
- Recruit at least two agencies to participate in a series of classes.

However, very few organizations actually link objectives to meaningful outcomes like growth, sales, or productivity. This is a gap that the best-run companies are beginning to bridge with data and analytical expertise. Organizations are hiring quants with advanced degrees to create new capabilities in human resources (HR). As an example, one of Canada's largest banks recently hired a team of PhD-level physicists into its workforce planning group to design tools that will help managers be more proactive in providing feedback to employees.

There can be unintended consequences when the future impacts of performance management decisions are not well understood. One consequence is organizational swell. Organizations tend to swell through the natural cycle of promotions and turnover, year over year; this can evolve a nimble, efficient workforce into one that has an expensive middle or is top-heavy. Very much like athletes, it is important for companies to ensure they are in ideal shape to deliver on their objectives. This is a challenge, as the profile of a workforce is constantly in motion. To stay ahead of this, leaders need to understand how these changes impact their ability to deliver on a strategy and the best options available to correct course.

Our approach is twofold: First, assess the workforce required to deliver on future objectives. Then, proactively manage employees to align their development with high-level objectives. Relative to current practice, this will focus employees' growth where it will have the biggest impact and help to ensure that the workforce evolves in a sustainable way.

Traditional Performance Management

Current practices typically involve an annual review and promotion cycle, with semiannual check-ins to assess performance. Objectives are set annually and measured formally once a year. This practice emerged as more qualitative scorecard-based performance systems developed to consolidate manager ratings into a single score. This approach involved time-intensive interviews, project reviews, and group meetings.

Performance ratings and promotions are typically determined by individual success relative to goals. Success can be very tangible (e.g., sales, cases reviewed, billable hours) or more difficult to measure (e.g., leadership, team contribution, problem solving). In most cases, performance is assessed as a combination of tangible metrics, perception by management, feedback from colleagues, and performance reviews. The labor-intensive and qualitative approach to assessment meant that reviews were performed only once or twice a year (see Figure 9.1).

Leveraging Analytics to Drive Business Performance

An analytical approach that utilizes data enables performance to be assessed at a much more granular level (monthly, or even daily) relative to objectives (see Figure 9.2). The point-in-time data underlying

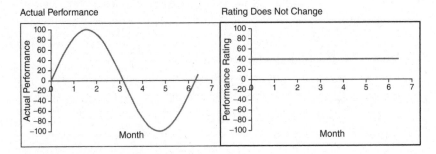

Figure 9.1 Annual Performance Evaluation

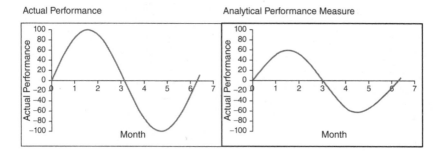

Figure 9.2 Continuous Performance Evaluation

performance provides employees with transparent feedback as to why their performance increased or decreased. Ratings also reflect current conditions rather than a consolidated year of work. This also reduces the impact of the psychological bias that managers have, including the provision of greater credibility to more recent work in their ratings.

GENERAL ELECTRIC: WHY PERFORMANCE MANAGEMENT VIA AN APP IS THE NEW NORM

Demographics changes in the workforce propelled by the emergence of millennials forced companies like Accenture, Adobe, and Microsoft to move away from their old annual performance review system to adopt a more ongoing and frequent management review via apps.

General Electric (GE), one of the pioneers in annual performance, joined the team by sun-setting its old annual performance review. GE's longstanding annual performance review, known as the "vitality curve" or "rank and yank," segmented employees' performance down to a number on which they were judged and ranked against peers. The bottom 10 percent of underperformers were then let go. The company got rid of this style of annual performance review to adopt a new way of measuring performance via an app called PD@GE, which stands for "performance development at GE." According to a *Quartz* article, with the management via app system, employees can give or request feedback at any point

(Continued)

(Continued)

through a feature called "insights."[1] The feedback isn't limited to the employee's immediate manager or even his or her division head.

Using apps is becoming the new norm for performance management across leading organizations.

Although continuous monitoring of performance does provide the most accurate current assessment of performance, a hybrid approach is typically preferred—one that incorporates greater historical data and structural changes in the business. This has the effect of balancing the long-term and short-term performance measures.

Employee performance is critical to success or failure at an organization. An approach that leverages analytics enables leadership to respond faster to problems and promote success on an ongoing basis.

CASE STUDY

GOLDCORP: FRONTLINE STORY FROM THE MINING INDUSTRY

A great illustration of a transition from the traditional view of performance to one that leverages Big Data analytics is the way that mining corporation Goldcorp is looking at its health and safety performance metrics.

Health and safety metrics are closely monitored by all North American mining companies, including Goldcorp. Through traditional approaches, Goldcorp had achieved a 75 percent drop in incident frequency rates over six years; however, fatality rates remained unchanged. Goldcorp utilized an advanced analytics platform to review 792 million data points at an employee-day level in an effort to find patterns among high-impact incidents. Information on behavioral factors such as month of the year, marital status, age, or compensation structure were the most important predictors of incidents. These insights are being used to enhance procedures and training to change behavior and are being monitored to proactively mitigate the risk of injury.

DEFINING PERFORMANCE MEASURES

The first step in defining performance measures is to define success. Then, assess measurable ways that each employee contributes to that success. The extent of the employee's contribution is used to assess performance and eventually promotion.

Most organizations have in place enterprise-grade systems that track employee plans, and enable monitoring and evaluation. They have metrics such as "client impact" or "quality" that are underpinned by concrete goals that are proposed by employees and reviewed by management. In current practice, the link between outcomes and the system is presupposed. Implicit in this system is the assumption that quality will actually improve as a result of employees' achieving their goals for the "quality" metric.

Traditionally, quality of work was far easier to measure than impact. This is particularly true for internal processes at large companies and for those in the public sector. Consider the function of compliance at a bank. Employees in this role review documentation, application processing, regulatory filings, and the like. They play a critical role, and their value is priceless when compared to risk associated with fraud and noncompliance. Traditionally, investigators in this role evaluated based on the number of reviews performed, issues identified, branches inspected, quality of documentation, and similar process-based measures. However, measuring the degree to which an action was performed relative to expectations is not the same as measuring the impact of that action. This approach to assessment *assumes* that high-quality work reduces compliance risk.

A distinguishing characteristic of our analytical approach is a lack of this assumption. An alternative way to measure performance is to assess actual fraud and noncompliance, and review results *ex post* relative to the activities performed to mitigate the risk of these outcomes. This approach leverages historical data and assesses performance relative to actual results.

There are three ways that organizations measure performance using analytics: quantitative, qualitative, and passive.

Quantitative

The most meaningful measures of employee performance are often not obvious. Three principles that often describe the best quantitative performance measures are:

1. **Physical:** Something that actually happened, such as sales, fraud, injury, turnover, growth.
2. **Individual:** Can be associated with one and only one employee.
3. **Connected:** Can be tied (e.g., via a database) to the outcomes of other individuals.

Measures of performance that meet these specifications can be tracked and monitored in a granular way (daily or monthly) to provide insight into an employee's performance as it evolves. This enables managers to be more proactive with regard to performance. Physical metrics are transparent, and ratings can be evaluated monthly to reward hard work when it happens or take corrective action quickly, if required.

Qualitative

For all of the hype, data is not perfect—there some things that simply cannot be measured. Passion and a drive to innovate are both invaluable and nearly impossible to quantify. Short-term performance measures are sensitive to failure and can encourage a very shortsighted approach to management. Qualitative measures such as 360-degree feedback, self-assessment, and project performance reviews provide a meaningful dimension of performance and should be considered to balance quantitative measures.

Think of the qualitative input as a performance measure dampener. It tempers the highs and lows generated by a purely outcomes-based performance score. This qualitative approach helps to put performance measures in context with feedback.

Passive

This is Big Data and leading edge. Organizations collect an astounding amount of data passively on their employees. Examples include every website visited, instant message sent, e-mail dispatched, document opened, log-in, Facebook post, keystroke, vacation day taken, training course completed, and ID badge swiped. This data is typically retained for at least three months. Millions of data points are collected on each employee through the course of employment.

Looked at collectively, this data paints a very clear picture of each employee on each day worked. In a recent study, a prestigious management consulting firm in Australia performed analysis of every e-mail sent by every employee for a period of three months. Their study was able to identify key people in the organization who connected different groups and encouraged collaboration. The activity of collaboration was previously very difficult to quantify, but now is transparent and easy to quantify.

Our Approach

Keep it simple. To monitor performance, it's important to use both a qualitative and a quantitative approach that is driven by data and relevant to desired outcomes. All measures should enable active measurement and be relevant at the most granular level (e.g., individual). Ensure that all measures make simple business sense, and be skeptical of obscure metrics that seem like a silver bullet. Create performance metrics with the intent that they will be shared transparently with those they're designed to monitor.

Digging into passively collected data takes time, but can yield a competitive advantage in terms of identifying performance drivers (e.g., highly connected influencers in Australia). Most organizations that utilize Big Data do so through an elite skunk-works type of operation of highly skilled, creative individuals.

PERFORMANCE INCENTIVES AND PROMOTION

Using data to assess performance enables incentives to be more closely linked to desired behaviors and outstanding performance. Most organizations adjust salaries on an annual basis, and this is an antiquated approach that grew out of annual review cycles and the traditional approach to performance management.

A major benefit of utilizing an outcomes-based analytical approach for assessing performance is that the value of each employee can be evaluated at any point in time. This is a distinguishing feature that provides a significant advantage in terms of flexibility and talent retention. This approach enables organizations to more closely align compensation, level, and value delivered by an employee. An approach where compensation is closely tied to performance will reward employees more on months (or quarters) when they are delivering greater value and less when they deliver less value. Value contributed is measured in terms of performance measures, which highlight the importance of ensuring that these measures are grounded in quantifiable metrics that are linked to business outcomes.

Knowing when an employee is ready for promotion is exceedingly difficult because, in addition to compensation, the role of the employee also changes. With the right data, analytics can add clarity to the selection process by assessing each employee for the characteristics identified in those who are successful at the next level. Promotion into a new role can involve a steep learning curve. The metrics used to identify employees for promotion also provide insights into their strengths and areas where they need to grow. From a mentoring perspective, this information can be used to provide informed and tactical assistance in a proactive way to new managers.

A proactive approach to performance and promotion also tells managers how many employees they will need at each level in the coming years. It helps manager to address questions such as:

- Which employees will be successful if promoted?
- What training would an employee need before getting promoted?
- What team members are required to ensure success of newly promoted employee?
- How long should an employee work for your organization before he or she gets a promotion?

This also helps leading organizations to predict employee promotion paths.

This information can be used to mentor and grow high-potential candidates in ways that will fill identified gaps in the future. Integration and analysis of HR performance measures provide further clarity to the skills needed in the future. Once the gaps have been identified, the next step is incorporating them into the objective-setting process for current employees. The goal is to ensure that the current workforce is grown and mentored to fit into areas of need in the coming years.

Consulting can be a notoriously intense industry, often involving long hours, weekend work, and travel. A well-known predictive analytics firm discovered that it could fight fatigue, increase retention, and boost morale by paying certain employees more during times when they were intensely busy, and less through slower cycles. The approach was simple; compensation increased during long hours and decreased when employees worked less. This also provided the firm with justification at the end of its annual review cycle for avoiding large pay increases, as its employees had technically already received that compensation when the firm was operating at full capacity earlier in the year. The strategy employed was enabled by good data that was available monthly and very transparent performance metrics that linked in a credible way to profitability.

PROVIDE INSIGHT TO SENIOR MANAGEMENT

Senior management defines the objectives for an organization and relies on managers and staff to deliver based on senior managers' guidance. From their perspective, performance management ties very closely to workforce planning in that organizations need to assess the staff profile required at each level to deliver on a plan. We'll define the profile of an organization as its distribution of senior leadership, management, and operational resources. This profile is typically measured at multiple levels and varies based on level and function in the organization. Most companies simply let their profiles evolve by inertia through hiring, promotion, and termination. This passive approach can have unintended consequences with regard to organizational shape. More important, it does not in any way seek to maintain the right number of people in the places where they can be most effective.

By leveraging historical data and the right technical expertise, organizations can understand the impact that their shape will have on future performance. This is an exercise that correlates the proportion of employees at each level to key metrics such as revenue, profitability, and growth to identify an optimal profile for each business unit. Once the target state has been defined by senior management, basic ratios can be used to compare subgroups with their associated target state to distinguish optimal and suboptimal profiles. It's important that this analysis incorporate at least a five-year projection of staff levels adjusted to incorporate retirement, hiring, and termination expectations. Best practice is also to use multiple scenarios (worst, expected, best) to provide recommendations that incorporate uncertainty about the future.

Coupling workforce planning, simulation, and an understanding of target profiles enables management to identify gaps both today and in the future at multiple levels of the organization. Google performed this analysis and found that if it maintained its current hiring practices it would be a middle-heavy organization. Its solution was to reduce new hiring into senior-level positions and instead promote internally, even in the case of management departures.

An understanding of future needs and the implications of HR decisions is invaluable when planning for the long term. Insight into the staff and management profile needed in the coming years enables managers to be more proactive. The number of promotions can be determined by need rather than tenure and relationships. Career growth is determined by anticipated demand for people at different levels in addition to aptitude. This data can be fed back to employees so they are aware of expected gaps in leadership and can plan to grow into positions. Tactically, managers can use this information to plan for the longer term and be more transparent about promotion and performance evaluation.

Employees' performance is best measured relative to broader organizational objectives. Their performance and related goals should link directly to an outcome. This is a challenge, as each employee has unique performance metrics that are constantly in motion. This can make identifying patterns at the employee level nearly impossible. One way to tackle this problem is to group performance measures in a way that enables them to be tracked as a whole. Performance measurement categories can be mapped across the organization to facilitate a comparison among different employees. The performance categories can be viewed as natural overlays atop concrete measures. Grouping measures assists management in comparing the contributions of employees fairly relative to those of their peers on a similar plane.

BENEFITS OF ANALYTICAL PERFORMANCE MANAGEMENT

To the business: An analytical performance management (APM)-driven approach jointly benefits the business, HR function, and employees (see Table 9.1). The benefits to the business are generated by an improved focus on high-level objectives, including product development, safety, or efficiency. The APM approach ensures that management can actively monitor employees to make sure that they are focused on what counts on an ongoing basis at a granular level.

To employees: Employees become more engaged when goals and accountability are transparent. Utilizing concrete data for performance reviews provides transparency to the review process and enables management to reward employees based on performance when performance is high, rather than 12 months later. Employees benefit from this approach of active reinforcement. Further, transparency in

Table 9.1 Traditional Approach versus Analytical Performance Management

	Traditional	APM
Promotion	Qualitative Tenure-driven Opaque	Quantitative Performance-based Transparent Graph theory Analytics-driven career pathway
Compensation	Reviewed annually Determined by rating Limited assessment	Continuously reviewed Determined by impact Broad assessment
Employee Feedback	Annual review cycle Reactive Higher level	Monthly review cycle Proactive and responsive Granular and specific Review/feedback via an app

the review process will enable top performers to shine and provide evidence-based feedback to all employees.

To human resources: In most organizations, the HR function relies on feedback and relatively soft metrics to review employees. This results in performance metrics and promotions that, however justified, can be difficult to defend. Another impact of their reliance on softer data is that it can be difficult to quantify the value of HR. An APM approach can resolve both of these challenges. A data-driven approach to promotion and performance management will add transparency to the product and enable HR to clearly articulate the evidence and rationale for promotion. Through a more thorough understanding of employee performance and its impact on the business, HR can also more accurately estimate the employee's value to the business and justify further investment.

BEST PRACTICES

There are three areas that distinguish organizations that do a fantastic job utilizing their data to increase performance from those who do a very poor job:

1. Link people to the business.
2. Use data and think ahead.
3. Continuously evaluate.

Best practices start by answering the question "Which employee performance measures are meaningful to the business?" Create a list. Then begin to collect data and continuously evaluate and provide feedback to promote an alignment between employees and objectives set by management. Be proactive in managing a workforce to ensure that the profile remains lean.

Do:

- Capture granular data on employee performance.
- Evaluate employees with metrics that can be linked to business outcomes.

- Use data to drive decision making.
- Use an app to manage performance.
- Use predictive analytics to anticipate promotion success.
- Adapt to your workforce demographics.

Do not:

- Remove the guesswork and the human element of people management.
- Define metrics that employees cannot effect.
- Rely on data in isolation from the broader context.
- Use old annual performance reviews.

PREDICTIVE ANALYTICS AND GRAPH THEORY TO OPTIMIZE CAREER PATHWAYS AND EMPLOYEE PROMOTION

Some forward-looking companies we spoke with are already harnessing their talent data using graph theory coupled with predictive analytics to determine whether a given employee will be successful if promoted to a senior-level position. In fact, those companies that are using such predictive models and graph theory analytics recorded 33 percent more success from their newly promoted employees than those who are not leveraging these insights.

So, how does it work? These new workforce promotion and career pathway models use digital mapping of companies' global resume databases and employee profile data to perform a comprehensive analysis of every candidate or employee. The program also profiles the digital representation of every job and every skill required for those positions. By comparing the data, the models provide insight based on past performance as to whether that particular individual has the skills and track record that will lead to success. The models then assign a final promotion success score to each employee based on current career level, experience, skills, and network graph information.

Similarly, career pathway models are also used to provide advice to employees and even job seekers who would like to transition to other positions—which can be particularly useful to those who are considering a new or an alternative career path. Some companies are using these solutions as orientation tools to provide counsel on what the best next career transition could be for a particular employee.

While still nascent, Big Data graph theory and predictive analytics models will definitely be useful once fully connected to large employment institutions, such as universities or the U.S. Bureau of Labor Statistics, as they will provide actionable insights in regard to training, learning, and development, but, more important, they will also provide even greater data intelligence to those working and competing for global talent.

KEY TAKEAWAYS

- Performance analytics is required to remain competitive.
- Promote and reward based on impact to the organization.
- Evaluate performance and promotion globally and proactively.
- Performance review should be an ongoing, evolving, and transparent process.
- Leading companies are retiring their old annual performance to adopt management via an app to meet their workforce needs and preferences.
- Predictive analytics and graph theory should be used to predict employee promotion path and support employee promotion.

NOTE

1. Max Nissen, "'It's a Millennial Thing': Why GE Had To Kill Its Annual Performance Reviews After More Than Three Decades," *Quartz*, August 13, 2015, http://qz.com/597812/who-will-win-davos-2016/.

REFERENCES

Agut, Sonia, Marisa Salanova, and Jose Maria Miero. "Linking Organizational Resources and Work Engagement to Employee Performance and Customer Loyalty: The Mediation of Service Climate." *Journal of Applied Psychology* 90, no. 6 (2005): 1217–1227.

Arthur, Jeffrey. "Effects of Human Resource Systems on Manufacturing Performance and Turnover." *Academy of Management Journal* 37, no. 3 (June 1994): 670–687.

Davenport, Thomas, and Jeanne Harris. "Competing on Analytics." *Harvard Business Review*, January 2006.

Kehoe, Rebecca, and Patrick Wright. "The Impact of High-Performance Human Resource Practices on Employees' Attitudes and Behaviors." *Journal of Management* 39, no. 2 (February 2013): 366–391.

Menezes, Lilian, Stephen Wood, and Garry Gelade. "The Integration of Human Resource and Operation Management Practices and Its Link with Performance: A Longitudinal Latent Class Study." *Journal of Operations Management* (2010).

Powell, Thomas, and Anne Dent-Micallef. "Information Technology as Competitive Advantage: The Role of Human, Business, and Technology Resources." *Strategic Management Journal* 18, no. 5 (May 1997): 375–405.

Walumbwa, Fred, David Mayer, Peng Wang, Hui Wang, Kristina Workman, and Amanda Christensen. "Linking Ethical Leadership to Employee Performance: The Roles of Leader–Member Exchange, Self-Efficacy, and Organizational Identification." *Organizational Behavior and Human Decision Processes* 115 (2011): 204–213.

CHAPTER 10

Employee Lifetime Value and Cost Modeling

Pasha Roberts
Chief Scientist, Talent Analytics, Corp.

How far would Moses have gone if he had taken a poll in Egypt?

—Harry S. Truman

UNDERSTANDING THE MOST EXPENSIVE ASSET

Practically every business shares the same biggest cost—employees. This makes sense, because even in this age of robots and computers, human talent is behind everything that a company does. People are the source of innovation, growth, and competitive edge for every company.

Given this importance, it's a bit strange that data science is only beginning to look inward at the workforce. We have measured the consumer behavior from every angle. We can quote the lifetime value (LTV) of our customers to three decimal points, though we don't really know them. Our employee relationships are deeper, longer-term, stickier, and more laden with potential value than customers in almost every industry.

But most hiring and employee development happen by intuition or chance. Long-term workforce planning is done at only a very high level for very common roles. Rules of thumb and industry benchmarks from magazine articles dominate employee strategy. However, there are more rigorous and methodical methods available.

ARE EMPLOYEES COSTS OR ASSETS?

From the perspective of generally accepted accounting principles, most employee expenditures are considered to be costs. Employees are not subject to depreciation, as are machines, for example. This isn't changing anytime soon.

But from a management point of view, employees are more like a portfolio of assets—with interlocking strengths, weaknesses, and capacities. If you run a call center, your staff is your primary tool for processing calls, arguably more important than the phone switch. Likewise for a software development group or a marketing department and their tasks.

In this sense, employees are key assets, much like machines, for getting work done. If you hire or develop a more efficient and long-lasting employee, production will go up. We encourage employers not only to value their workers as human beings, but also to think of people as productive units that can be intelligently optimized for targeted outcomes.

THE BASIS FOR ADVANCED ANALYTICS

In this chapter we present a powerful first step to advanced employee analytics. We will walk through a cohesive framework for measuring the cost, performance, and attrition of a workforce.

These three key metrics (cost, performance, attrition) combine in interesting ways to inform decision making. Most important, the metrics are a quantitative baseline for predictive analytics exercises. Only with these metrics will we be able to learn how to apply predictive models or whether the models are improving operations.

Note that each of these three metrics is not a single number, but a series of values across the lifetime of an employee. Technically they are a time series or vector, but we will use the terms *metric* and *curve* interchangeably to describe them.

Employee Lifetime Value

One notable takeaway from this chapter is a lifetime value of an employee in a role. The lifetime value of a *customer* is often defined as "a prediction of the net profit attributed to the entire future relationship with a customer."

Our calculations of employee lifetime value (ELTV) refer to "a prediction of the net profit attributed to an employee through the employee's tenure in a given role." If someone changes roles, say from Customer Service III to Internal Sales IV, a new lifetime value will apply.

We limit our analysis to one role at a time—say Underwriter I, or Teller II, or Customer Service III. We don't attempt to predict an employee's promotion path or ultimate journey through the company.

ELTV is probability-weighted by the risk of attrition from the role. Because it is risk-weighted, the ELTV is an excellent roll-up number to compare programs or scenarios, with a direct tie to the bottom line.

Key Outcomes

We address employee cost, performance, attrition, and lifetime value to bring the practice of human resources (HR) into the information age. Only with these metrics will the actual value and dynamics of our HR be known. We imagine a future where enterprise software dashboards commonly report this information, and the curves are routinely used in planning. With this kind of information innovation, business operations will be able to routinely measure and apply productive gains from advanced analytics.

Executives will learn key workforce measurement concepts that will enable a new level of business intelligence (BI). With these key metrics in focus, executives will be able to lead predictive analytics efforts throughout the enterprise.

HR, recruiting, and staffing professionals will learn to measure what happens to new hires after they leave the HR funnel and enter the workplace. Intelligent feedback from workplace performance or attrition can effectively inform hiring efforts to be smarter and more targeted.

Line of business managers, such as sales operations or call center managers, will learn to format their employee operations into enterprise-relevant information.

Data scientists, analysts, and information technology professionals will learn the business context for their analysis. These analysts can apply the knowledge to identify information sources and formats for dashboards and predictive analytics.

Three Vital Metrics for Every Employment Role

One Role at a Time

First, it is only meaningful to evaluate one role at a time, one company at a time. The curves and dynamics for accounting will be very different from those for inside sales. Likewise, so-called industry benchmarks are next to useless—companies differ, regions are different, and enterprises evolve over time. It is easy enough to gather this information for your own company's roles, and we suggest investing the time to simply do so.

Some roles have more volume and size than others. A call center or underwriter role will have plenty of data for great accuracy. Executive leadership is a small sample with less turnover—not as useful for analytics.

Time Frame

Often this exercise comes about in response to attrition or training issues, which manifest in the first year or two. The simplest of all is an entry-level position that automatically promotes after a year or two.

These short-term cases are easier to calculate than long-term employees. Beyond a few years, cost and performance factors get more complicated with raises, equity, inflation, and the time value of money. Long-term employees also vary in performance patterns—some continue to learn, while others coast or check out.

Three Commonsense Numbers

Three commonsense questions underlie our three metrics (see Figure 10.1):

1. How much does it **cost** to find, train, and keep an employee in this role?
2. How much does an employee in this role **contribute** to the business's top line?
3. How long do people tend to **stay** in this role?

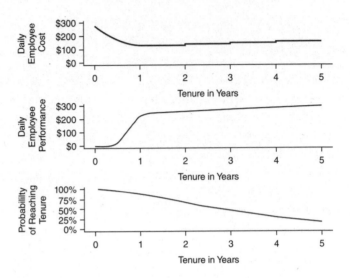

Figure 10.1 The Three Curves

These calculations are usually done at a high level, aggregating costs and performance for everyone in a single role. More advanced approaches seek out clusters or individual patterns across thousands of employees. These Big Data approaches are more useful for transaction- and revenue-related roles.

The cost curve tracks how much money is spent on an employee in the role over time. It is like a daily log of costs for a new employee, from day one. After a flurry of recruiting, orienting, training, and onboarding costs, the expenses typically level out as salary and infrastructure.

The performance curve estimates the contribution an employee makes to the company, starting at day one. Typically until training and orientation are complete, that number is zero. Employees typically ramp up to productivity after weeks, months, or years. After ramp-up, that level may plateau, increase gradually, or even bow downward after years. The ultimate level of contribution can be calculated directly for some roles, or estimated for others.

The attrition curve shows the probability of an employee's being in the role at different points of tenure. On the first day, that number is close to 100 percent. This number is the flip side of turnover—if a role has 40 percent annual turnover, there is a 60 percent chance of still being on the job in a year. The full curve is easily calculated from the HR system of record, and is a powerful tool.

The three curves in combination are exceedingly powerful.

The Employee Cost Curve

It is simple enough to document the hard costs that make up the initial stages of the employee life cycle. This section will walk through the major cost areas, but the specifics will depend on the role at hand. We don't suggest modeling soft costs such as morale or engagement, as they are easy to manipulate and difficult to defend.

Typically, a small number of meetings and accounting queries are all that is needed to put a simple aggregate together. It is a good practice to assemble the costs in a shared spreadsheet for the involved parties' approval.

Recruiting Costs

HR spends a great deal of time and effort to fill one position. Typically a recruiter will screen, interview, and reject many candidates before finding the right person. What does this cost?

Such costs often include the following:

- Job boards
- Social media networks
- Print ads
- Job fairs
- Employee referral fees
- Skills assessment
- Predictive scores
- Drug testing
- Background screening

In addition, managers and staff spend time interviewing candidates. This is usually well documented, consisting of phone or video interviews, panel interviews, and final individual interviews. They cost money, including:

- Recruiter time
- Manager time
- Parking/transportation

These costs are surprisingly consistent. Some items, like drug tests, have fixed costs. HR works hard to keep the hiring funnel efficient and full. There is usually a fixed set of job fairs, advertising, and job board usage per year.

All of these costs get aggregated and averaged for the role, and applied to the first day of a new hire's job. It is not unusual for this acquisition cost to be quite high.

Onboarding Costs

What are the costs to bring one employee on board? Some companies have regular orientation events to welcome new hires.

Such costs often include the following:

- HR paperwork
- Orientation event—parking, staff
- Shirt, gifts
- Days of shadowing workers on the job

Employee salary typically starts during orientation. As with recruiting costs, these onboarding costs simply go into the spreadsheet on the proper day.

If termination costs are significant, you may want to include them here on day one. Essentially, we are accounting for the *prior* employee's termination.

Training Costs

What are the costs to train one employee?

Such costs often include the following, averaged per hire:

- Trainer salary divided across students
- Transportation
- Food and venue

How many days, weeks, or months does the training take? Is there a test at the end, and if so, how many pass the test? Is the new employee paid at full salary during the training?

As before, these costs are relatively fixed and can be filled into the spreadsheet.

On-the-Job Learning

Even after training, employees are not fully productive. The actual ramp-up is not a cost, but part of performance. We will cover that in the next section—it is important not to double-count.

But during ramp-up, most new employees consume the attention of managers and peers. Often this is the expected procedure, and can be modeled into the costs like everything else. For example, a bank supervisor may watch every transaction of a new bank teller until milestones are met.

Where peer attention is significant and structural, it makes sense to build simple rules to factor it in. For example, a model may include 20 percent more of a supervisor's time (and therefore salary) for the first month. Again, we roll this into the model, day by day.

Base Salary, Benefits, and Infrastructure

In most large organizations, employee salaries for a role fall within a reasonably tight band. In an entry-level position, such as a call center, the first-year salary may be completely standardized. Even in positions with large individual variances, the long-term patterns are often quite stable. The goal is to build a reasonable model of the salary for one new employee in this role. If there is a probationary salary, simply model it in.

Sales commissions and other bonuses are performance-based. They can be either included here or deducted from performance numbers in the next section. Commissions can be dominant in a role or a secondary effect. The important thing is to be consistent, and not double-count costs versus performance.

Add in other fixed, ongoing costs for the employee, such as health insurance or other benefits, at the time that the new hire starts. If benefits start later in the cycle, simply model that in.

Some infrastructure is appropriate for inclusion—incremental ongoing fees, such as electricity or building usage. However, do not include infrastructure that is reused when the employee is replaced; for example, a computer or desk will be used by a replacement employee.

Once the employee is at full productivity, costs are typically limited to salary, benefits, and infrastructure. For long-term roles, we model in raises and bonuses. When an employee is promoted, he or she has effectively left the role of this analysis.

Summing Up the Cost Curve

The result is a list of daily costs for having an employee on board in this role. If the employee ends up terminating, the costs will stop. But this metric does not handle terminations—that comes later.

It isn't necessary to cover edge cases, like lawsuits or medical emergencies. These are exceptions—a distraction from the overall patterns that will emerge.

A typical curve for an entry-level role may resemble the one in Figure 10.2—a high spike at the outset, followed by a slow stair-step pattern.

The Employee Performance Curve

Employee performance is the amount that an individual contributes to corporate revenue. We use the word *performance* because *benefit* can

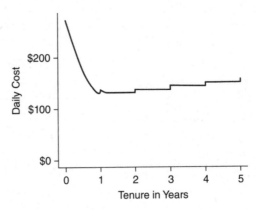

Figure 10.2 The Cost Curve

become confused with *benefits*. But more important, the *performance* term underscores the fact that an employee is an asset, here in your company to deliver daily value.

There are three aspects to this curve:

1. The ramp-up from zero to full performance.
2. The fully ramped-up level of contribution.
3. Where does performance go after this? Flat, up, down?

We will address each in turn.

The Ramp-Up

People are generally not productive on their first day—often it can take months to get up to speed. The ramp upward may not even start until training or certification is complete. We have seen jobs where financial advisers train for months for the Series 7 exam. Until they pass Series 7, it is illegal for them to take a single phone call. In this case, the upward ramp begins months into the employee tenure.

The easy, informal way to gauge the size of this ramp is to ask line managers, "How long does it take someone to get up to speed?" Experienced managers will have an informed opinion, the average of which will be useful. The answer will be anything from "three months" to "a year and a half" or more.

The middle route is to look at aggregate or anecdotal data to test the managers' statements. With sales data, we can measure average sales performance at three months, six months, nine months, and one year to build our own ramp curves.

And, the long way is with Big Data, as covered in a following section in this chapter. Very strong results can be gained with the easiest route, simply talking with operational managers.

The shape of the curve will not make a large difference. An S-shaped ramp is intuitive and quantitatively pleasing, but a straight ramp is easier to model (see Figure 10.3). Basically, every day the new employee gets better at the job and contributes more to the company.

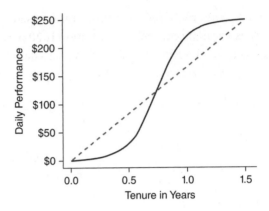

Figure 10.3 Performance Ramp Shapes

The Fully Ramped Performance Level

Some roles, such as sales or industrial production, are more directly connected to revenue. When a sales representative makes a deal, a solid portion of the deal can be attributed to the sales rep's work. When a machinist builds a car door, it is not difficult to apportion the worker's productivity to revenue. A management consultant will always have billable hours and rates high on his or her mind. Brief consultations with accounting or senior management can determine a percentage to allocate to each unit.

For example, perhaps we allocate 20 percent of a software sale's value to the sales rep who sold the software. On an aggregate level, a sales group with 200 reps may sell $100 million worth per year, so each rep is responsible for ($100M × 20%/200 employees = $100,000) per rep per year, or $410 a day. In real life, reps differ in performance—but we don't know how a new rep will perform on the first day, so the average is our expected value.

Other roles, such as an accountant, a CEO, or a software developer, have a less tangible connection to the top line. There are two ways to estimate these. First, we can allocate a portion of revenue to each department and divide by the number of employees. For example, in accounting, ($100M × 1%)/20 accountants = $50,000 per accountant per year, or $205 per day.

Second, we can simply estimate a profit ratio based on salary. For example, we may estimate that the contribution is 20 percent over salary. So, a daily salary of $100 would imply a $120 daily contribution. For companies with unusually low revenue, this may be the only way to do it.

Ongoing Performance

The focus of this analysis is usually on attrition and the first years. But the approach can be extended to evaluate the contributions of long-tenured employees as well.

Several shapes are possible: Employees may plateau at their full level—arguably a five-year underwriter may not be more productive than a two-year underwriter. Employees may "dome" after the full level—after a certain level of tenure, they may not work as hard. Employees may continue to learn, grow, and contribute—slowly ramping upward forever. (See Figure 10.4.)

The Final Performance Curve

The result of these three elements is a curve much like the cost curve (see Figure 10.5). For every day of tenure, we show a dollar contribution for a new employee in the role.

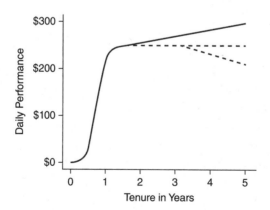

Figure 10.4 Long-Term Employee Performance Curves

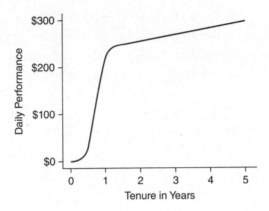

Figure 10.5 The Performance Curve

Human Resource Accounting

There is a subfield of accounting called human resource accounting (HRA) that delves more deeply into these valuations, rigorously treating employees as assets instead of costs. When scaled to the entire enterprise, HRA can be prohibitively complex. For a single role, we need not dig as deep—simple heuristics can build the curves very well.

Quantitative Scissors and the Hockey Stick: Net Employee Value

Now it is time to put the cost curve and the performance curve together.

Daily Breakeven

Figure 10.6 shows a stylized cost/performance plot for one employee across five years of tenure. At first, costs from recruiting, onboarding, and training are high while performance is zero. Every day the employee comes in, the business loses money. At nine months the lines cross—and for the first time, the employee delivers a net positive contribution. This is called the "daily breakeven (B/E) point."

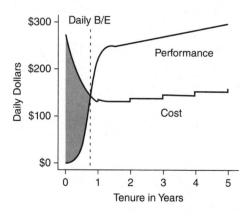

Figure 10.6 Cost and Performance for One Employee

Beyond this point, a long-term pattern of net positive contribution, endures. These crossing curves are sometimes called the "quantitative scissors"—the shaded zone on the left is an inescapable reality of doing business. To decrease the overall costs due to employee churn, *something* has to budge on these curves. However, daily B/E is not the full story.

Cumulative Breakeven

We must account for the debt incurred by training and early costs. The cumulative sum of daily losses or surpluses brings us the cumulative value chart.

The cumulative value generally falls into a familiar hockey stick shape as in Figure 10.7. The plot shows the net value accrued by an employee once he or she gets to a specific tenure. It shows us when the debt from recruiting and training costs is paid off, and the line crosses zero. This point is called the cumulative B/E.

The cumulative value curve is a valuable business object. The shaded region on the left shows how terminations before this point are a cost to the business.

In this stylized example, the employee starts providing daily value after nine months, and has not paid back the startup debt until 24

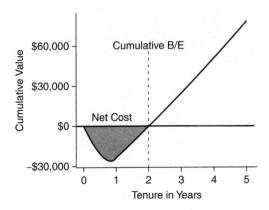

Figure 10.7 Cumulative Value for One Employee

months. An employee who leaves at nine months represents a net cost of more than $25,000 on average in lost start-up costs. By comparison, we often see impressive attrition after just three to six months.

In calculations that span very long tenures, it may be advisable to adjust values for inflation.

Replacement Cost

When an employee must be replaced, the business has lost a functioning asset, a valuable team member. A proper replacement should be considered as a fully trained, fully ramped-up employee, ready to take on the work.

For such calculations, we sum up the costs under the cost curve to one of three places, depending on internal policy (see Figure 10.8):

- Up to the daily B/E point
- Up to the full productivity point
- Up to the cumulative B/E point

We count the costs only, to identify the total additional outlay that the business is forced to make upon losing a staff member. The full productivity point is the most intuitive, stable, and defensible option. This number is typically thousands of dollars even for entry-level positions.

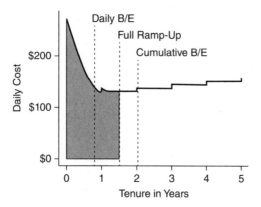

Figure 10.8 Replacement Cost Cutoffs

Employee Tenure in a Survival Analytics Framework

With a cumulative cost curve in hand, we now turn to evaluate attrition. We hope to illustrate a far more intuitive and useful visualization than annual attrition, the popular business metric. Annual attrition is but a single point on this easy-to-understand business tool.

Survival Analytics

Employee attrition falls into the same class of survival problem as machine failure rates or medical research. This domain has brought us solid statistical innovations, including a visualization known as the survival curve. The risk of a particular employee terminating from a job is much the same as figuring when an industrial machine is going to stop working, or how long a patient may live with a given disease. In all cases, we are estimating *when an event will happen* while we're in the middle of normal operations.

Calculation

In measuring employee attrition or any survival analytics problem, there is a complication. We don't know when a current employee will terminate—it could be tomorrow or years in the future. Since current employees are a significant part of our sample, we have to compensate.

It is not statistically correct to simply average or regress employment tenures, for this reason. Likewise, it is technically wrong to tally or predict terminations without regard to tenure or staffing level. There is a subtle interplay between tenure and termination that must be handled properly.

This adjustment is done with the Kaplan–Meier Estimator, which mathematically removes current employees from calculations beyond their tenure. Born decades ago from medical research, the Kaplan–Meier calculation is standard in many fields. The function is built into most modern statistical software, such as the "survival" package in R. It can even be done in Excel, with a bit of setup.

The Hazard Curve

Once Kaplan–Meier has been properly adjusted, we can show attrition in at least two ways. The first is called a "hazard curve," which is the chance (hazard) that the event (termination) will occur on any given day during the employee's tenure. In Figure 10.9 we see hazard curves for two hypothetical locations, Chicago and New York. We see that early termination is more likely in New York.

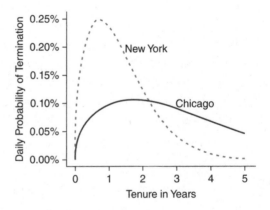

Figure 10.9 Hazard Curves—Daily Probability of Termination

We will use these hazard curve values later for risk weighting, but it is not the best visual tool.

The Survival Curve

The best visualization of employee attrition is the survival curve, as shown in Figure 10.10. It is a sum of the probabilities in the hazard curve, up to each point in tenure. It shows nuances, bulges, trends, and differences far better than any simple attrition figure. We have found that the survival curve is accessible for most business users, and hope someday to see it on BI dashboards everywhere.

Across the horizontal x-axis we see tenure, from zero to many years. On the vertical y-axis we see the probability of an employee's surviving to that tenure. Although some people don't show up on their first day of work, on day one survival is nearly 100 percent. Statisticians will recognize the survival curve as (1 − CDF) of the hazard curve (CDF is cumulative distribution function).

Attrition for All Periods

The business-familiar annual attrition number is here—at the one-year mark on Figure 10.10, we see 86 percent survival for the Chicago curve, which subtracts from the top for 14 percent annual attrition.

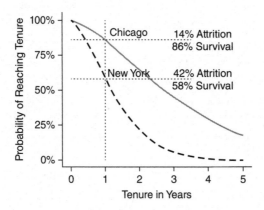

Figure 10.10 Survival Curves—Probability of Reaching Tenure

Likewise, the New York curve shows 58 percent survival at one year, which subtracts to 42 percent annual attrition.

But one year is somewhat arbitrary. Remember that our break-even point is two years, so arguably that is a more useful threshold. At this 24-month breakeven point, we see 65 percent remaining in Chicago, but only 21 percent in New York.

One of the great strengths of survival curves is that we can compare multiple groupings. On one chart, we can compare geographic regions, as in Figure 10.10. Likewise, we can compare managers or multiple job roles. In predictive hiring work, we compare survival curves before intervention versus after intervention.

Rolling It Up: Employee Lifetime Value

One important application of these curves is to obtain the lifetime value of an employee in the role.

We can look up the cumulative value at an arbitrary date, say five years. The chart shows that an employee at that tenure is worth $78,851. However, not all employees last five years—only 18 percent in Chicago and 0.2 percent in New York.

Risk Weighting

Borrowing a technique from finance, we will risk-weight the cost curve to give our answer. A 5 percent chance of getting $100 is effectively a $5 expected value. In a similar manner, we will multiply every probability in the hazard curve, Figure 10.9, with the matching dollar value in the cumulative value curve, Figure 10.7.

Then, we sum these expected values into a single number. This is called a dot-product, available in Excel as "DOTPRODUCT" or in R as simple multiplication. This dot-product gives us a proper risk-weighted lifetime value.

Be careful to use the hazard curve, the daily probability of termination, and not the survival curve, the cumulative probability of survival. Also, take care to use the entire hazard curve, extending far into the future—the sum of probabilities under that curve should equal 1.

The Lifetime Value of an Employee

In this sample, as shown in Figure 10.11, a Chicago employee's lifetime value is $31,487, while the New Yorker's lifetime value is a loss with –$9,343, a far cry from the potential $78,851 lifetime value of a five-year tenure. These groups have the *same* cost curve but *different* survival curves—which makes a significant difference.

This is more like the lifetime value of a new employee in a given role than the lifetime value of a specific employee. We are not attempting to predict whether a specific person will someday rise to become president of the company, or if they will take a lateral move to another department. When they enter a new role, they enter a new set of calculations.

A Useful Rollup Number

The lifetime value figure is sensitive to changes in attrition as well as costs or performance. It encompasses most foreseeable financial aspects of employees in that role, and allows fair comparisons of value.

While these numbers may never show up on a financial balance sheet, they are a strong estimate of how a set of employees will play out into the future.

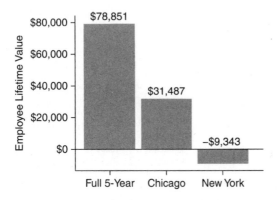

Figure 10.11 Comparison of Employee Lifetime Value

Big Data Approaches to Employee Development

The preceding approaches assume that all employees are the same, and average performance results. This is not entirely unreasonable, since we often have no prediction of what kind of candidate is joining the company. But certain roles give us enough data that we can evaluate the many paths to success and the relative value of each. We can even begin to predict which of several performance paths a new candidate may take.

Rather than building a monolithic example of sales based on averages, we can use large-scale tools like Hadoop or SAP HANA to do better. Consider a sales example, in which we have data for every single transaction sold by every rep for 10 years. Consider that we sort through these millions of transactions involving thousands of sales reps.

Then, we evaluate the sales that each rep made from his or her first day. How did all the sales reps do? Instead of one performance curve, we have thousands.

- Did they start strong and then plateau?
- Did they slowly grow and learn to sell over time?
- Did they start strong, fizzle out, and terminate?
- Did they never get it and consequently terminate early?
- Or something else?

We can use clustering algorithms to find groupings of sales rep performance—that is, how different reps ramped up. Now, instead of thousands of performance curves, we may have three to seven well-traveled clusters or patterns.

In the sections that follow, we would calculate different B/E points and different lifetime values for each of these types of sales reps. Does the business prefer a slow learner over a strong-start-then-plateau sales rep? The data will tell us; at the simplest level we just need to compare lifetime values of each curve type. There are strategic and teamwork considerations as well, and a complete comparison would move into Monte Carlo simulation.

It also moves us far beyond the scope of this chapter. This Big Data analysis lays the groundwork for predictive work to identify the propensity for candidates to follow one of these sales performance paths. More advanced applications will span multiple performance variables. This is a simple, single-performance-variable example of what is possible with transactional data and a good amount of effort.

Practical Applications of Employee Metrics

After all of this work, we are left with several useful assets for a role:

- Daily cost and performance (the quantitative scissors)
- Cumulative net value (the hockey stick)
- Replacement cost
- Daily and cumulative B/E points
- The survival curve
- ELTV

Here are a variety of business applications of these metrics.

Measuring the Cost of Attrition

Everyone knows that attrition is expensive, but what is the actual cost? The relevant number is the amount that the business must spend to handle the problem (i.e., the replacement cost).

We find the number of attrition-related hires per year—for example, say a company with 1,000 agents that has 40 percent annual turnover and a replacement cost of $11,000. This implies that 400 agents need to be replaced every year, if the company is holding steady or growing. Simply multiply 400 agents by the replacement cost for the annual attrition cost.

In this case, attrition costs $4.4 million a year. If the company halved its attrition rate, it would save $2.2 million.

Scenario Planning

Employment, and business in general, is not a laboratory environment. We don't get do-overs for failed scenarios, and our ability to try things out is limited. Customer analytics is slightly more amenable to A/B testing, just because the relationship is thinner, and there are many customers.

With this model of lifetime value, we can simulate the impact of programs. What happens if we:

- Increase wages by x percent, and assume that doing so will shift survival curves up by y percent?
- Reduce wages by x percent, and assume it will shift survival curves down by y percent?
- Spend $\$x$ more on training, and assume it will accelerate learning by y percent?
- Spend $\$x$ more on coaching, and assume it will help New Yorkers stay y percent longer?
- Hire x percent more employees in Chicago?

Any of these business changes would impact any or all of the underlying three curves. The outcomes of these scenarios can be estimated, compared, and prioritized.

Consider a change in training:

- More training would increase the first part of the cost curve.
- More training would (hopefully) speed up the ramp-up period on the performance curve.
- More training may decrease attrition, moving the survival curve up a bit.

The combined effect of these changes would be seen in two ways:

1. A different cumulative B/E date—hopefully lower, if the ramp effect overpowers the increased cost.
2. An increased lifetime value—with a higher survival curve and more ultimate performance.

If the three underlying curves are modeled properly, they will be sensitive to any operational change.

Impact of Hiring Changes

Hiring changes are more complex. Consider a new hiring program to find candidates with lower attrition. This means that the new program would find new candidates with higher survival curves. The cost and performance curves would remain the same, but the lifetime value of the new hires would be higher, due to a lower risk of attrition.

Two calculable outcomes would bring value to the company:

1. **Fewer early terminations:** Fewer of the new hires would terminate while still in the red on the cumulative value curve.
2. **More good candidates:** The new hires would tend to last longer past the B/E point, accruing more lifetime value.

These numbers can be calculated and tested. In the first case, fewer early terminations, the models would estimate a new turnover rate, implying perhaps 40 fewer pre-B/E terminations. As before, say the replacement cost is $11,000. So the company would save 40 times $11,000, or $440,000 in the first year as it transitions to a lower attrition rate.

In the second case, we compare lifetime value in the role, before and after the change. We multiply the increase in lifetime value by the number of new hires, to show an increase in the stock of employee value in the role. Perhaps the lifetime value increased by $3,100 and we hired 400 agents; therefore, we will increase the value of employees in this role by $1.24 million.

Predictive Analytics Thresholds Tuning

Models can be designed to score predictions of future employee attrition or performance, even before someone is hired. Such models are commonly deployed as part of the hiring process to find better candidates. This advanced form of analytics raises employee models from rough averages to a very granular, individual-based view of employment.

All of the previous calculations feed directly into such a modeling exercise, and become the method by which we judge the success of a model. If we want to increase performance, we expect to see an increase in the performance curve. If we expect to decrease attrition, we would see an increase in the survival curve. A successful model will bring higher lifetime value.

Attrition-based models often use survival curves directly, and aim to shift the curves upward. All predictive models create a score—your credit score is an example. The survival curve becomes the basis for a range of acceptance thresholds for the model. The plot in Figure 10.12 is an example of a survival curve with multiple predictive bands.

Employee Costs, Survival, and Business Intelligence Dashboards

Most of these figures are prime candidates for monitoring in a business intelligence (BI) framework, particularly interactive dashboards. Imagine a few possibilities:

- **Survival curve dashboard:** Consider a dashboard with survival curves for every major role in the company. Users could drill in to compare attrition across departments, regions, managers, and roles. Managers could find the areas with the most pain, as measured by turnover. Researchers could identify and discover outliers.

- **Key performance indicators and alerts** could be implemented to keep groups on track. New hires and the results of predictive hiring could be tracked in real time.

- **Costs, performance, and lifetime value across the enterprise:** Likewise, the single-role cost curves and performance

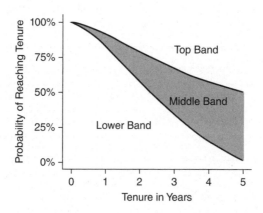

Figure 10.12 Predictive Thresholds in a Survival Model

curves could be combined, drilled into, and split up across the enterprise. Users could compare training costs between geographical regions. Researchers could investigate the impact of training or onboarding changes. Breakeven points and lifetime value could be directly compared. Scenarios could be tested directly in the BI framework.

KEY TAKEAWAYS

- We believe that survival curves along with cost and performance curves are three vital tools that should be produced by every HR or finance department for every high-traffic role. These three numbers capture the essence of the role's impact on the company, and are the basis of powerful calculations.

- We believe that three key metrics (cost, performance, and attrition) combine in interesting ways provide inform decision making. Most important, the metrics are a quantitative baseline for predictive analytics exercises in ELTV building.

- HR is known for having inward-facing metrics, like cost per hire or time to fill. The metrics that we have introduced here—cumulative employee value, survival curves, and ELTV—go beyond HR to serve enterprise goals. They are key indicators of how employees—the people whom HR hired—are lasting and performing. These metrics are especially valuable for high-volume, high-turnover roles. They are the measuring stick for improvements to hiring selection, engagement efforts, and performance improvements. Is it time for your organization to begin using them?

CHAPTER 11

Using Retention Analytics to Protect Your Most Valuable Asset

Amel Arhab
Senior Manager at Deloitte
Consulting, LLP

John Houston
Principal at Deloitte Consulting, LLP

Your number one customers are your people. Look after employees first and then customers last.

—Ian Hutchinson

I n today's complex, global, and extremely competitive world, talent is top of mind for most CEOs. While concerned about acquiring and retaining the best and brightest, executives are also worried about nurturing, engaging, and advancing their star performers. As simpler jobs get offshored and the demand for highly skilled individuals continues to rise, competition for the critical remaining pool of talent is fierce. Additionally, millennials bring up another set of challenges by setting new employee preferences for health and environment, purpose and community, and hard work with balanced lifestyles. As a result, the talent puzzle seems to be as multifaceted as it has even been.

Perhaps it is not surprising that retention and attrition may be the biggest challenges of all. In a recent Deloitte survey, over 70 percent of respondents expressed "high" or "very high" levels of concern about retaining critical talent over the next 12 months, along with 66 percent who had the same concern about retaining high-potential talent.[1] Robin Erickson, PhD, Vice President of Talent Acquisition Research at Bersin, reminds us that employee retention is a top concern of most business and HR leaders now that the global economy is improving. "High-performing employees can look for jobs passively just by having their job histories on a social networking site. And, according to Deloitte's 2014 Global Human Capital survey, 83 percent of the organizations surveyed do not believe they are ready to respond."

TRADITIONAL APPROACHES ARE FAILING

Many traditional human resources (HR) methods for understanding and improving retention (or attrition, its antonym) are typically reactive and slow to produce results. They cater to a past generation and associated organizational structures where employee movement was slow and laborious. They typically consist of blanket (not individually targeted) retention campaigns aimed at attacking the latest attrition driver identified from someone's gut feelings acquired over many years of experience. One example is an across-the-board compensation increase for every employee by the same amount, when variations and customizations (by level, department, skills demand, etc.) are typically needed. The focus for these programs also often seems to be on a handful of high-demand top personnel with the most critical skills, with little to no attention given to the rest of the employee base that has the potential to impact retention ratios in a more major way.

Clearly, the aim of traditional approaches can be uncertain and slow in action, so their return on investment (ROI) is extremely difficult to quantify. Exit interviews may contain crucial information, but their confidentiality and low frequency hinder their use in an efficient manner, and they are used only anecdotally. It is, therefore, no surprise that many of these traditional methods are quickly becoming obsolete and ill-suited to an increasingly mobile workforce in which individuals can easily surf the web for job postings tailored to their published skills on social media sites, get e-mail notifications of open positions by their social media network, or respond to direct mobile text messages from various recruitment sources.

WHAT IS RETENTION, ANYWAY?

The inability to calculate an ROI has hindered the understanding of what employee retention truly is. Erickson continues, "Retention has long been believed to be a squishy theoretical concept when it truly is not. Retaining employees requires a combination of real and concrete things that include career growth opportunities, fair compensation, regular performance feedback, learning and development opportunities, focus on employee engagement, and trust in leadership—ultimately, retention can be measured by regretted voluntary turnover, whether your employees stay or go."

More and more, we have observed sophisticated companies, both big and small, move toward advanced analytics and Big Data to help them understand their retention issues, quantify them, and become more agile in solving them. These companies are seeking analytics not to help them identify a silver lining, but rather to be used as a tool to continuously fine-tune their understanding of retention issues and, almost in real time, to propose nimble and novel solutions to curtail retention. From machine-learning techniques and building algorithms that continuously learn behaviors to the use of Big Data to integrate as many multidimensional facets of the individuals as possible, ROI for these types of HR retention solutions has become cutting-edge and quantifiable.

WHAT YOU NEED AND HOW IT WORKS

The building blocks of retention analytics solutions are similar to those of any other analytics initiative. They consist of:

- **Data:** This is the first building block of any analytics initiative and needs to contain instances where employees were retained and others who have attrited. This is so the model can be trained to recognize the differences, discern and learn the patterns of each, and be able to make accurate predictions. The more varied the data sources (i.e., capturing every angle of the employee, business, working conditions, economic climate, etc.), the better the model accuracy is likely to become as it has more information to draw upon for its analysis. Of course, data is to be manipulated and used with care, and most data manipulation leading practices are in the public domain today.
- **Intelligence:** Creating insights from the first building block, intelligence is about extracting, interpreting, and acting on the data. This involves people as well as methods and processes.

- People are needed to develop the crunchy questions, interpret what the statistics are suggesting, and decide what to do with this knowledge. In the context of retention analytics, various subject matter experts are needed: data wranglers and statisticians, retention specialists and end users, HR team leaders and executives, and other peripheral HR practitioners who can help in designing the appropriate actions to take to avoid attrition by individuals, in addition to crafting these solutions to fit within current everyday work flows.

- Statistical methods and routines are needed to process, cleanse, and assemble the data, quantify correlations and data signals, and perform validation testing. Leading practices in statistical modeling are in the public domain and need not be of extreme complexity to yield real and meaningful results.

- **Technology:** This is software to support the data and intelligence building blocks, and can range from basic database management tools to house the data (e.g., Microsoft Office tools, text files, etc.) to the most customized statistical packages for data mining and predictions (e.g., SAS, SPSS, or R).

  - We have noticed that technology can be an accelerator but not necessarily a differentiator. In other words, the sophistication of the technology used need not be of highest complexity to yield real results. However, care should be taken so that whatever technology is used doesn't create new burdens for the end users.

These blocks come together to build the foundation of retention analytics solutions. Data, which contains mountains of information and insights, needs to be organized and mined for insights by intelligent tools and people. Once those insights are extracted, interpreted, and acknowledged, business strategies need to be carefully identified by HR retention experts and put into action. Only once put into action can these solutions realize value by reducing the retention ratio and deterring employees from leaving.

THE BUSINESS CASE

Beyond the fight for the critical and small pool of talent that is increasingly sought after, there is a real economic driving factor behind this move toward sophistication. Losing an employee means at the very least a transfer of knowledge and experience to, perhaps, a competitor, as well as a real loss of productivity, and a shift, even if momentary, of personnel morale. Beyond the well-known costs of searching for replacements (social media adds, headhunters, etc.), finding a suitable candidate (interviews and trial periods), training (learning curves and training costs), and finally hiring (hiring costs, relocation packages, sign-up bonuses, etc.), turnover can quickly become a large business cost to a company. According to Josh Bersin, principal at Bersin, "the cost of losing one employee is 1.5 to 2.0 times the person's annual salary. And if you are talking about a senior executive or highly skilled individuals this cost is quickly increasing beyond twofold!" That is because the pool of people who could replace this individual is small. Therefore, more investment needs to be made to find, attract, hire, and train these individuals than in the case of a lower-level position that can easily be filled.

Can Retention Be Practically Analyzed and Impacted?

As Big Data and advanced analytics are customarily used in other services industries (e.g., customer retention), they have quickly been borrowed by the HR industry. In the analytics world, a large emphasis is being placed on developing crunchy (not soft or easy) questions and getting to answers that will return value on investment, such as "What motivates a high performer to stay or leave?" "How can I know it in advance?" "If I do, is there something I can do about it?" and "What are the options?"

It turns out that, yes, it is possible to identify multiple drivers of attrition, and most of them are actionable. And, assuming that these drivers are identified before the decision of leaving is made (timing is paramount, as most research shows that employees start thinking about leaving 9 to 12 months before they resign), then some customized and impactful actions can be made to prevent that attrition. John Houston, a principal at Deloitte Consulting LLP, says, "In my 18 years of service, I have found that when employees have made the decision to leave and communicate the decision, it is often too late to change their minds. Getting to them three-plus months in advance of that decision is crucial to be able to impact it. People tend to want to leave for compensation, career opportunities, or even because they don't enjoy what they are doing. These are not things you can solve on the spot; they take time to identify, think through, and put the right solution in place to convince the person to stay."

A Concrete Business Study

Impacting the consulting world where retention can be an issue, Deloitte used Big Data and advanced analytics to understand retention issues. From analyzing time sheets and figuring out how many hours are being worked, vacation days taken, client impact, efforts spent, and additional firm projects tackled, to paying attention to travel entries, including frequency and distance of travel, number of nights spent in hotel rooms, and airports visited per week, Deloitte has tackled a large amount of employee data and various sources, including geodemographic factors (city of residence) and economic conditions (prevailing unemployment rates).

Quantify What Is Already Known, Discover What Is Unknown

Clear and intuitive patterns have emerged: For example, if an employee consistently works long hours every week or takes a small amount of vacation yearly, then probabilities for that employee's departure the next year are increased manifoldly. This all makes sense, and we don't need complex analytics to figure out that being overworked and not taking enough rest is bad for retention. However, with analytics not only can we prove something by the numbers, or disprove someone's gut feeling or deeply ingrained traditionally acquired knowledge, but we can also quantify it. And digging even deeper actually lets you see more subtle patterns than the prior belief: Hours worked is actually

U-shaped, meaning that if one individual works a large number of hours and another works very few, then attrition rates are increased in both cases.

We found that excessive travel tends to raise departure rates, which is intuitive since hotels and airport time can take a toll on a person's energy level and morale rather quickly. Similarly, not only could this relationship be confirmed and quantified by the numbers, but subtler patterns also emerged: The excessive travel impact completely breaks down for younger generations and nonexperienced hires. These practitioners enjoy traveling.

We have also analyzed the size of project teams, their locations, managerial composition, individual-to-team performance, and more. We found that managers' actions and behaviors play a very impactful role in a staff project experience. This pattern turns out to be rather negligible on smaller projects, but is manifoldly more important on mega projects (large teams and multiyear engagements), so those projects need to be staffed a lot more carefully with the right number and fit of managers to staff.

Go Deeper in Studying Factors

With advanced and powerful statistics, it has been found that recency is of utmost importance. Looking at excessive travel or poor fit within a project months in advance shows a great deal of correlation with future potential retention issues. But if you look at these or most other characteristics with a year's delay, this correlation starts to break down significantly. This shows that today's workforce is very agile and fast adapting: If they are unhappy, they either change their current circumstances if they can or choose to leave only months later if they can't.

Equally important is the extremeness of drivers. Heavy hours, not enough vacation, or excessive travel do start to trigger voluntary departures; and the more extreme these are, the more departures they will cause—and faster. This is important because when it becomes time to impact these about-to-leave employees, tackling these extreme cases with priority will likely make a greater impact than blanket actions.

Social Factor and Media Effect

Social media and network analyses of individual employees are also being contemplated more closely. Text and sentiment analyses applied on social media posts and other blogging material can infer motivation levels at the workplace through engagement analytics. In addition, studying one's social media network and identifying types and proximity of influencers can identify the likelihood of an employee's being agile about employment change or indicate stickiness at the current workplace.

Now What?

This is all very nice in theory, but do these predictive algorithms actually work outside a classroom and in real life? Yes, they do. Statistical models using a wide range of data sources have been known to identify in the top decile (10 percent) those individuals who have a likelihood of leaving 330 percent more than the average as identified in the previous Deloitte case study. In addition, focusing on the top two deciles (20 percent) of the employee population may capture 65 percent or more of the population likely to leave. These impressive numbers speak to the predictive power of these models using thousands of data points, multiple years of experience, and a variety of information sources. Specifically, they identify who, when, and why:

- Identifying the population at high risk of attrition. For an organization of, say, 50,000 individuals, finding the few hundred higher performers who are likely to leave in the next term can be powerful and insightful.
- It is of crucial importance that this identification can be done a few months before the actual attrition, so as to provide time to act and, it is hoped, avoid the attrition.
- Identifying the likely reasons for attrition for each individual is useful since those are the specific issues the organization needs to think about resolving in order to avoid the attrition.

Knowledge Is Power—or Is It?

But identifying who is at risk of leaving and the reasons why is only half the battle. What to do then? Are these reasons always actionable? Will they impact attrition decisions? What if they are not actionable at all?

If the reasons for leaving are specific enough (i.e., at the individual level, recent, and combined with other close factors), they can be influential. If overwork with excessive travel is leading an individual to think about leaving, then a close look at the individual's career and project assignments with tailored changes (e.g., local project and a rest period) may be enough. If model drivers are pointing to a superstar who draws significant competitor curiosity through social media and recent performance data suggests a beginning of disengagement (e.g., as measured via survey collections), then compensation coupled with highly customized career and leadership development may be worth the investment (e.g., consideration for fast track, project assignment with top management, top leadership training, or shadowing). See Figure 11.1.

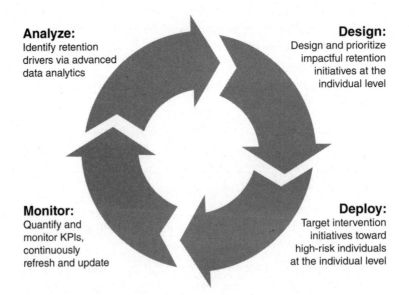

Analyze:
Identify retention drivers via advanced data analytics

Design:
Design and prioritize impactful retention initiatives at the individual level

Monitor:
Quantify and monitor KPIs, continuously refresh and update

Deploy:
Target intervention initiatives toward high-risk individuals at the individual level

Figure 11.1 Illustrative Talent Retention Framework

But even if the model drivers seem not to be actionable (e.g., an individual who wants a complete change of career path, or one who wants to stay home and start a family), even in these instances knowing these moves before they occur can give the organization some lead time. These organizations are able to anticipate the change and prepare for it more smoothly than if they did not know about it. The about-to-leave individual can, in fact, help to find a suitable replacement, assist in training firsthand, and help avoid the gap in productivity as well as any emotional toll the change may take on the team.

Why Should I Care?

If it still isn't clear, let us revisit the issue in numbers. The same corporation discussed earlier with 50,000 employees and an average voluntary turnover rate of, say, 5 percent loses 2,500 individuals a year. With an average salary of $100,000 and a cost of attrition of twice the annual salary, the organization is losing $500 million a year. If predictive models help move the 5 percent attrition rate down to 3 percent, this generates a savings of $200 million.

If this number seems too big, let us cut our assumption for the cost of attrition in half, and the predictive model is able to move the attrition rate to only 4 percent, down from 5 percent. The annual cost is now $50 million. Therefore, the calculations on tangible cost savings can mount up very quickly.

These costs are compounded manifoldly for highly skilled individuals and critical high-potential employees, as the timing assumption of finding and replacing individuals is elongated and costs accumulate over time. And all of this is, of course, excluding all the intangibles, the likes of which are loss of interim productivity, employee morale, brand recognition, loss of intellectual property, and investment in training and development. "Another great intangible loss that we see is loss of network," says Houston. "All the collaboration and web relationships that were built and nurtured run the risk of collapsing with a single individual leaving. And that can take years to rebuild and even more years to become effective at prior levels."

DEPLOYING RETENTION ANALYTICS . . . PIECE OF CAKE?

With the implementation of any business analytics solution, the secret is often in how well it is being deployed rather than how complex and advanced the tools or methods are: "The main pitfall I have seen," says Houston, "is people and organizations getting extremely excited about this new shiny tool that produces real-time scores and cool visualization dashboards, while not spending enough time to work with the business community and end users to understand how this will help them do their jobs more effectively. Too often, these solutions ultimately are given to folks with not enough thought around best integration, and end up adding to one's daily workload versus alleviating it. And with today's fast world of quick apps and everything at our fingertips, we all have even less patience and attention span to tolerate add-on work."

According to a study from Bersin by Deloitte,[2] only 5 percent of Fortune 1000 companies use predictive analytics in HR. Even if the concept of predictive modeling is still new in HR, other areas of businesses such as finance, manufacturing, and marketing have embraced it. In fact, these industries have been relying on predictive modeling to proactively reach out to customers at risk, target the most profitable customers, optimize their supply chains, and improve their overall customer relationship management.

Approaches and techniques similar to those used in the aforementioned industries could be applied to help anticipate employee attrition. Predictive models provide HR teams and managers with actionable insights to proactively put in place initiatives and strategies to address company business objectives such as:

- What are your most important talent issues?
- Which employees are at risk of leaving your organization? When and why?
- What is the profile of employees most likely to leave?
- What is the risk to the organization if employees leave?
- What is the current pulse of your employees? And how is it trending?

- What are the main drivers of attrition for your organization? How do they map by various subsets of employees?
- Who are your star performers and critical employees? Which ones are most likely to leave in the next three to six months and why?
- What is the risk/impact of this attrition?

HOW TO IMPLEMENT PROACTIVE TALENT RETENTION MODELS

The key to successful analytics lies in the "implementation" or "deployment"—this is where we have seen some companies succeed while others have failed. The most advanced and complex predictive model will realize little to no value if it ends up sitting on a shelf. Therefore, let's turn to the ingredients of successful analytics implementation. As discussed in the previous chapters, predictive analytics has proven to provide actionable insights in anticipating outcomes such as who will click, who will vote, who will buy, who will convert, and who will lie. Applied to HR, predictive analytics could help to anticipate who will quit, when, and why. To do this, you will need the data, the quant or data miner, and a statistician or business analyst to build an appropriate attrition model needed to provide you with the key drivers and actionable insights to address your talent attrition.

As a quick overview, predictive models encompass two types of variables in addition to an equation (link function) that bring the two together:

1. Input variables, also called independent variables, are factors that you include in the model in order to test and assess their relationship with the outcome event. Input variables also provide their impact in predicting the outcome.

2. Output variables are the elements you are seeking to predict. In this case, it would be the attrition status: 1 = attrition and 0 = no attrition. These may also be known as dependent or response variables.

The goal of the predictive modeling exercise is to build the quantitative relationship between input and output variables based on past learnings as encompassed in the data. Basic but market-leading statistical assumptions and methodologies are to be used to build this relationship. It is generally enough to use these basic statistical techniques as most of the lift may be realized with simple regressions or decision trees. The iteration process is similar to any statistical exercise in other industries and applications.

Predictive models also tell how strong each variable is in terms of explaining why an employee will leave based on statistical tests. Figure 11.2 illustrates an employee attrition model that can be explained using three major data sources as discussed in Chapter 2: company data, publicly available talent data, and labor market data.

Predictive models applied to the aforementioned data help to determine the statistical impact of every data element, whether it is company human resources information system (HRIS) data, labor market data, or publicly available talent data.

Companies we spoke with during our research for this book mentioned not having access to all the data or having access to just part of it. In the next main section, we will explore what types of variables should be included in employee attrition predictive models in order to assess their relevance and impact.

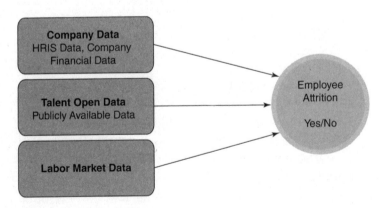

Figure 11.2 Talent Attrition Predictive Model

PROFILE

▼ **Interview with Arun Chidambaram, Director of Global Workforce Intelligence, Pfizer**

JP Isson had the opportunity to discuss talent retention analytics with Arun Chidambaram.

Isson: Can you explain how Pfizer has been leveraging Big Data analytics for talent retention?

Chidambaram: When we approach talent retention, we treat each market uniquely. [He explains that, with nearly 80,000 employees, the company has devised a strategy that leverages the power of HR data, publicly available information, and quantitative data to optimize and tailor its talent retention tactics for its offices throughout the world.]

Isson: What is the incremental value of publicly available data for Pfizer?

Chidambaram: Only looking at internal data creates a limited and myopic approach toward talent retention, so Pfizer is adopting models that are dynamic and adjusted by country and region. As a result, the company is able to:

Gradually reduce employee turnover in specific areas by leveraging a proactive approach to pinpoint driving factors of talent attrition.

Provide a comprehensive picture of risk factors to better understand how internal and external factors impact Pfizer's talent market supply chain and identify the best actions for the company to maintain workforce stability.

Prioritize investments in programs that are working and help the company to maintain its competitive edge by keeping its most important asset—its talent.

By implementing these new methods, each talent market is considered uniquely. When it comes to hiring and retaining the top employees, companies cannot rely on a one-size-fits-all solution.

DATA FOR TALENT ATTRITION PREDICTIVE MODELING

As noted in JP's interview with Chidambaram from Pfizer, it is important to remember that there is no one size fits all when it comes time to discuss predictive model drivers in HR. Each company has its own issues, from culture to employer and employee value propositions. Today, thanks to Big Data, we have access to more talent data than ever before. For the scope of this book, we will look at four major sources of data to test in the model:

Internal data includes data from HRIS compensation data learning and development training system applicant tracking systems.

Company data includes financial performance, company revenue, growth, number of customers, company brand, company social media scores, company reviews and rankings such as those on Glassdoor and opinion sites, and company online reputation.

Labor market data includes data from a vast array of sources that cover trends such as:

- Gross domestic product (GDP) by industry location and company size.
- Unemployment rate by industry location and company size.
- Cost per hire and turnover rate by industry location and company size.
- Company stock market trend indicator.
- Stock market indicator (e.g., Dow Jones Industrial Average, Standard & Poor's 500).
- Supply and demand data (is your company in an industry with high demand for its skilled workers such as STEM fields?).
- Online job postings (analysis of all job postings available online).
- Regional and global financial risks.

Publicly available talent data is the most important piece of talent data and is a complete game changer because this data 10 years ago was not available. Open talent data or publicly available data includes the digital footprint that your talent leaves on the web, on social media sites like Twitter, Facebook, or LinkedIn and on niche sites such as GitHub or Stack Overflow.

According to some studies, this publicly available talent data is linked to:

- Profile updates tracking
- Profile photo changes
- Having or not having a profile on social media
- Education level
- Years of experience by occupation
- Social media posts, updates, and mentions
- Followers and number of following influencers
- Groups
- Influencers

In some industries, this external data can explain 50 percent of attrition. This means that half of your employee attrition could be explained by this type of information. Now you see what we mean when we say that this data is a game changer! It holds statistically significant insights and explains voluntary talent attrition.

 Interview with John Callery, People Analytics Director, AOL

PROFILE

JP Isson had the opportunity to discuss the impact of publicly available data in talent retention analytics with John Callery.

Isson: What is the impact of publicly available data on talent attrition/ retention predictive models?

Callery: Without publicly available data, your talent and talent retention equation is incomplete. We need to capture that piece of information to enrich our internal talent retention data. By leveraging publicly available quant data and HRIS data, AOL has a unique

(Continued)

(*continued*)

approach that is not just focused on overall retention rates, but on specific areas of the business where proactive retention makes the company more competitive.

Armed with this talent retention knowledge, AOL created actionable insights and changed the way they do business, manage people, and address "push factors," or those elements that explain talent supply-and-demand fluctuations, and those aspects that can cause employees to become unhappy and lead them to begin looking for another job.

Isson: What were the benefits of your predictive models on proactive talent retention strategies?

Callery: AOL used their data to devise strategy and after implementing it, the company has seen impressive results that exceeded their expectations in the following areas:

- **Business value:** Creating a plan for proactive talent retention provided AOL with actual business value that comes from tying retention to real dollars and the overall workforce performance.

- **Culture:** By proactively retaining employees who are at risk for leaving helped AOL strengthen their company culture, because it lowered level of turnovers, which improved morale and strengthened internal teams.

- **Talent brand:** By creating a strong culture, AOL also fortified its talent brand, which helps and provides the company with actionable insights needed to attract and retain great talent in the future.

Callery closes with, "Our benefits not only include a significant decrease on our attrition rate on those target areas and groups. We are also seeing significant benefits on our business value, our culture, and our talent brand."

Table 11.1 provides a summary of the most common variables that could be assessed in your model.

Table 11.1 Variables for Talent Attrition Predictive Model

Sociodemographic and Geodemographic Data	Motivation: Work–Life Balance	Development: Personal and Professional	Talent Market Attractiveness
Gender	Relationship with manager	Specialization and development of technical skills	Unemployment rate by industry and by occupation
Age group	Clarity of goals	Development of management skills	Unemployment by education level
Age at hire	Confidence in management	Professional development offered	Job openings
Minority	Fit with company culture and value	Training or continuing education fees allowance	Job openings by occupation
Job level and category	Type of projects	Conference attendance	Job openings by region
Education	Variety of projects	Speaking at conference	Online job openings by occupation, region, and industry
Experience on current occupation	Project completions	Training outside and inside the company	GDP by industry
Location	Ad hoc versus long-term projects	Opportunity to develop as a whole person	Cost per hire
Distance to work	Manager feedback frequency, recency, and style	Opportunity to fully use skills at work	Quits by industry and occupation categories
Distance to commute	Job satisfaction factors	Perceived company support for career development or opportunities offered	Salary benchmark by roles, occupations, experience, and location
Parking	Bonding with teammates and colleagues	Development for roles and occupations	Supply-and-demand ratio by occupation, by education level, by region, and by industry
Commute type (public transportation, own car, or other)	Recognition (reward, trip, or simple thank-you event)	Performance review ranking	Talent shortage indicator
Length of service	Work schedule	Performance review rewards	Competition's offer to attract similar talent
Salary	Flexible hours (arrival, departure)	For public organizations, stock options ownership	Talent open data
Skills			Online presence
Time to position			Social media presence (LinkedIn, Twitter, Facebook, GitHub, Stack Overflow)
			Social media behavior
			Profile change (photo, experience, expertise, education, certification, career)
			Profile update
			Online posts
			Followers/following influencers

PUTTING YOUR EMPLOYEE ATTRITION FINDINGS TO WORK

It is important to keep in mind that there is also not a one-size-fits-all approach when it comes to addressing churn, so prioritization should happen based on roles such as:

- Revenue-generator roles
- Customer-facing roles
- Mission-critical, non-customer-facing roles

Once you get actionable insights from your predictive models and can identify high-value employees who are at risk of quitting, the reasons why they might leave, and the time frame, one approach we suggest is to leverage strategies used in other industries to prevent this outcome. To optimize your action plan and strategies, the attrition score should be combined with the lifetime value (LTV) of the employee (for more information on these topics, see Chapter 10).

You should calculate each employee's lifetime value (grouped into high, medium, or low segments, as discussed broadly in Chapter 10) and his or her risk of leaving, also called attrition score (grouped into high, medium, or low attrition segments) using predictive models and suggested recommendations for retention strategies.

In the end this would look like Figure 11.3.

1. Attrition Score: Low Medium High

2. Life Time Value: Low Medium High

3. Recommendations: A series of suggested retention actions based on predictive model insights. It also provides you with employees' lifetime value, using survival analysis and other advanced analytics sophisticated approaches. Combining attrition predictive model scores with the employee lifetime value scores will provide you with a 360-degree view of your employee base.

Figure 11.3 Actionable Employee Value and Attrition Risk Segmentation

THE SEGMENTATION STRATEGY OF TALENT RETENTION MODEL INSIGHTS

To effectively leverage the predictive insights from your attrition model, we recommend tying the attrition score to the employee's LTV score. When it comes time for strategic discussions with your business and executive team, leverage the quadrant segmentation approach to help you develop your human capital strategy for each quadrant defined in Figure 11.4.

The resulting quadrant approach with its four segments provides HR and managers with the following five benefits that help them to:

1. Identify employees who are more likely to quit by LTV segment.
2. Identify when they would quit.
3. Identify the patterns that lead to voluntary attrition.
4. Apply those patterns to the employee population to identify employees likely to quit.
5. Develop incentives to retain desired employees and put together succession planning for medium- and low-performing employees.

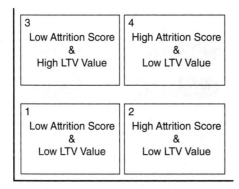

Figure 11.4 Talent Retention Grid

A Look into the Future of Retention Analytics

With data being collected about nearly every facet of our lives (credit card purchases, phone usage, web clicks, wearable technologies, etc.) and analytics being increasingly used with ease, it is intuitive to imagine that retention analytics will continue to develop and become more and more sophisticated. Josh Bersin envisions the avenue of a *quantified* employee. "We will reach a point in the near future where HR departments will be flooded with data about their employees from internal and external sources, from real-time project feedback to e-mail traffic, social interactions, wearable technologies, and more. Executives will be much more equipped to make quick, positive decisions about their employees to engage them, retain them, and keep them healthy, productive, and safe."

 KEY TAKEAWAYS

- Retention is not a squishy theoretical concept but a combination of real and concrete things that include compensation, performance, feedback, learning and development, and trust in leadership that can in the end be measured by the mere action of leaving or staying. A quantified ROI helps make the leap.

- Advanced analytics and Big Data are being heavily introduced into employee retention solutions because many traditional methods are failing and no longer fit our fast-paced world. These solutions help identify attrition risks in terms of who, when, and why.

- Why should you care? The business benefit is clear and economically favorable to the bottom line. You don't believe us yet? Cut all your assumptions in half and you are still working with large benefits.

- Employee attrition can be addressed by leveraging similar predictive modeling approaches that other industries, such as finance, manufacturing, and marketing, have been using so that you can proactively address human capital issues and help your organization to keep and protect your talent.

- When working on talent attrition, there is no one-size-fits-all approach. Instead, always "think global, but go local," even if you're a global organization. There are cultural differences that could be driven by the location, industry, and size of your organization.

- When you put your churn predictive model into operation, we recommend you prioritize your retention activities and strategies, meaning start with the cream-of-the-crop revenue generators and mission-critical roles.

- Attrition is not always a bad thing, but attrition of your star players is where you should first focus your strategy.

- Predictive modeling combined with employee lifetime value model scores help you to identify your workforce trends and anticipate changes before they happen. They also help you to identify your talents who are at risk of leaving, enabling you to proactively put in place retention, leadership development, and succession plans.

- When addressing attrition, it's paramount to factor in other elements such as the lifetime value of employees; their high, medium, or low value; why they would leave and when; and what you should do to keep and protect your most valuable asset: your talent.

- Predictive analytics is one of the best vehicles to help HR become more strategic in assisting organizations keep and protect their human capital investment and in positively impacting the company's bottom line.

- In today's explosion of digital information where we have more data than ever before, publicly available talent data combined with advanced analytics from quants can help HR to become a strategic department through predictive modeling.

NOTES

1. Alice Kwan, Jeff Schwartz, and Andrew Liakopoulos, "Talent Edge 2020: Redrafting Strategies for the Uneven Recovery," Deloitte University Press, January 1, 2012, http://dupress.com/articles/talent-edge-2020-redrafting-strategies-for-the-uneven-recovery/.
2. Josh Bersin, "HR Analytics Maturity Model," Bersin by Deloitte, www.bersin.com/Lexicon/Details.aspx?id=15302.

CHAPTER 12

Employee Wellness, Health, and Safety to Drive Business Performance and Loyalty

*Always do what's right; this will gratify some and astonish
the rest.*

—Albert Einstein

I n the previous chapters of this book, we discussed how people are
the most important asset of any organization; they lead, innovate,
and drive performance. Your workforce helps your organization
to compete in an aggressive marketplace and ultimately succeed.
In order to accomplish this critical mission of delivering the best
performance and productivity possible, companies need to provide
their workforces with high standards of wellness, health, and a safe
environment.

While some organizations still view employee wellness programs
as just a nice-to-have perk, a cool extra, another costly employee
benefit, or, according to Lewis and Khanna,[1] "an employee control
tool" and "a marketing tool for health plans," other organizations are
fully integrating wellness programs as a strategic business imperative. According to a 2013 RAND study[2] commissioned by the U.S.
Department of Labor and the U.S. Department of Health and Human
Services, today nearly 80 percent of people who work for organizations with 50 or more employees have access to a corporate wellness
program.

Immediately following the 2008 financial crisis, the number one
priority for the majority of companies was to get back to productivity and profitability as soon as possible, and they did this by focusing
solely on meeting their financial objectives and goals. We all witnessed
the shift in corporate structuring, as companies requested even more
results from their downsized workforces, putting the numbers first
and, in some cases, completely forgetting about taking care of their talent through employee wellness programs. Some CEOs we spoke with
told us that when your employee wellness is front and center, your

workforce is more likely to drive performance and hit their numbers; however, if you keep focusing only on the numbers, your employees will probably miss their marks. As marketing strategist Andrew Benett states in his book *The Talent Mandate*,[3] only truly "talent-centric" organizations are destined to thrive in our fast-changing economy.

In today's global, multigenerational workforce, competition is fierce. By 2020, millennials will make up more than 50 percent of the workforce, and baby boomers will continue to retire at increasing rates. For prospective employees, work–life balance, employer branding, and a value proposition that promotes great workplace wellness can make the difference when choosing a company for which to work. To optimize their talent management life cycle, forward-thinking companies have been integrating workplace wellness and health programs into their talent management and are leveraging Big Data analytics to help them demonstrate the outstanding return on investment (ROI). They are also benefiting from the economic value they are creating for their business by capitalizing on workplace wellness, health, and safety.

These leading-edge organizations, also known as Best Place to Work companies, have demonstrated that there is not only a correlation, but a causation, between employee morale, wellness, health, and safety, and profitability; and their data analytics on their wellness programs provide evidence on this relationship between workplace wellness, employee productivity, and their company's bottom line. For instance, Google offers its employees an array of services, such as on-site massage rooms, nap pods, free food, and bowling alleys. SAS Institute employee perks include an on-site natatorium, gym services, a recreation room, on-site physicians, artists-in-residence work space, and a laundry list of personal enrichment courses. Zappos, the online seller of shoes and clothing, has a unique culture that includes spontaneous activities such as a stage parade because it's Monday, free pet adoption services, or a CEO car raffle to a lucky employee. Johnson & Johnson offers a private concierge service to employees whose children are enrolled in affiliated day care facilities, and also has paid sabbaticals. For these companies, workplace wellness programs are not simply a nice extra or perk; they are an integral part of the corporate culture.

Companies that have successfully implemented wellness programs are able to demonstrate ROI and how that investment has led to tangible rewards, which enables them to compete on talent analytics. They can also measure the impact of these programs against their employees' performance and overall company bottom line. This is a key to their success because, as Peter Drucker, the famous management consultant, said, "if you can't measure it, you can't manage it."

Leading organizations that leverage data, identify wellness as a strategic business imperative, and place it at the forefront of their employee value proposition will see improvements in their ability to compete successfully in the global talent marketplace. In the following sections, we will cover employee wellness, health, and safety programs, looking at case studies and examples from the front lines and identifying best practices and key takeaways for successfully integrating these programs into your organization. Our hope is that this will spark some heated debates around the benefits of these programs in organizations of all sizes, and help change the attitude that they are just "nice to have" into the understanding that they are a key pillar for forward-thinking companies that are competing and winning with talent analytics.

WHAT IS EMPLOYEE WELLNESS?

Based upon conversations with a variety of industry leaders who have successfully implemented corporate wellness programs, we define an employee wellness program as any employer-sponsored program that focuses on proactively improving the well-being, safety, and health of employees and sometimes their families and that, as a result, also helps the organization increase productivity, efficiency, performance, and its bottom line. Workplace wellness encourages employers to focus on preventive health care initiatives and lifestyle changes, such as:

- Increasing physical activities
- Improving eating habits
- Reducing stress
- Reducing or ceasing tobacco use

- Reducing absenteeism
- Increasing employee morale
- Increasing engagement
- Lifestyle coaching
- Nutrition counseling and biometric screening
- Gym memberships

Workplace wellness programs consist of a variety of behavior-changing and educational initiatives to help employees, and sometimes their dependents, achieve a healthier lifestyle.

A study from Weiner, Lewis, and Linnan[4] found that some of the most effective activities involved in wellness programs include support groups, exercise classes, healthy eating habits counseling, and annual physical checkups.

WHY SHOULD YOU CARE ABOUT WORKPLACE WELLNESS?

According to an article from Rosen and Spaulding titled "Best Practices for Wellness Programs,"[5] 50 percent of a person's health status is a result of behavior, and 75 percent of health care costs can be prevented, delayed, or curtailed through lifestyle modifications. Findings from this study also demonstrate that an increasing number of forward-looking organizations are encouraging employees to improve their healthy behaviors through the adoption of corporate wellness programs designed to decrease health care expenses related to unhealthy employee lifestyles, and to increase employee productivity.

Happy and Healthy Employees Create Satisfied Customers

When one of this book's authors, authors, JP Isson, worked as a senior manager of customer behavior modeling for the largest wireless service provider in telecommunications in North America, he spent a lot of time working closely with the customer services team, providing them with two major lists of customers: a scored list of customers to proactively call because they were at risk to churn, and a second list that included customers to try to up-sell with new products. To determine the efficacy of these lists, we conducted an experiment, tracking the performance of the 600 service reps and crossing their performance against their employee satisfaction scores and their Net Promoter Scores (NPS). We discovered that the customer services agents who recorded the highest employee satisfaction and NPS scores also topped the list in terms of customer satisfaction, customer retention rates, and customer up-sell metrics. In fact, on average, they were able to deliver a retention rate that was 37 percent higher than the rates of those reps who had low satisfaction scores; additionally, they were up-selling 63 percent more than those reps with low satisfaction scores.

The key learning for us was that customer satisfaction and employee satisfaction were strongly related. We found that, all things being equal, our customer services reps' satisfaction was the key differentiator between our best performers and our lowest performers. In fact, employee satisfaction drives customer satisfaction, and when a customer is satisfied with your service or product and decides to come back and to do business with you, the likelihood that he or she will increase their wallet share or average order size is higher. Because you have established a good relationship, your business has won their trust, and they are more receptive to your suggestions and product offerings. The key takeaway here is that employee satisfaction, particularly as it relates to customer-facing roles, and is a key area that can have significant impact on your organization's bottom line.

According to a *Harvard Business Review* article,[6] "Competing on Talent Analytics," leading entertainment company Harrah's used metrics to evaluate the effects of its health and wellness programs on employee engagement and its bottom line. Preventive-care visits to its on-site clinics have increased, lowering urgent-care costs by millions of dollars over a 12-month period. One executive we spoke with succinctly articulated the correlation between employee satisfaction and customer satisfaction, saying: "How can we ask employees to take care of customers when they aren't empowered to take care of themselves?" And, because Harrah's understands the important relationship between employee engagement and top-line revenue, it can evaluate the program according to its revenue contribution as well.

The direct impact of workplace wellness programs on employee productivity, overall health care costs for companies, employee morale, and absenteeism also has a positive impact on the overall company bottom line. The wellness and productivity of employees are essential for a company's economic success, and there is a strong correlation between a person's health and efficiency. According to studies, employees with a higher number of health risk behaviors can lead to elevated health care costs and lower levels of work productivity due to absenteeism,[7] so encouraging healthy habits is good for your company, as well as your workforce. According to one Gallup survey, unhealthy and overweight employees account for 450 million days of work lost over the course of an average year. To put this in perspective, that's roughly three days of work lost for every single person in the U.S. workforce.[8] And multiple studies from the Centers for Disease Control[9] have demonstrated that health-promotion programs paid for themselves; not only did they decrease health care costs, including absenteeism, disability, and workers' compensation, but, more important, every dollar invested in those programs resulted in a $3 to $6 increase in ROI.

Leaders we spoke with who have successfully implemented wellness programs in both large and small companies also noticed that healthy employees take fewer sick days and are more productive at work. According to a study from Pittsburgh-based business health consumer provider Highmark Inc.,[10] workplace wellness pays off for small businesses as well as large ones; in fact, small business employers can save up to $1.65 in health care costs for every dollar invested in workplace wellness programs. It's a win-win situation that benefits your employees, your business productivity level, and your bottom line.

The ROI of workplace wellness programs is well documented. A *Harvard Business Review* study[11] shows that since 1995, the percentage of Johnson & Johnson employees who smoke has dropped by more than two-thirds, which has meant that the incidence of employees with high blood pressure has declined by more than half. This is wonderful health news for these employees, but it also was great news for Johnson & Johnson leaders, who estimate a cumulative savings of $250 million on health care costs over the past decade. From 2002 to 2008, the return was $2.71 for every dollar spent. Based on this study, wellness initiatives save an employer an average of $394 per employee per year, while the programs cost an average of only $159 per employee per year—an ROI of $3.36 for every $1 spent.

Employee health and satisfaction is a critical issue that is linked to a number of positive outcomes for both employees and organizations, including reduced health care costs, improved quality of life, and higher employee morale. Over the past couple of years, the explosion of digital information, the expansion of digital employer branding, and the availability of online company value propositions have taken workplace wellness programs from mere hypothetical scenarios discussed in dry, academic HR journals to a key pillar of recruitment and a sought-after benefits that prospective job candidates seek out as they make their job selections. Today's workplace wellness programs are one of the most valuable assets of a company's value proposition and can significantly enhance company attractiveness. Studies show that implementing such initiatives impacts talent acquisition by showcasing the investments the company has made in its employees and demonstrating how leadership cares about the workforce. This is a key component for retention, because wellness benefits are both consciously and unconsciously factored into an employee's decision whether to leave or stay with a company. While a study published in the *Harvard Business Review*[12] found that employee wellness programs are often viewed as a nice workplace perk but not necessarily viewed as a tactical imperative, a growing body of data suggests otherwise. In fact, the article also points out that the ROI on comprehensive, well-run employee wellness programs can be as high as 6 to 1.

Following is a frontline story of SAS Institute's successful employee wellness program.

Impact of Employee Wellness and Health on Talent Retention and Productivity: An Interview with SAS Institute

While it's important to have a deep understanding of the type of data you must have to build a successful employee wellness program, it is also equally important to hear practical advice from other companies that have done it in the past three decades.

JP Isson had the opportunity to speak with two executives at the SAS Institute: Jenn Mann, Vice President of Human Resources, and Gale Adcock, Chief Health Officer, to hear their perspectives and gain insights on how SAS, the world pioneer and leader in analytics solutions, has made employee wellness and health programs part of the company's DNA over the past 31 years—and, as a result, has seen significant impact on employee retention and loyalty, talent acquisition, and productivity, as well as overall health care cost savings.

Isson: What made SAS decide to invest in a workplace wellness program?

Mann: From a culture perspective, it is just the way SAS views our employees. We take a real holistic approach to thinking about our people. It wasn't kind of like a movement. It was simply part of our DNA from the very beginning. While some companies may have had an event, committee, or culture change that ignited that kind of effort, at SAS this was simply the right thing to do for our employees. . . . At SAS we have been a pioneer into two areas: One is analytics and the second one is investing in our people and culture. This was important at the very beginning.

Adcock: [Gale Adcock has been with SAS for 24 years, working on building and enhancing the health care plan.] We have been running on-site health care for 31 years. It seems like a big deal now. There were maybe a few changes that led to an on-site health care culture. It became like the most logical thing to do. There was no ROI or return on stock evaluation or analysis; it was as simple as "What can we do next to help employees with health care services?"

(Continued)

(*Continued*)

We built out what they said. This is very much the SAS model of how we build our software. We ask our customers about what they need. For our employees it was "What do you need to get your work done efficiently?" That was how we built our Health Care Center. We built a program that became simply kind of the smart thing to do. It wasn't directed by any financial meaning; it was just the most logical thing to do for our employees.

Mann: The Health Care Center is a place employees then go to be seen and treated. This is a full view of work and wellness. It is a full service for employees and their families.

Even with changes with health care, we are still very competitive in the type of services we give and cover. We provide physical amenities and recreational and fitness facilities as we have for 31 years, and just made an investment in expanding those services to meet the needs of our growing population and provide services for various demographics. SAS has increased some of its wellness and health programs, including Pilates, yoga, and progressive classes for those of younger age.

Adcock: At SAS, wellness is everybody's business. It's a very comprehensive approach. [Some people have asked where wellness resided. She always answers, "Everywhere."]

Isson: Even if the initial goal was not to track ROI, how do you measure that the wellness plan is working?

Adcock: We actually do measure the impact we have on our employees in terms of what they say when they come to the Health Care Center. Our model is unique in the country. When employees and their families come, they don't pay anything; our program is self-funded. We do measure some financial impact. And after 30 years we are getting more sophisticated tracking metrics such as:

- How much business we do in a year.
- How many times employees come to the Health Care Center.
- The cost of services compared to the industry.

We look at the street costs versus our Health Care Center, and know how much employees save, meaning financial input for the care data.

Mann: In terms of ROI, we look at things like where we might have to anticipate some spike in medical costs or prescription costs, putting programs in place that help to drive costs down and shift dollars to other areas. We look at the total rewards velocity.

Two years ago we added an on-site pharmacy that is part of the Health Care Center facility. That has been an incredible and convenient benefit for employees.

Adcock: The last four years we have begun to look at 25 years of data in addition to saving money every day for people who use our health care plan and service instead of going with another community center provider. The goal was to figure out what are other ways to utilize our health care plan in a smarter way.

- Early intervention for chronic illness.
- Preventive approach to illness.
- Do we have some way to utilize data in a smarter way?
- We try to figure out things like a predisposition for hypertension and diabetes.
- We looked at claims data for three years, and we found the following benefit:
  - For our patient employees who use our health care plan on a regular basis versus those who use it occasionally or not at all, we found a significant financial difference ([i.e., a benefit] if they use our health care plan).
- Our private patients who use our Health Care Center with their families recorded:
  - Fewer emergency room visits.
  - Fewer hospitalizations for conditions that do not require emergency treatment or hospitalization.

We believe we are having an impact on a day-to-day basis with health care.

Mann: There is a bigger saving in terms of quality of life: having a majority of employees going to the emergency room without hospitalization, and on a long-term view being the employer of choice.

(*Continued*)

(*Continued*)

The SAS Work/Life Center is also staffed with professionals and social workers that focus on any area that could help employees reduce stress:

- Provide elder care workshop.
- Help new parents with advice for newborns and teenagers.
- Provide employees with support whether they are raising children or taking care of elders.

The wellness program enables an emotional connection between our employees and the company. And some tangible outcomes are in talent retention/turnover, employee satisfaction, and engagement with the company.

SAS's turnover is 3 to 5 percent while the industry turnover is 15 to 16 percent. This is a legacy for us. SAS has been in the GPTW [certified as a Great Place to Work] since its inception. And in recent years SAS has been part of the top list of Great Place to Work companies. [SAS really is off the chart is when it comes to a healthy and safe environment. SAS scores in the 90s all the time for those factors. As to the financial ROI, last year SAS updated the ROI for its health facility and found that for every $1 invested there was about $2.40 to $2.50 ROI, measured in value and saving employees' time.]

Isson: What advice would you give to someone starting a wellness program? What are some dos and don'ts?

Adcock: From the health perspective, it's important to address the overarching question: What is the culture from the get-go? In the case of SAS, this has been part of our DNA, asking ourselves: "What should we do next for our employees? What is the most logical thing to do?" You should also evaluate what you are already doing that you could leverage, and then craft something based upon employee needs and wants—their overall feedback. Understand where they are already spending their health care dollars. On health, SAS built its wellness program based upon continuous feedback. "If you do this, would they come?" The company also has a survey.

Build something that is consistent with your company culture and scalable. Don't build something that is not financially sustainable.

Mann: The culture component has been there from the very beginning. We really focus on what type of culture and work environment and freedom employees need to do their jobs, and what cool work and project they would like to work on to impress our customers. We engage our employees with our customers. We don't micromanage. We have a work environment that is pleasant to work in.

SAS used to do a health care satisfaction survey, but stopped it to focus on continuous health dialogue. The company prefers a one-on-one personal touch that helps SAS to improve service delivery.

As part of overall wellness and satisfaction, SAS runs an employee satisfaction survey every 36 months—not every year, because the company deeply analyzes the survey using SAS software to [not only] capture employee feedback but more importantly to act on the survey findings accordingly. They look at employees' feedback and develop programs and training based upon that feedback.

SAS also found that there is a strong correlation between the wellness program and talent acquisition and talent retention. Today employees are very mindful and are looking for the overall package when it comes time to work for a given company; and our wellness program helps us to increase the satisfaction of our employees, helping to improve the quality of life by providing tremendous support to employees and their families.

Mann: The wellness and health care program helps the SAS brand not only to attract talent but also to retain them.

Isson: What's the future of wellness programs?

Adcock: What SAS is doing in terms of being a great place to work and retaining talent is not happening in a vacuum. It is happening in the economy and people. The time is changing, and today we have a lot of opportunities to put people in control. They have all the ways to track their workout, what they eat, how that impacts their lives, and the quality of life.

Today employees ask themselves where they want to be and who they would like to work for. It takes a different type of workplace to appeal to the latest generation. We have more info than we ever had. People come to the Health Care Center with more information because they are all

(*Continued*)

> (*Continued*)
>
> connected, and this helps the whole equation of improving the quality. We continue to update our wellness program to meet and exceed the needs and preferences of our employees.

EMPLOYEE WELLNESS PROGRAM BEST PRACTICES

Like any major initiative involving people and behavior change, the successful implementation of workplace wellness programs is a journey. Based on our discussions with industry leaders and executives who have developed corporate wellness programs, there are a few basic tenets that are keys to success.

Executive Leadership Sponsor

Your executive leadership team must recognize, support, and actively participate in and lead the workplace wellness program across all levels of management. A lack of sponsorship will result in eventual failure, so this team must lead the wellness program by example—for instance, by showing the value of health in their own lifestyles or work habits. According to the Wellness Council of America,[13] "For any organization change initiative to be effective there has to be a champion. When CEOs value healthy lifestyles and openly practice good health habits, the rest of the organization is likely to follow in their footsteps. To be genuine in promoting health, CEOs need to embrace health as an individual priority." The CEO, along with the leadership team, should ensure that health and wellness are kept top of mind, and every leader at the organization should work hard to tie all wellness activities back to a broader company strategy. You need to secure your organization executive team's commitment and support as champions who will tout the mental and physical benefits of the wellness program. All levels of management within your organization should be open and onboarded to promote the benefits of wellness, safety, and health, and wellness should be instituted as a company value.

Understand the Profile of Your Workforce

The starting point for any successful wellness program is to get a comprehensive understanding of your workforce's health status, as well as present health risks. You should leverage data to proactively identify potential segments of your workforce with health risks and develop a made-to-measure program to help remediate these risks. It is important that you also evaluate your employee base to gauge if they are ready to change before implementing a program. Performing this assessment will enable your organization to design effective plans and choose interventions that are most likely to engage and benefit members. Some preliminary data sources that can help you better understand the profile of your employee population's health include claims data such as medical claims, pharmacy and lab work, and employee survey data on their health conditions. It is also paramount to understand the demographics of your workforce before putting together strategies that will meet and exceed the needs, preferences, and values of each segment of your employee population.

Communication

Implementing a workplace wellness program requires precise execution in order to enable insights and actions that allow you to accurately address critical business challenges. The way you align your staff and roll out and communicate your wellness program can significantly impact the program's effectiveness. Failing to do so can result in wasted time, frustrated employees, reluctance to participate, and hard pushback, so proper communication is critical.

Your communications strategy and messaging must be compelling and designed to create awareness, increase interest, motivate, and improve engagement rates. Without a proper framework, your program can backfire; for instance, poorly delivered messaging about eating habits or physical activity can be misconstrued as being offensive or intrusive, which can lead to employee turnoff in regard to the program. Generally speaking, employees are receptive to wellness programs and see them as a benefit that improves their well-being, as long as these initiatives are correctly positioned and introduced—not presented as an effort to intrude on their privacy or as merely a way of saving money on their health coverage costs.

Beyond the wellness program, having a great communication environment is also part of employee well-being. Companies that foster open dialogue typically have employees who feel empowered to express their views, and get more involved and engaged in the culture and mission.

Collaboration and Support across Organizational Groups

Successful wellness programs require collaboration, participation, and adoption across the organization. Because they are designed for employees, your workforce should be part of the building process. They should not perceive the wellness program as a top-down initiative, something managers have put together and want them to adopt. Instead, they should be involved from the very start; they should own the program and help build the key components of it. Asking for employee feedback regarding the program is important, and you should ensure that this feedback is reflected in your wellness policies.

Measure and Track the Outcome against Benchmark and Baseline

Your wellness program must have metrics and measurement in order to track progress and success. And, more important, it needs a benchmark against a baseline. These metrics will translate the business challenges into operational programs that can be monitored over time, not only for the wellness impact on your employees, but also on your overall productivity and bottom line. It's important to remember that this is a dynamic process, and your wellness program's management team should monitor performance, evaluate effectiveness, and make adjustments as needed.

If the metrics are well designed, they will be objective means by which your company can track progress and business impact. Your company should use them to quantify broad business objectives such as being acknowledged as a Great Place to Work, as well as other measurable objectives, such as:

- Increased employee satisfaction
- Increased employee morale
- Increased employee health conditions
- Providing preventive health and lifestyle program
- Reducing stress
- Increasing physical activities
- Improving eating habits
- Decreasing tobacco use
- Increasing productivity
- Reducing long-term health care costs
- Increasing your company's bottom line

In the era of data analytics, it is important to set clear goals that engage employees and measure the outcomes at the appropriate time. Some companies adopt incentives such as awarding a bonus to employees who quit smoking, or provide insurance plans that cover health maintenance services and tobacco cessation.

Human Capital and Change Management

Implementing wellness programs effectively requires a dynamic multidisciplinary team to be in place and available so that your organization can achieve the ultimate goal of executing the plan and reaching your business objectives. Resources and talent are necessary in order to deliver on every phase of the business solution. We suspect that for some small organizations, getting the funding to implement a full-fledged wellness program could be a challenge, as they will not be able to install a gym on-site and hire a full-time wellness coach or physicians. There is good news, however. Small-to-medium-size business leaders we've spoken with have mentioned there are less expensive ways to make a difference in the health of employees without spending a fortune. Best practices include implementing a no-smoking policy or a walking program, replacing the box of candy in the lunchroom with fresh fruits and vegetables, offering on-site flu shots, encouraging employees to take the stairs rather than the elevator, buying healthy foods for meetings, subsidizing healthy options in vending machines, providing pedometers and walking club challenges, and encouraging personal health and safety practices like seat belt use, sleep, hygiene, and stress management. All of these small initiatives add up and can make a huge difference.

Employee Experience and Accessibility

When it comes to wellness programs, taking the employee experience into account should be at the forefront of your strategy. Consider how employees will adopt the program, and what it will take for them to embrace this culture change. What will be the major hurdles? How will they interact with the program? How will they get access to the solutions as well as learn about the program's features? To this end, convenience, privacy, and ease of use are central to the value proposition of a successful wellness program implementation.

Employee buy-in can make or break a wellness program and ultimately affect the overall success of the organization. This is why it's important to gather employees' feedback and adjust your workplace wellness program accordingly. Employees should feel like they are part of the team that helps design program features, particularly as they are the ones who are participating and who will be changing their lifestyles, habits, and behaviors.

Integrated Process

To ensure a successful implementation, your wellness program should be integrated into your company structure and value proposition tools and systems. It should be aligned with and tied to other corporate initiatives and groups, including workplace safety, benefits, human resources, and other infrastructure elements. For instance, the program should provide employees with a standardized set of tools to monitor physical activities, record workouts and health challenges, and enable them to access health information, communications, and program schedules, as well as gain access to wellness support experts, including coaches, or online resources and tools.

OPTIMIZING YOUR EMPLOYEE WELLNESS HEALTH AND WORKPLACE SAFETY WITH PREDICTIVE ANALYTICS

Data analytics helps demonstrate the impact that a successful employee wellness program can have on an organization, both by reducing the rising health care costs as well as increasing employee productivity and the company's bottom-line performance. Data analytics would also help to address measurement goals stated in the previous sections.

If you work in an office setting, workplace safety might not be a top-of-mind concern; however, if you work in construction, mining, or health care, the physical safety of the workforce is definitely paramount in your business strategies.

In 2012, the American Association of Occupational Health Nurses, Inc. conducted a web-based membership survey of 5,138 members to identify occupational health and safety issues facing them. A total of 2,123 members responded to the survey (41 percent response rate), and of that total, 61 percent reported health risk appraisal priorities for 2012, with the top three areas identified being weight management/nutrition/healthy eating; physical activity; and mental health/ stress management.

For people working in the mining and construction industries, injuries or accidents could be fatal and dramatically impact the company's overall supply chain and production lines. For instance, predictive analytics can be used to help anticipate some key business challenges, including:

- Which employees are more likely to get injured?
- What extraction sites are more likely to experience system failure?
- Which employees are more likely to take sick leave?
- What trucks would require preventive maintenance to avoid failure?

- What tractors will experience failures?
- What pipeline is more likely to be at risk of leaking or exploding?
- From what industry will you have an increase number of injuries and number of claims?
- When should you expect claims to spike?

Following is a frontline story showing predictive analytics in action for employee health and safety.

Interview with Dr. Eugene Wen, Vice President and Chief Statistician, Workplace Safety and Insurance Board

The Workplace Safety and Insurance Board (WSIB) of Ontario (Canada) is a 101-year-old government agency that focuses on workers' compensation and employee workplace safety. The WSIB is one of the largest workplace insurance organizations in North America. Managing more than CAD $4 billion in premium revenue each year, and with close to 4,000 staff, it provides employers with no-fault collective liability insurance. For workers who are injured or contract an occupational disease at work, the WSIB provides return-to-work and recovery services and loss-of-earnings benefits, and covers the costs of required health care.

JP Isson had the opportunity to speak with Dr. Eugene Wen to understand how the WSIB leverages predictive analytics to provide the best services to employers and employees.

Isson: Why has the WSIB decided to leverage predictive analytics?

Wen: The WSIB was set up for workers' compensation and takes care of workers after they have suffered work-related injuries and illnesses by providing health care and loss-of-earnings benefits, and by helping them get back to work. To do that, the WSIB makes more than one million decisions each year. The WSIB has decided to use predictive analytics to support both strategic and operational decision making in order to optimize service outcomes and help injured and sick workers return to work. With predictive analytics, we can better understand the key factors affecting injured workers' return to work, predict potential outcomes of the injury, forecast upcoming trends, support better resource allocation, and improve service quality. When injured workers get back to work, their families, employers, communities, and our whole society all benefit from the efforts.

Isson: How does society benefit from these efforts?

Wen: The workforce is the fundamental driver of the economy. Investing in prevention and return to work helps employers maintain their workforce and helps employees get back to work, and in so doing helps keep society productive. Over the years, a great amount of resources and efforts by employers, employees, and WSIB have been put into new technology, safe practices and workplaces, better health care, and return to work. These are tremendous investments in the entire workforce supply chain. Because of these joint efforts, Ontario saw two million fewer working days lost to workplace injury and illness in 2013 than it did in 2009. Considering average workforce productivity in this province, that would translate to nearly $1 billion saved from potential loss to the economy.

Armed with insights and knowledge, decision makers can optimize their workforce planning accordingly and can prepare for potential system failures; and can adjust their resources, workforce, and human capital supply chain to remain competitive and successful.

KEY TAKEAWAYS

- Workplace wellness programs are a key component of company value propositions and can be used as an incentive to attract and acquire new talent (by promoting the wellness program to prospective job candidates) and as a retention tool to keep and protect existing employees.

- Business outcomes of successful wellness programs for employees and organizations include lower absenteeism, higher employee morale, higher job satisfaction, higher employee retention, increased work productivity, lower health care costs, improved quality of life, and better business performance.

■ Although previously considered just nice-to-have workplace perks, workplace wellness programs have been demonstrated, in data from a variety of studies, to be a strategic business imperative. Investing in wellness program pays off; in fact, some studies suggest that the ROI of a well-run workplace wellness program can be as high as 6 to 1.

■ When implementing a wellness program, it is effective to start small first, which will let you evaluate challenges and opportunities and reduce the cost of failure. Test and learn before expanding, and track performance and results to make any necessary adjustments.

■ The successful implementation of a corporate wellness program requires leadership sponsors and commitment, a good understanding of your workforce health conditions, a compelling communication strategy, collaboration from employees and managers, an integrated process, a tremendous user experience, and well-defined key performance indicators to track progress and program outcomes.

■ Predictive analytics helps to assess the ROI of wellness programs and, more important, provide employers with proactive insights needed to mitigate any health and safety events that could impact the organizations' resources, supply chain, or productivity.

■ Employee health, happiness, and productivity at work are deeply related, and to remain competitive and succeed in today's competitive marketplace, companies should foster all three—this is a shared mission to cultivate a healthier workforce that benefits everyone.

NOTES

1. Al Lewis and Vik Khanna, "The Cure for the Common Corporate Wellness Program," *Harvard Business Review*, January 30, 2014, https://hbr.org/2014/01/the-cure-for-the-common-corporate-wellness-program/.

2. Soeren Mattke, Hangsheng Liu, John P. Caloyeras, Christina Y. Huang, Kristin R. Van Busum, Dmitry Khodyakov, and Victoria Shier, *Workplace Wellness Study Final Report*, RAND Health, http://aspe.hhs.gov/hsp/13/WorkplaceWellness/rpt_wellness.pdf.

3. Andrew Benett, *The Talent Mandate* (New York: Palgrave Macmillan, 2013).

4. B. J. Weiner, M. A. Lewis, and L. A. Linnan, "Using Organization Theory to Understand the Determinants of Effective Implementation of Worksite Health Promotion Programs," *Health Education Research* 24, no. 2 (April 2009): 292–305.

5. Michael Rosen and Todd Spaulding, "Best Practices for Wellness Programs," *Occupational Health & Safety Online*, July 1, 2009, http://ohsonline.com/Articles/2009/07/01/Best-Practices-for-Wellness-Programs.aspx.

6. Tom Davenport, Jeanne Harris, and Jeremy Shapiro, "Competing on Talent Analytics." *Harvard Business Review*, October 2010, https://hbr.org/2010/10/competing-on-talent-analytics.

7. J. Kuoppala, A. Lamminpää, and P. Husman, "Work Health Promotion, Job Well-Being, and Sickness Absences—A Systematic Review and Meta-Analysis," *Journal of Occupational and Environmental Medicine* 50, no. 11 (November 2008): 1216–1227.

8. "7 Best Practices for an Effective Wellness Program," Blackhawk Engagement Solutions, June 11, 2013, www.bhengagement.com/7-best-practices-wellness-program/#sthash.0DtFrKX0.pdf.

9. *Reducing the Risk of Heart Disease and Stroke: A Six Step Guide for Employers*, Centers for Disease Control, www.cdc.gov/dhdsp/pubs/docs/six_step_guide.pdf.

10. B. L. Naydeck, J. A. Pearson, R. J. Ozminkowski, B. T. Day, and R. Z. Goetzel, "The Impact of the Highmark Employee Wellness Programs on 4-Year Healthcare Costs," *Journal of Occupational and Environmental Medicine* 50, no. 2 (February 2008): 146–156.

11. Davenport, Harris, and Shapiro, "Competing on Talent Analytics."

12. Ibid.

13. "WELCOA's 7 Benchmarks of Success," *Absolute Advantage* 6, no. 1 (2006). https://www.welcoa.org/wp/wp-content/uploads/2014/06/aa_6.1_novdec061.pdf.

CHAPTER 13

Big Data and People Analytics

Whatever has happened in my quest for innovation has been part of my quest for immaculate reality.

—George Lucas

B ig Data continues to be touted as the next wave of technology and analytics innovation. From our perspective, the next wave of innovation is less about Big Data and more about how companies leverage Big Data analytics to take action and optimize their business. Having data is not enough; it needs to be leveraged effectively to drive and optimize business action that is coordinated at all levels of the organization. As it relates to People Analytics, Big Data is critical to providing real-time insights to businesses regarding how to maximize the value of the talent for the organization, as well as maximize the organization's value for the talent it intends to retain and develop. In this chapter, we revisit our Seven Pillars of People Analytics Success in the context of Big Data, providing examples for each pillar to help illustrate the concepts you've read about so far throughout this book.

WHAT IS BIG DATA?

Big Data is one of those buzzwords that can mean so many different things, and, as a result, it has the potential to be meaningless. However, to most people, the concept of Big Data is the notion that certain data comes at us so frequently, in so many different forms, and at such high volumes that it's difficult for a single human to make sense of or analyze it efficiently and effectively. For example, a daily temperature reading over the course of one year is not, by most, considered Big Data. However, if you imagine temperature readings collected every minute across a thousand different types of thermometers placed around the globe—that would be considered Big Data. Most location data such as that provided by WiFi or GPS tracking is considered Big Data because there's an ongoing stream of it over time.

Big Data is the hottest buzzword to hit the tech and Internet world since *social*. So, what does it mean? *Big Data* tends to be a broad and

332

overused term that is varied and ill-defined when you actually ask people to explain what it means to them. Some people define it as web data, whereas others define it as a large data set that cannot be handled by traditional database software; still others define it as data that flows in real time. All definitions have their weaknesses, but we like the one first formulated by Gartner analyst Doug Laney that asserts that Big Data has volume, velocity, and variety.[1] Although we can argue with some aspects of this definition, it's a helpful way to think about and understand how Big Data may differ from other data sources and how you need to think about it differently.

Volume is the attribute most people mention when they think about Big Data. The idea here is that you are dealing with large quantities of data, usually larger than a normal person can get one's head around or larger than can be processed using traditional tools. The exact criteria for what is considered large volume is a moving target as the technology is improving so rapidly that yesterday's large-volume data set is today's typical-size data set. For instance, the online engagement marketing platform Constant Contact has always dealt in very high-volume data. Each year Constant Contact facilitates 65 billion marketing communications on behalf of customers. This type of activity creates unimaginable flows of data volume. The main appeal in using larger volumes of data is that doing so allows you to predict behavior using statistical models with much more accuracy that smaller volumes of data can provide.

However, volume presents unique challenges of its own to many conventional information technology tools and systems. Data volume calls for scalable storage and a distributed approach to querying. It's more common for companies to have large amounts of archived data stores, but they often lack the capacity to process that stored data effectively. Companies that can process large volumes of data rely on more than conventional relational database infrastructures. They must rely on, for example, parallel data processing architectures such as Hadoop and Spark. Hadoop is a platform for distributing computing problems across a number of servers that was first developed and released as open source by Yahoo! It implements the MapReduce approach pioneered by Google in compiling its search indexes, and involves three steps. The first step is the "map" stage, where data is distributed among multiple servers and compiled. The partial results are then recombined in what is known as the "reduce" step in order to simplify the data. The last step is the "retrieval" step in which the data models are retrieved from the Hadoop file system and utilized. For example, Hadoop is one of the tools Facebook uses to be able to personalize its site experience for you.

The second element of the definition put forth by Laney is that Big Data has velocity. Velocity simply means that data has an ongoing flow and fast speed coming into your organization, sometimes referred to as "streaming." Unfortunately, as volume of data has increased dramatically across the enterprise, so has velocity. This is primarily due to the growth of the Internet and mobile usage such that data is flowing 24/7 every day of the year. Therefore, if you are an Internet company, your data architecture and tools must accommodate the processing of high data velocity and volume all the time, nonstop. As a result, companies such as online retailers are able to compile large histories of customers' every click and interaction, not just the final sales. Successful companies are able to utilize that information in real time by recommending additional products and services. For example, Walmart began using a 10-node Hadoop cluster as a way to analyze the online shopping experience and to make it more personal. It worked so well for the company that Walmart is moving to consolidate 10 different data processing platforms into one 250-node Hadoop cluster to deal with the increased streams of data it needs to process in order to create the strongest possible online customer experience.[2]

The third important concept to consider in Big Data is variety. In today's complex world of multiple points of customer interaction and data streams, data comes in a standardized form and ready for processing. Given this, a common theme in Big Data systems is that the data sources and formats are widely diverse and don't fall into consistent structures that can be easily utilized by a company for processing or analysis. Examples of the variety of Big Data flows with high volume and velocity might include customer comments on a social media website, search terms on a website, click-stream data from an online shopping experience, location data from GPS or WiFi tracking, and image or video uploads, among others. The critical advancement in the data management world related to the principle of variety in Big Data is that traditional structured data is now able to be joined with semistructured and unstructured data. In Big Data, variety is just as important as volume and velocity. Put all three of those concepts together (volume, velocity, and variety), and you start to understand the challenges and opportunities of Big Data.

There is another V that we believe is paramount when addressing Big Data. That fourth V stands for value: the business value that you can create from your data. Big Data without business value is simply noise. Your goal is to find out signals from your deluge of data. That's why the value is extremely important for Big Data to be relevant to your business.

Big Data efforts require the right people, processes, and systems to execute at a highly skilled level. As companies struggle to get the most business value from their Big Data initiatives, ABI Research forecasts that global spending on Big Data hardware, software, and services will continue to grow at a compound annual growth rate (CAGR) of 30 percent through 2018, reaching a total market size of $114 billion.[3] Additionally, IDG Enterprise research indicates that companies are intensifying their efforts to derive value through Big Data initiatives, with nearly half (49 percent) of respondents already implementing Big Data projects or in the process of doing so in the future, with the average enterprise organization expecting to spend $8 million on Big Data–related initiatives in 2015.[4]

As a reflection of how rapidly the Big Data landscape is evolving, IDC issued the following 10 predictions for the future of Big Data. This list is taken from the IDC FutureScape for Big Data and analytics report.[5]

1. Visual data discovery tools will be growing 2.5 times faster than the rest of the business intelligence market. By 2018, investing in this enabler of end-user self-service will become a requirement for all enterprises.

2. Over the next five years spending on cloud-based Big Data and analytics (BDA) solutions will grow three times faster than spending for on-premise solutions. Hybrid on/off-premise deployments will become a requirement.

3. Shortage of skilled staff will persist. In the United States alone there will be 181,000 deep analytics roles in 2018 and five times that many positions requiring related skills in data management and interpretation.

4. By 2017 unified data platform architecture will become the foundation of BDA strategy. The unification will occur across information management, analysis, and search technology.

5. Growth in applications incorporating advanced and predictive analytics, including machine learning, will accelerate in 2015. These apps will grow 65 percent faster than apps without predictive functionality.

6. Seventy percent of large organizations already purchase external data, and 100 percent will do so by 2019. In parallel, more organizations will begin to monetize their data by selling it or providing value-added content.

7. Adoption of technology to continuously analyze streams of events will accelerate in 2015 as it is applied to Internet of Things analytics, which is expected to grow at a five-year CAGR of 30 percent.

8. Decision management platforms will expand at a CAGR of 60 percent through 2019 in response to the need for greater consistency in decision making and decision-making process knowledge retention.

9. Rich media (video, audio, image) analytics will at least triple in 2015 and emerge as the key driver for BDA technology investment.

10. By 2018 half of all consumers will interact on a regular basis with services based on cognitive computing.

BIG DATA AND PEOPLE ANALYTICS

Throughout this book, we have provided multiple examples of companies undertaking People Analytics initiatives using Big Data analytics across the scope of talent management challenges that companies are facing. Now that we have covered a lot of ground throughout this book, we thought it would be helpful to revisit our Seven Pillars of People Analytics Success, and provide a real-life example of Big Data analytics in action for each one. We believe this will help solidify understanding of the pillars as well as how Big Data analytics can be applied to each in order to address key business challenges associated with each pillar.

The rise of Big Data and analytics is changing the way the world does business, and this applies to talent management as well. When you combine the way technology has changed the speed at which people communicate with the vast insight available on human behavior, you get Big Data that can be applied to the workforce. Big Data around workforce behavior and attitudes can help us predict behavior, identify valuable talent like never before, match capabilities to market needs, retain the best people, and act on proven insight to drive business outcomes.

As the complexity of workforce challenges continues to rise, so too does the demand for more quantitative approaches to address the increasingly difficult people-related questions central to organizational success.

The power of People Analytics is in its ability to challenge conventional wisdom, influence behavior, enable human resources (HR) and business leaders to make and execute smarter and more strategic workforce decisions, and ultimately impact business outcomes. To realize value from investments in People Analytics, organizations need to understand:

- The relationship between their workforce strategies and their business challenges.
- The approaches at their disposal.
- The capabilities required to translate raw HR data into defensible action.

Many organizations have built the capability to produce basic HR reports and metrics, and some have begun to use analytics to reveal and understand historical trends and patterns. However, a 2014 IBM study of 342 chief human resources officers reveals that less than 16 percent of companies report having the ability to use data to make predictions and take action on future workforce issues.[6]

LEVERAGING PEOPLE ANALYTICS

The ultimate goal of our Seven Pillars of People Analytics Success framework is to focus your attention on those areas that are keys to talent management success and will lead to the greatest return on investment. People Analytics is at a relatively early stage, and this framework should be used as a starting point for your organization. There is no specific order to use to follow the pillars because the challenges each company faces will differ. For instance, one organization may have a great talent acquisition strategy but be really weak in employee retention. However, you will find there are natural inter-relationships between the pillars within the framework, as well as the underlying analytics. Take the Acquisition/Hiring Analytics pillar, as an example. A bad candidate selection could also lead to an increase in turnover rates or high retention costs, which is represented by the Employee Churn and Retention pillar. Depending on the maturity of your company's People Analytics, each pillar could possibly be addressed separately without following a specific order.

The framework could also be adjusted based on your organization's most pressing needs. It should help to master the talent management life cycle propelling it with the power of analytics that could be:

- **Descriptive:** What happened in the past?
- **Diagnostic:** What is happening now and why?
- **Predictive:** What will happen and why?
- **Prescriptive:** What should you do, knowing what will happen?

In the next sections, we revisit each of the seven pillars introduced in Chapter 3 and provide a real-world example of where a company has used Big Data analytics to tackle each.

As discussed in Chapter 3, our 7 Pillars of People Analytics Success include:

1. Workforce Planning Analytics pillar
2. Souring Analytics pillar
3. Acquisition/Hiring Analytics pillar
4. Onboarding, Culture Fit, and Engagement pillar

5. Performance Assessment and Development and Employee Lifetime Value pillar

6. Employee Churn and Retention pillar

7. Employee Wellness, Health, and Safety pillar

WORKFORCE PLANNING ANALYTICS PILLAR

Generally speaking, workforce planning refers to the process that helps identify what talent your organization will require to achieve its business goals and business objectives—from current needs to future needs and succession planning.

Planning should start with a clear definition and understanding of your company mission, and most pressing business goals and objectives. As with any large undertaking, it is important to be transparent and include all internal stakeholders and executives in the process to ensure full organization-wide support. They should understand from the get-go what their role is, how finding the right talent at the right cost will impact the company's objectives, how HR functions and activities relate to business challenges, and how the business return on investment (ROI) of the initiative is demonstrated.

The Workforce Planning Analytics pillar is about leveraging analytics to proactively plan for the right number of employees with the right skill sets, at the right place, at the right time, and at the optimal cost. It is one of the most important pillars of talent management because it is highly connected to the other pillars. For instance, turnover, resume triaging, and retention insights will feed the Workforce Planning Analytics pillar. It is influenced by the quality and accuracy of the model used to predict churn or employee turnover, both voluntary and involuntary, as well as talent acquisition and promotion models.

Workforce planning analytics helps organizations to create economic value from their human capital planning processes. When properly executed, this approach enables your organization to reduce labor costs (through acquisition, onboarding, retention, and cost per hire), increase productivity, and drive business performance by providing organizations with the right knowledge and tools to be proactive in managing their most valuable asset: their employees.

A great example of a company applying Big Data analytics to workforce planning comes from FedEx. FedEx Corporation is synonymous with overnight delivery, an industry the company developed during the 1970s and one it continues to dominate. FedEx is now composed of five major operating companies: FedEx Express, FedEx Ground, FedEx Freight, FedEx Custom Critical, and FedEx Trade Networks. Operating in 211 countries and employing over 375,000 associates, FedEx is the world's largest express shipping company. Every business day FedEx makes almost five million physical shipments and processes more than 100 million electronic transactions. FedEx thus uses its planes, ground vehicles, and electronic technologies to speed up transportation so that companies and individuals can transfer time-sensitive material across vast distances in virtually seamless fashion.

As you can imagine, it's critical that FedEx's talent management strategy be grounded in Big Data analytics, and workforce planning is no exception. Workforce planning for FedEx is more complex than simply planning for the number of new hires for the following year or two. FedEx needs to also consider the current skills and capabilities that can be leveraged across vast business units spanning multiple geographies. For example, before FedEx acquires a company, its HR department uses Big Data analytics to aggregate employee data from the acquisition target, including employee engagement survey results, and compares them with FedEx data. "Our analysis provides management with another data point before they make their decision," says Bob Bennett, chief learning officer and vice president of HR. "I try not to use the term 'Big Data.' It scares people away," Bennett says. "The important message is that now, more than ever, deriving value from data is critical in the business environment. HR has an important role because it has to use data to drive employee behaviors, making sure those behaviors are measured, monitored, and shaped to achieve business goals."[7]

Other frontline stories include companies like Dow Chemical, Black Hill, Bullhorn, and Société de Transport de Montréal that we broadly covered in the workforce planning chapter. Those companies have successfully leveraged predictive analytics and Big Data to optimize their workforce planning.

SOURCING ANALYTICS PILLAR

Once you've completed your workforce planning stage, you will have a solid plan of how you will help your organization achieve its business goals. At this stage, you will also start investigating how you will staff your plan, and what channels you can use to accomplish this. Sourcing analytics is about harnessing all the data and talent information available to optimize your sourcing results.

Successfully searching for candidates in today's globally competitive talent market requires an approach that leverages the power of analytics to identify and locate candidates, assess their potential, and engage with them. The Sourcing Analytics pillar is about harnessing all the data and talent information available to optimize your sourcing results, including how to determine staffing resources and what channels will be most effective to engage potential candidates. We define talent sourcing as a talent management process that consists of proactively searching for candidates to fill specific positions (clearly defined from your workforce plan), leveraging job boards, employee referrals, staffing firms, headhunters, and offline, online, and social media tools and resources.

The Sourcing Analytics pillar is also about understanding and capturing data from both the employer's decision journey and the candidate's decision journey to optimize your outcome. It can help a business address questions such as:

- How can a business move a candidate from passive or visitor viewer to a job applicant?
- What are key candidate decision points during job consideration?
- What sourcing channels will optimize candidate search results?
- Where are the best places to search for a specific niche of candidates with tech skills such as those in science, technology, engineering, and math fields?
- How can a business best allocate searching spend and efforts?

A great example of a company applying Big Data analytics to sourcing comes from Wells Fargo. After Wells Fargo bought Wachovia Corporation in 2010, the company began to centralize recruitment functions for its community banking division. The new team would recruit for Wells Fargo's 6,200 retail branches, call centers and online functions, business banking for customers with up to $20 million in annual revenues, and wealth management for customers with up to $1 million in investable assets. Overall, the newly centralized team recruits between 50 percent and 70 percent of Wells Fargo's 270,000 employees, including most of the customer-facing roles.

To aid in standardizing recruitment across the company, Wells Fargo implanted Big Data analytics to narrow the sourced pool of candidates to a more manageable volume of candidate flow the bank believed were more likely to succeed if they made it through a full selection and interview process. The bank attempted to focus on the most qualified candidates for teller and personal banker positions based on their background experience, career motivation, performance, and life/work skills.[8]

The predictive sourcing model Wells Fargo developed focused primarily on easy-to-identify or answer things that can reasonably be verified, such as "How many jobs have you had? How long have you stayed in those jobs? How many promotions have you had? What is the highest level of education that you've completed?" The bank ended up with 65 questions that each candidate for Wells Fargo's teller and personal banker positions would answer online and that would be scored in real time. If candidates score high, then they are automatically scheduled for an interview as soon as they complete the assessment.

From the start of the rollout through the end of the year 2012, Wells Fargo collected roughly one million job seeker records and found statistically significant differences in performance metrics and retention rates between those team members that the tool would prioritize for hire and other team members whom Wells Fargo would just hire without the early screening step.

Other frontline stories include companies like Facebook and Bloomberg. For example, Facebook uses StrengthsFinder in a clever way to deploy talent efficiently. Regardless of the job openings it has available, Facebook simply hires the smartest people it can find, and then uses StrengthsFinder results to understand their talents and create a job tailored to each new hire. On the other hand, Bloomberg leverages its People Analytics attribution model to efficiently source for candidates and to help assess the performance of every source of hire, whether it is the company's career site, traditional job boards, social media, employee referrals, or university campuses. Armed with this data, the talent management team can anticipate what source should be leveraged for specific positions within the company and can adjust the tactics and hiring budget accordingly.

ACQUISITION/HIRING ANALYTICS PILLAR

Whether you have a small company or manage a large organization with thousands of employees, choosing the wrong candidates can have a lethal impact on your business. So ensuring that your organization makes wise talent investments is critical to both long-term and short-term success.

The Acquisition/Hiring Analytics pillar uses analytics to optimize the interview process, helping to determine the best ways to vet candidates, to set up interview questions, and to create some tests that can be used to analyze the correlation between a candidate's performance during the interview and his or her performance in a particular job function.

By applying advanced analytics to talent data and to the information generated through talent acquisition, businesses can better address talent acquisition questions, including:

- What are the best sets of questions to ask during an interview?
- Is there a correlation between interview performance and job performance?
- How many interviews should we conduct before hiring?
- What is the impact of candidate experience and the interview outcome?
- Do referred candidates tend to perform better than other candidates?
- Which job applicants should you meet for an interview?

A great example of a company applying Big Data analytics to hiring is Transcom. Transcom is a global company providing customer care, sales, technical support, and credit management services through a network of contact centers and work-at-home agents. The company employs more than 29,000 customer experience specialists at 54 contact centers across 23 countries, delivering services in 33 languages to more than 400 international brands in various industry verticals. As a result, the effective hiring and retention of high-performing service professionals is a key component of Transcom's business strategy.

Using Big Data analytics, Transcom discovered that the trait of honesty was actually a good predictor of future performance.[9] As a result, the company conducted a pilot project to improve hiring and selection using data analytics. It screened for softer traits like honesty by asking candidates how comfortable they were working on a personal computer and whether they knew simple keyboard shortcuts for a cut-and-paste task. If they answered yes, the applicants were later asked to perform that task. Those who scored high on honesty typically stayed in their jobs 20 to 30 percent longer than those who didn't.

According to Neil Rae, an executive vice president of Transcom, in the call-center world 5 percent attrition a month (60 percent a year) is great performance. Dropout rates are relatively high in the industry and are calculated at 30-day intervals. Also, it takes from four to six weeks to train a worker, so the cost to hire a replacement for one customer service person who leaves is about $1,500.

Transcom was able to hire fewer people using this analytical approach (about 800 instead of a more typical 1,000 hires) to get 500 workers who were still on the job at least three months later. The big payoff, he says, should come in cost savings and better customer service with less worker churn in call centers. "This makes hiring more a science and less subjective," Rae says.

Other frontline stories include companies like Microsoft, CISCO, Xerox, and Bloomberg that we broadly covered in Chapter 6. Those companies have successfully leveraged predictive analytics and Big Data to optimize their talent acquisition. Bloomberg, for instance, uses Location Intelligence People Analytics Solutions that tells them things like:

- How popular is a specific skill set?
- How popular is a specific skill set within a certain function?
- How popular is a specific skill set with a certain experience level?
- How many companies are looking for similar roles?
- What schools are nearby that teach courses relevant to those roles?

ONBOARDING, CULTURE FIT, AND ENGAGEMENT PILLAR

Once the right candidates have been hired, they need to be properly onboarded to ensure they are aligned with primary business goals and the overall mission of the company. New hires need to have the best first impression of you as a manager and of your company. Depending on the role and position of your new hire, this should be accomplished within the first 6 to 12 months (depending on the role and candidate) by assisting the new employee with a list of resources and tools along with clear guidance on expectations and goals.

We define talent onboarding as an ongoing talent management process that consists of introducing, training, mentoring, coaching, and integrating a new hire to the core values, business vision, and overall culture of an organization in order to secure new employee loyalty and productivity. Analytics from the Onboarding, Culture Fit, and Engagement pillar can be used to enhance a new hire's first impression and create business value from your onboarding activities and efforts. It will also help your organization address vital talent management questions, including:

- How can a business improve time to performance?
- Does your new employee fit with company culture?
- What is an appropriate talent onboarding budget?
- What impact does talent onboarding have on employee turnover?
- What is the impact of talent onboarding on employee loyalty?

In this diverse workforce demographic where multiple generations have to work together, cultural fit is critical for the successful integration of your new hire; and employee and company value mismatches are one of the major reasons for early turnover.

For a great example of a company applying Big Data analytics to onboarding, let's revisit our Wells Fargo example. As part of the plan to improve the effectiveness of its sourcing through simple candidate questions grounded in real-time Big Data analytics, Wells Fargo gathered a lot of valuable information during the sourcing process to help with onboarding its new hire classes. The bank was able to get a sense of the areas of best fit, as well as the areas that needed more training and education for each candidate. This enabled the bank to create personalized onboarding experiences that make it more likely that each candidate will succeed in his or her role.

"This has given us the ability to say that, for those team members we are bringing on board who may not have the in-depth experience and life skills that we would want, we will coach them to help them be more successful," says Sangeeta Doss, senior vice president, recruiting manager for community banking. "We can determine if we need to give them a different onboarding experience or a stronger coach, and/ or buddy them up with other team members for mentoring."[10]

Wells Fargo measured the retention rate after each of the hires was on board for six months and found that teller retention improved by 15 percent and personal banker retention improved by 12 percent.

USING PEOPLE ANALYTICS TO IMPROVE COST PER HIRE AND BUSINESS OUTCOME OF CUSTOMER SUPPORT

Meredith Lazar, Senior Manager of Talent Acquisition, Constant Contact

When hiring customer engagement specialists for our Waltham, Massachusetts, office, we realized that the market is a lot more competitive than it had been in recent years; more companies in the area are also looking for people with specific customer service or customer support background. We used analytics to help us uncover that a customer-focused aptitude in a candidate was actually more predictive of future customer support job success than prior years of experience in a customer service role. Therefore, to fill the top of the funnel in this talent market, we updated our recruitment strategy to include candidates who may not have the ideal work experience on paper, but they have the right competencies and motivations.

Based on this People Analytics approach, we are now focused on targeting candidates who are customer focused and have the aptitude and attitude to learn the role and be successful. We are looking for people who are coachable, flexible, and tech savvy, and someone who is a good listener and a multitasker. Every potential candidate does not necessarily have to come right out of another customer service or support role in a call center type of environment; they may just work in hospitality or retail or simply be a people person who is customer service oriented, looking for a position in a fun, fast-paced environment.

Also, to prepare the customer support team leaders to interview someone without the specific customer service skill set we usually seek, we added specific interview questions to uncover the specific traits we are targeting in order to increase the potential talent pool. It's early in our process, but we have already seen the ratio of interviews to hires increase from 36 percent to 75 percent.

PERFORMANCE ASSESSMENT AND DEVELOPMENT AND EMPLOYEE LIFETIME VALUE PILLAR

To stay competitive, it is paramount to keep your employees fully engaged in order to meet and exceed your customers' expectations and achieve your corporate goals. A key component to accomplish this is to monitor the engagement level of your employee population.

We define an engaged employee as happy, enthusiastic, and motivated, and as an individual who eagerly relishes the challenges of her job. Analytics helps to understand the various drivers of employee engagement that deliver happier, more productive workers, and decrease unplanned turnover. It can also help human capital management teams sift through data and talent information to better understand employee engagement and help address some talent management questions such as:

- What are the key drivers of employee engagement?
- How does employee engagement affect productivity and financial bottom lines?
- What is the impact of hard-to-fill positions or hard-to-find skill sets on employee engagement?
- How do talent engagement elements, such as relationship with manager and confidence in leadership and company, affect turnover?

Talent engagement analytics can also provide insights on methods for increasing employee engagement via existing channels such as performance appraisals, the voice of the candidate, industry standards, and other metrics that can boost employee satisfaction and assist in paving career pathways. This pillar can also help organizations assess the correlation between engagement scores and employee performance in the past, present, and future—which is important information for reducing and mitigating the cost of bad hires and ultimately optimizing employees' lifetime value.

A great example of a company applying Big Data analytics to engagement and performance comes from The Container Store. Founded in 1978, The Container Store operates a chain of more than 60 retail stores in 22 states carrying over 10,000 home organization and storage products. It also provides design and installation services and sells its products online.

The Container Store full-time staffers receive 263 hours of training during their first year, compared to the 7-hour retail industry average, and its salespeople reportedly make 50 to 100 percent more than the industry average. The Container Store also looks for ways to empower its retail staff with technology, and is currently using wearable tech. Although the technology is designed to improve communication within its stores through the application of Big Data analytics, it is also used to monitor employees when they're at work to ensure engagement and performance.[11]

Using this technology, store management can access performance data, including how employees communicate with coworkers and customers and where they spend most of their time. Applying these Big Data analytics to employee performance can also help The Container Store identify and acknowledge top performers, along with workers who may be struggling in their positions.

Other frontline stories include companies like Goldcorp and GE that we broadly covered in Chapter 9. Those companies have successfully leveraged predictive analytics and Big Data to optimize their employee performance management. Goldcorp utilized an advanced analytics platform to review 792 million data points at an employee-day level in an effort to find patterns among high-impact incidents.

Information on behavioral factors such as month of the year, marital status, age, or compensation structure were the most important predictors of incidents and helped the company to anticipate potential performance issues and apply appropriate adjustment to mitigate the risk and maintain its overall workforce performance.

EMPLOYEE CHURN AND RETENTION PILLAR

Your ultimate goal with all employees, both new and existing, is to earn their trust, commitment, and engagement, so that they can fully achieve their goals and help your organization be successful. However, some of your employees will be high-value creators and the top performers of your organization. Others may require multiple trials in order to address performance issues, which can have a negative impact on your organization. The separation with your employee, whether it is voluntary or involuntary, is called churn or turnover. Voluntary churn occurs when an employee decides to leave an organization due to favorable conditions elsewhere, for instance to work for the competition. Involuntary churn, or attrition, refers to the termination of a position. Leveraging employee churn analytics will help to create business value from employee attrition knowledge by analyzing internal and external talent data intelligence, and help an organization address major attrition questions, including:

- Which employees will experience performance issues?
- Who are the top performers that are at high risk of leaving, and why?
- When are they more likely to quit?
- What proactive actions could be done to retain employees?
- What is the cost of losing top performers?

Employee retention is about proactively identifying and understanding which of your valuable employees are employees at risk of leaving, and when and why they would leave. Analytics can help to marry employee data, company data, and market data to predict and interpret top-performing employees' behaviors, giving you competitive insights for your retention strategies.

A great example of a company applying Big Data analytics to workforce churn and retention is Omnitracs. Omnitracs provides fleet management solutions based on software as a service to transportation and logistics companies in North America and Latin America. It provides technologies, including solutions for safety and compliance, fuel efficiency, driver retention, fleet productivity, GPS fleet tracking, and fleet maintenance. The company's mobile fleet management solutions and information services help users to manage assets, handle fuel management, reduce costs, retain drivers, and stay safe on the road. Omnitracs helps more than 40,000 private and for-hire fleet customers manage over 1.5 million mobile transportation assets in more than 70 countries.

Omnitracs also has a strong focus on Big Data analytics on behalf of its customers and does a lot of work to help clients address personnel issues—a big driver of success in the transportation industry. In the trucking industry, a lack of drivers means less revenue and more trucks sitting idle. Omnitracs is a believer that Big Data analytics can provide some powerful insights into driver retention.[12] Predictive models can help indicate when a driver is likely to quit and why, so the employer can improve the situation and prevent the loss of behind-the-wheel talent. Part of this equation is driver satisfaction. Raising the satisfaction within the driver workforce not only mitigates the cost to hire and train a new driver (estimated at $8,000 to $23,000), but prevents a negative ripple effect into the interactions your drivers have with customers when delivering shipments.

As an example, an Omnitracs client's trucking carrier with 1,400 drivers was experiencing high driver turnover. By using a custom Big Data–powered predictive model, they were able to prevent 290 truck drivers from quitting—reducing driver turnover by half and saving the company $1.2 million. Without knowing anything about any particular driver, the predictive model could analyze thousands of real-time data points and determine with high probability when a driver might be ready to quit for any number of reasons, like frustrations with a fleet manager, a skills gap, or family or financial problems. And, armed with that knowledge and with specific dialogue directed toward a solution, fleet managers were able to connect with their drivers at the right time and in the right way, so that their drivers felt heard and supported.

Other frontline stories include companies like AOL, Google, Deloitte, and Pfizer that we broadly covered in Chapter 11. Those companies were able to optimize their talent retention activities by leveraging the power of Big Data and predictive analytics, demonstrating significant ROI to the business.

EMPLOYEE WELLNESS, HEALTH, AND SAFETY PILLAR

To be successful, organizations have to create and design an environment and culture that promotes the safety, health, and well-being of their employees. This means finances and resources need to be allocated to support these endeavors, which requires a demonstrable linking of investments in employee health, safety, and well-being to company business performance. Best practices include proactive activities such as wellness visits, preventive checkups, and vaccinations to avoid the high cost of urgent reactive procedures.

Leveraged properly, this pillar provides a competitive advantage that can assist organizations in differentiating themselves from their competition, and further showcase the impact of that investment on their bottom lines by addressing questions such as:

- What is the impact of employee well-being and health on company productivity?
- What is the impact of employee satisfaction on customer satisfaction?
- What is the impact of employee health and well-being on company retention and acquisition metrics?

By investing in programs that promote the health, well-being, and safety of their workforce, companies can proactively increase the happiness of their employees. This boosts engagement and improves the quality of services they provide to the customers they serve. Ultimately, the result is a healthier company bottom line.

We can turn back to our Omnitracs example for an illustration of a company using Big Data analytics to improve workforce health and safety. In the trucking industry, everything comes down to safety and ROI. From Omnitracs' perspective, truck and driver safety improvements will be the most immediate benefit of Big Data technologies for the trucking industry. Any time you can prevent an accident, that's a good thing—and Big Data will make that possible.

For example, when fleet managers understand when drivers are stressed—and why—they can talk to their drivers about the right topic at the right time, resulting in happier, well-rested drivers who are content with their jobs, produce more miles, earn more money, burn less fuel, and have better safety records. Yes, carriers may be excited about preventing car–truck crashes at the outset, but they'll quickly find that relieving driver stress becomes less art and more science, returning big benefits for drivers and carriers alike.

To help transportation carriers identify drivers at risk, Omnitracs created an analytics model for accident prediction.[13] They took driver logs and turned each one into about a thousand distinct data points— from the amount of time the truck driver drove each hour of the day, to how many hours of sleep that driver got and when those hours occurred, to how many times that driver drove through sunrise. Then, they took 27,000 severe accidents from their customers' data sets and reverse-engineered a severity model, which allowed them to identify predictive data points in a particular driver logbook that indicated the potential for a bad accident. The model is so precise that they can take any driver's logbook and predict the likelihood of a bad accident each hour of his or her day.

Other frontline stories include companies like SAS Institute and WSIB that we broadly covered in Chapter 12. Those companies have successfully leveraged predictive analytics and Big Data to demonstrate ROI of employee wellness health and safety on their company bottom line as well as the overall talent management key performance metrics.

As a tool for summarizing our approach, Table 13.1 lists some of the key items of information needed in order to have analytical impact (see our IMPACT Cycle framework from Chapter 2) across the seven pillars, as well as examples of companies excelling in each.

Table 13.1 Applying the IMPACT Cycle to the Seven Pillars of People Analytics

IMPACT Cycle applied to the Seven Pillars of People Analytics Success	Pillar 1 Workforce Planning Analytics	Pillar 2 Sourcing Analytics	Pillar 3 Acquisition/Hiring Analytics	Pillar 4 Onboarding, Culture Fit, and Engagement	Pillar 5 Performance Assessment and Development and Employee Lifetime Value	Pillar 6 Employee Churn and Retention	Pillar 7 Employee Wellness, Health, and Safety
Identify the business challenges	1. What staff would you need in the next 12, 24, or 60 months ?	1. What sourcing channel delivers the best return on investment?	1. What candidate should you hire (who will stay long and perform well at job)?	1. What is the impact of a talent onboarding program on early turnover? 2. What is the impact of employee engagement on turnover and performance?	1. What is the breakeven point of your new employee? 2. What is the lifetime value of your employee? 3. Which of your talents will be successful if promoted?	1. Which star employees are at risk of leaving, and when and why?	1. What is the impact of the employee wellness program and health on employee retention and performance?
Master the data	1. Integrate internal and external talent data. 2. Build scenarios models for the supply/demand.	1. Integrate candidate data, company data, and labor market data. 2. Build predictive models to identify the best source of hire.	1. Integrate candidate data, company data, and labor market data. 2. Build predictive models to identify which candidates will be loyal and perform well on the job.	1. Integrate internal and external onboarding engagement and survey data. 2. Build predictive models to assess the impact of engagement initiatives on outcomes such as: time to productivity, turnover loyalty, and performance.	1. Integrate employee data and company data. 2. Build employee lifetime value and cost models of your employee population.	1. Integrate talent data (internal and external), company data, labor market data, and publicly available data. 2. Build predictive models to identify which employees are at risk to leave, and when and why.	1. Integrate all HRIS data, wellness data, and health data. 2. Build models to anticipate and assess the impact of employee wellness program on retention and performance.

(Continued)

Table 13.1 (Continued)

	Pillar 1	Pillar 2	Pillar 3	Pillar 4	Pillar 5	Pillar 6	Pillar 7
IMPACT Cycle applied to the Seven Pillars of People Analytics Success	**Workforce Planning Analytics**	**Sourcing Analytics**	**Acquisition/ Hiring Analytics**	**Onboarding, Culture Fit, and Engagement**	**Performance Assessment and Development and Employee Lifetime Value**	**Employee Churn and Retention**	**Employee Wellness, Health, and Safety**
Provide the meaning	Articulate, clear, and concise interpretations of the data and visuals in the context of the critical business questions that were identified.						
Act on the findings and recommendations	Provide thoughtful business recommendations based on your interpretation of the data. Even if they are off-base, it's easier to react to a suggestion than to generate one. Where possible, tie a rough dollar figure to any revenue improvements or cost savings associated with your recommendations.						
Communicate	Focus on a multi-pronged communication strategy that will get your insights as far and as wide into the organization as possible (e.g., an interactive tool others can use, a recorded WebEx of your insights, a lunch and learn, or even just a thoughtful executive memo that can be passed around).						
Track the results	Set up a way to track the impact of your insights. Make sure there is future follow-up with your business partners on the outcome of any actions: What was done, what was the impact, and what are the new critical questions that need your help as a result?						
Real-life applications	General Electric, Dow Chemical, Black Hills, Bullhorn, FedEx	General Motors, ManPower, CVS Aviation, Wells Fargo, Facebook	Bloomberg, Xerox, AT&T, Microsoft, CISCO, Google, Transcom	BestBuy, Lockheed Martin, Wells Fargo, The Container Store, Starbucks	Goldcorp, General Electric	AOL, Deloitte, Google, Bloomberg, Hewlett-Packard, Sprint, Omnitracs	SAS Institute, Workplace Safety and Insurance Board, Johnson & Johnson, Harrah's

KEY TAKEAWAYS

- Big Data encompasses three dimensions: volume, velocity, and variety. We added another V, which stands for the value of Big Data that we believe is paramount to showcase the business value of your data leveraging advanced analytics.
- Big Data analytics applied to People Analytics is gaining in popularity.
- The Seven Pillars of People Analytics Success can be used to identify companies from diverse industries and with diverse workforces that can apply Big Data analytics to talent management strategy challenges.
- Big Data analytics that brings multiple sources of data together and applies predictive analytics that are actionable is the best-in-class standard.
- To be successful, talent analytics requires an ongoing alignment with the organization's mission and goals.
- Frontline stories we discussed from leading organizations helped us to demonstrate the ROI of Big Data analytics applied to workforce management. People Analytics is already helping those companies to create business value from their talent data and to compete on talent analytics.

NOTES

1. Douglas Laney, "3D Data Management: Controlling Data Volume, Velocity, and Variety," META Group, February 6, 2001.
2. Interview with Stephen O'Sullivan, Walmart senior director of global e-commerce, GigaOM, March 23, 2012.
3. ABI Research, "Big Data Spending to Reach $114 Billion in 2018; Look for Machine Learning to Drive Analytics," www.abiresearch.com/press/big-data-spending-to-reach-114-billion-in-2014-loo.
4. IDG Enterprise, "2014 IDG Enterprise Big Data Research Study," www.idgenterprise.com/report/big-data-2.
5. "IDC FutureScape: Worldwide Big Data & Analytics 2015 Predictions," IDC webinar on December 10, 2014.
6. "Unlock the People Equation: Using Workforce Analytics to Drive Business Results," IBM Research Report, 2014.
7. Bill Roberts, "Cover Story: The Benefits of Big Data," *HR Magazine* 58, no. 10 (October 1, 2013).
8. Katie Kuehner-Hebert, "Predictive Analytics for Hiring," *Banking Strategies*, September 6, 2013.

9. Steve Lohr, "Big Data Trying to Build Better Workers," *New York Times*, April 20, 2013.

10. Kuehner-Hebert, "Predictive Analytics for Hiring."

11. Al Sacco, "How The Container Store Uses Wearable Tech to Think Outside the Box," *CIO Magazine*, March 6, 2014.

12. "Big Data Is about to Change the Trucking Industry as We Know It," Omnitracs, LLC, 2015.

13. Nicole Fallon, "Big Data: It's Not Just for Customer Insights," *Business News Daily*, September 9, 2014.

CHAPTER **14**

Future of People Analytics

Opportunity is missed by most people because it is dressed in overalls and looks like work.

—Thomas Edison

People Analytics is a growing area of data science that holds great promise for the future. It's likely to become a commonplace practice in the coming years as the people, processes, and systems mature and make People Analytics something that any organization can do. The field of People Analytics as a discipline at the intersection of business analytics and HR is still in relative infancy, and technology is finally beginning to catch up to fulfill the promise for what organizational leaders have wanted for many years. For example, some companies such as Starbucks, Limited Brands, and Best Buy can precisely identify the value of a 0.1 percent increase in employee engagement at a particular store. At Best Buy, for example, that value is more than $100,000 in the store's annual operating income.[1]

It's true that advanced analytic techniques of employee data that companies have at their disposal can help answer some of the critical questions surrounding the value of human capital, such as: How do investments in employee programs actually impact workforce performance? How can you motivate employees to succeed? and Who are your top performers? However, most companies are not currently able to answer these questions; they struggle with answering even basic workforce analytics questions, much less questions having to do with more sophisticated techniques. Futhermore, we believe the use of advanced People Analytics is intensifying and will soon become the new normal for businesses.

One day soon, people will stop discussing the merits of the emergence of People Analytics, which companies are using advanced People Analytics to optimize their human capital spend, or whether People Analytics is critical to their business. It will just be a given that every company must cope with the stream of Big Data from workers, and must have a People Analytics strategy, as well as use various data assets and tools to augment the data they collect internally. In other words, the formal use of People Analytics within HR and across business units will become as ubiquitous as data itself has become. In the same way that most companies have strategies for learning and development, onboarding, training, and resource planning, they will also have a formal strategy for People Analytics.

A wide range of trends are only just beginning to pave the way for advanced People Analytics, including improved technology, machine learning techniques, and data visualization. These trends are making applications of computational People Analytics possible that were not possible even five years ago. In this chapter we will discuss some of those, as well as other trends that will influence the future state of People Analytics.

We believe the future of advanced People Analytics is strong and that the future holds several key trends related to People Analytics, each of which we will discuss in the chapter. Specifically, we think that in a People Analytics future:

- There is a rise of employee behavioral data.
- People Analytics moves beyond the averages.
- Predictive analytics becomes the new standard.
- Big Data analytics becomes automated.
- Big Data empowers employee development.
- Models become the gold of People Analytics.
- People Analytics becomes more accessible to the nonanalyst.
- People Analytics becomes a specialized department.
- Employee data privacy becomes top of mind.
- There is quantification of HR.

RISE OF EMPLOYEE BEHAVIORAL DATA

Another future trend related to People Analytics will be the proliferation of various forms of employee data that can be tracked, analyzed, and modeled. The intersection of computer science, information technology, and psychology of how computers can effectively interact with humans is driving part of this new data on employee behavior. We are regularly gaining new knowledge on how humans can effectively interact with technology, as well as the tools to create that knowledge, which is being applied to the workplace more regularly. One of the oldest examples of this is GPS-based technology. GPS allows for the tracking of location and movement, and saw widespread usage initially in the shipping and logistics industry, where companies wanted to make sure drivers and packages arrived on time. And its use is on the rise. A 2014 study by the research firm Aberdeen found that 54 percent of companies that send employees out on service calls use some sort of location-based tracking system—and this is up from 37 percent found in 2012.[2]

What about employee behavioral data of the future? What types of technology are on the horizon to enable employees to be more successful and employers to use People Analytics to model successful outcomes? One example is eye-tracking technology. It's one form of human-centered computing whereby a camera can track the eye movement of someone viewing a computer screen, recording data about where and how often the person viewed different areas of the screen. It has been applied in areas as diverse as website usability testing, sports medicine, automobile testing, geriatric research, training simulators, and infant research. Some employers are already using it now to monitor whether employees are paying attention during training sessions.

As we look into the future, we expect more devices will interact directly with the human body and, as a result, generate data from those interactions in the workplace that needs to be analyzed. In terms of the future applications of human-centered computing, we think the following applications will be relevant for the field of People Analytics:

- Wearable computing/smart fabrics
- Consumer health informatics
- Brainwave measurement
- Facial recognition
- Emotional recognition
- Exercise informatics

- Body scan technologies
- Gesture-based interfaces
- Motion-detection devices
- Molecular computing

Furthermore, many of the hundreds of millions of mobile apps include some type of location-based tracking. Also, stores are experimenting with location-aware services that enable retailers to track and serve offers to users in a specific location. This same technology could be used to interact with employees based on their locations.

Certain companies are already creating multidimensional employee behavior tracking tools that are being used by some organizations. For example, imagine a tiny microphone embedded in the ID badge hanging from the lanyard around your neck. The microphone is gauging the tone of your voice and how frequently you are contributing in meetings. Hidden accelerometers measure your body language and track how often you push away from your desk. At the end of each day, the badge will have collected several gigabytes' worth of data about your office behavior. Sound like science fiction? It's not, and is being touted as the next frontier in office innovation by Boston-based creators Humanyze, which developed a badge that tracks employees' daily movements, how much they speak up during meetings, and whether they need a break or are going strong before storing nearly four gigabytes in data for employers to analyze at the end of the day. The company believes information like this will help with productivity in the office.[3]

As organizations begin to leverage employee behavioral data of different types, People Analytics will need to cope with policies about how to store, sort, analyze, and use this data for the benefit of organizations while respecting the privacy rights of employees.

PEOPLE ANALYTICS MOVES BEYOND THE AVERAGES

Analytics of any kind relies on describing patterns in the data. One such example of a metric that reflects the pattern in data is the "average," which is something most people learn during their early math education. To calculate an average, take all the data you have about something and divide the sum total into equal parts. Average is used frequently in People Analytics. For example, average cost per hire, average speed to answer, average time to productivity, average customer resolution rate, average talk time of a sales rep, and average hours worked are common metrics used to evaluate worker performance in organizations.

However, often the average doesn't do a great job at helping us understand the individual variations and nuances in your workforce. For example, if you have a customer service team of 100 and half of them have a very high talk time when helping customers and half have a very low talk time, calculating an average won't be very insightful. You'll end up with a metric that doesn't describe anyone in either group and, if used, would give a false sense of failure or success as you moved forward with initiatives to drive this metric.

A future trend in People Analytics will be to move beyond the averages and create analytical models that describe the complexity of the workforce. We think People Analytics will eventually move toward analytical models that help optimize each worker's performance such that analytical insights will help each person perform as best he or she can in a chosen career. Rather than being compared against a large population, the practical use of People Analytics will be to personalize our understanding of the unique qualities of each person, helping provide insights that benefit both the employer and the worker.

For example, imagine that we create an employee retention model that scores employees in terms of how at risk they are to leave the organization in the next 90 days. We might use metrics in the model such as absenteeism rate, hours worked, start time, projects delivered, and calls made, among others, to attempt to predict whether the worker is at risk of leaving the organization. If we used a simple average comparison of a specific person across an entire workforce, we might get a lot of false positives and think someone will leave when they won't, as well as fail to detect all those who are truly at risk of leaving. However, if we go beyond the averages and use, say, a ratio of the change in performance over time for *each* employee, we are much more likely to account for individual differences in how employees do their jobs. As a result, the key model inputs will be changes in how each employee works as a predictor of likelihood to quit, rather than evaluating how that employee compares to an average.

In the future, People Analytics will go beyond the averages and our models will be able to predict worker dynamics at an increasingly more granular level—even down to the level of a specific worker.

PREDICTIVE BECOMES THE NEW STANDARD

We provided overviews of predictive analytics and its importance throughout this book. We believe that as we progress toward the future, predictive analytics will become more widespread and evolve into the norm for all analytics. People-related analytical techniques will need to have a predictive component in order to be considered business-relevant or effective, not metrics to describe merely "what has happened," but to help describe "what will happen." This will require more sophisticated statistical techniques, data integrations, and more computational power, all of which are becoming possible. It will also require the expertise of analysts and HR that can develop people-related predictive models effectively and understand how to learn, test, and optimize using predictive analytical techniques. There are certainly many examples of predictive analytics applied to human capital, many of which you have seen illustrated in this book, and we expect to see it become the standard across all industries in the future.

AUTOMATED BIG DATA ANALYTICS

Machine learning is a branch of artificial intelligence concerned with the design and development of algorithms that allow computers to learn from processing real data and to become more proficient over time. In the future, artificial intelligence will start showing up in more and more unexpected places, including the software used by most employers. A major focus of machine learning research is to automatically learn to recognize complex patterns in Big Data and make intelligent decisions. Some examples of the current applications of machine learning include:

- Search engines
- Medical diagnosis
- Bioinformatics

- Cheminformatics
- Detecting credit card fraud
- Stock market analysis
- Classifying DNA sequences
- Speech and handwriting recognition
- Robot locomotion
- Aircraft autopilot
- Computational finance
- Sentiment analysis
- Recommender systems

Examples of automated Big Data analytics applied to employee data already exist. For example, Kanjoya, Inc. has developed sentiment analytics software that automatically sifts through thousands of open-ended employee comments to understand whether employees are satisfied or frustrated. For companies with thousands of employees in multiple locations, automated analytics like this can really improve productivity, letting leaders focus on changes to enhance employee engagement, rather than sift through data to understand it. Kanjoya's automated analytics, developed in collaboration with scientists at Stanford University, can also uncover subtle differences in opinions, attitudes, and sentiment in written conversations and can detect the earliest signs of workplace bullying, harassment, and discrimination.[4]

Machine learning is a rapidly evolving field that has the potential to have a great impact on People Analytics. However, what is not clear is how the future advances in machine learning will impact the need for trained analysts and other human resources. As machine learning models and techniques improve over the long term, it is possible there will be a reduction in demand for humans with that specialized skill set. Additionally, as sophisticated applications are developed, it will make it easier to run larger, more complex organizations with fewer people, possibly leading to corporate consolidation and the ability to do more with a smaller workforce.

BIG DATA EMPOWERS EMPLOYEE DEVELOPMENT

The days of the stressful annual performance review involving a big buildup of activity to get a long document written and delivered are starting to change. Going away are the days when feedback is given in large mega-doses that don't always lead to meaningful development. The availability of Big Data analytics is a key driver of this shift.

The broad trend is that companies will forgo the annual review process and traditional engagement surveys and replace them with a more flexible and ongoing feedback system enabled by Big Data management by apps. These systems will allow employees to give and receive feedback anytime throughout the year on a variety of issues. The new surveys would be shorter and more pointed than the long annual engagement survey. They'll also be designed for smartphones so they can be taken anywhere at any time. Companies like Adobe, Accenture, Starbucks, and General Electric have moved away from the old type of annual performance review to more open and ongoing feedback. Some of these companies are running their employee performance management by an app, from which employees can get feedback from their managers and peers and also communicate with them.

According to the head of human resources (HR) at Accenture, "you know the world is no longer working in yearlong cycles, so to set objectives at the beginning of the year and revisit them at the end of the year simply to see how people are doing is not really relevant any longer. Doing away with the annual review cycle really makes sense for us when you consider that two-thirds of our employees are millennials, who are used to giving and receiving constant feedback in their daily lives, whether it be through Instagram likes or writing and reading reviews on Amazon."[5]

Through leveraging Big Data analytics, companies will be able to analyze and identify, in real time, early signs of employee retention or morale issues, providing a closed-loop response to employees that empowers them and makes them heard rather than waiting around for the next annual performance review or employee survey.

MODELS BECOME THE NEW GOLD OF PEOPLE ANALYTICS

This may seem counterintuitive, but we believe data will become less valuable in the future. Even now, data are everywhere and people and organizations are overwhelmed with data. In the future, having a treasure trove of data about your employees will not, by itself, hold much value. However, we do expect analytical models to become *more* valuable at the same time the data by itself becomes less valuable. In other words, the companies that have the ability to create actionable knowledge-based tools from employee data, either using their own data or using someone else's data, will see the business benefits. This will take many forms: everything from applications that sift through employee data for nuggets of productivity insight to personalized algorithms that allow an individual employee to analyze his or her own behavioral performance data to help understand something about themselves and take action.

PEOPLE ANALYTICS BECOMES MORE ACCESSIBLE

Another trend that will shape the future of People Analytics is that analytical techniques will become more accessible to the general business user, enabling nonanalysts and people outside of HR to take an analytical approach to employee and human capital challenges. As general knowledge of analytics spreads and software providers automate the use of techniques (e.g., hide the actual steps of data analytics from the user, such as data modeling, text analytics, web analytics, and segmentation through automation), people with little or no analytical background will be able to run models and take business action from the results. We can already see instances of this occurring in certain analytical disciplines. For example, the rise of automated online survey tools over the past 10 years has led to people in all departments of organizations creating and analyzing their own customer surveys. This sometimes causes frustration for the marketing research experts, as survey questions are sometimes poorly worded or statistically significant differences or margins of error are not considered. However, we do believe this trend will be net positive for the influence of analytics, but we're sure there will be pain along the way. For example, untrained analysts are likely to apply analytical techniques improperly or in an inappropriate manner with incorrectly prepared data. As a result, there will be instances of confusion and frustration as those who know People Analytics help those who do not. However, we believe the social pressure that will result will eventually lead to People Analytics being used more effectively, not only by HR, but across the organization.

PEOPLE ANALYTICS BECOMES A SPECIALIZED DEPARTMENT

Although we expect that People Analytics techniques will become more available to nonanalysts across the enterprise, we also see the future of People Analytics being one where specialized departments are created to address the needs of People Analytics across the organization. In the current state, analytical professionals are often fragmented across the enterprise, frequently in different departments with labels such as business intelligence, statistician, survey researcher, web analyst, data scientist, and HR analyst. Furthermore, most companies have very few, if any, professionals who specialize in people-related analytics. We expect that most companies will move to centralize People Analytics expertise in a specialized department either in HR or in finance. The model for some companies may be to have People Analytics as a formal, centralized, shared service, and for others, as a center of excellence where People Analytics professionals are kept close to the business units they serve, yet have accountability to and participate in an analytics center of excellence. Regardless, the most successful companies of the future will recognize and prioritize the importance of People Analytics and related analytics professionals, making them into a formal business function in the same way that it is commonplace in many companies today to have such departments as engineering, marketing, customer service, technology, and finance.

EMPLOYEE DATA PRIVACY BACKLASH

Employee data privacy will be a hot topic in the future of People Analytics as employees continue to grapple with the notion that many of their activities are being tracked in great detail by their employer, both while they are at work and while they are at home if they're using work-provided equipment. Also, as analytics become more sophisticated and human-like, employees may get an uncomfortable feeling when they are given workplace insights and recommendations they didn't even know were possible. Recall the case we reviewed in Chapter 6 of Xerox's insight that customer service rep success is due, in part, to personality traits.

Already employee data privacy is a hot topic with many companies grappling with how best to use employee data. One position is that analytics software should be applied to data only where an employee has no expectation of privacy. For example, Intel is very thoughtful about only monitoring employees' sentiment through their communications in the workplace where privacy would never be assumed. "We're only going to do it where it's very clearly been an employee statement in a known public forum where they know their stuff is being looked at," says Intel's Richard Taylor. On internal Intel blogs, for example, employees must attach their real names to comments. In Intel's eyes, such posts would be acceptable for analysis. However, employee e-mails are seen as private and Intel won't analyze them. "We would lose the trust of our employees if we did that," he says. "That would be the worst thing" with this issue.[6]

The global economy will make the employee data privacy backlash even more complicated for multinational firms as different countries develop different standards regarding what is acceptable use and acceptable privacy rights of employee data. For example, an October 2015 ruling by the European Court of Justice makes it difficult to transfer employee data about a German worker outside of Germany without express permission. If the ruling stands, it may force all organizations that currently rely on the ability to access the data of their European Union (EU) partners and subsidiaries to seek alternate modes of data transfer or risk legal liability from being in noncompliance with EU data protection requirements.[7]

We expect that, as the future progresses and as data and People Analytics become more important in our workplace lives, there will be a data privacy backlash where employees will demand more awareness about what is being tracked and even more governmental involvement in employee data privacy standards and protection in the same way that Equal Employment Opportunity Commission guidelines have become an important role of the government. We do not know what form this will take, whether it will be a credit agency model whereby all information is centralized in a few organizations or it will be distributed across each employer whereby employees have the ability to decide which information about them is shared, hidden, or permanently deleted. Either way, the field of People Analytics must take note and engage in the conversation, as employer–employee dynamics will be directly impacted by any changes in data privacy policies and standards.

QUANTIFICATION OF HR

Another trend that will affect the future of People Analytics is what we call the quantification of HR. Those of you in HR leadership know you're under pressure: under pressure to quantify such things as people-related programs, demonstrate the ROI of training and development initiatives, and show efficient use workforce talent. This all takes hard data—data that you may not have, data that may be difficult to understand, and data that may be confusing to analyze. However, the CEO, CFO, and shareholders will continue to put pressure on the return from HR and how your organization knows it's getting the most from its people assets. Therefore, the future of HR looks a lot more like a quantitative discipline than just a people-friendly discipline.

So far, many organizations are already behind. The Sierra-Cedar HR Systems Survey, now in its seventeenth year, gathers information from more than 1,000 organizations across the globe that is validated against publicly available financial and market data. The longevity of the HR

Systems Survey affords a historical perspective that allows a look back year over year at factors that have an impact on business outcomes. As part of that survey, Sierra tracks the adoption and deployment of HR analytics solutions, gathering data on process maturity as well as the type and amount of data HR organizations are capturing.

The results are surprising. Although many companies used HR dashboards and reports of some kind, very few used true analytics, with workforce analytics used by only 16 percent, predictive analytics used by only 9 percent, strategic workforce planning analytics used by only 11 percent, and Big Data analytics used by only 9 percent.[8]

However, because Sierra is tracking business outcomes with its study, the analysts were able to compare the business outcomes of HR organizations that were data driven versus those that were not. They wanted to see whether organizations that gather more data, share that data openly, and leverage it in processes and decision making see improved outcomes from their efforts.

First, they had to define the quantified HR organization. Starting with key findings from the 2013–2014 survey results about business intelligence (BI) adoption, they determined that a quantified HR organization would be one that invests in HR measurement technologies, processes, and practices that enable it to improve workforce operations and achieve organizational goals in an environment of data-driven decision making. Specifically, they identified several selection criteria that were based on an organization's leadership in four areas:

1. Business intelligence process maturity.
2. Managers' direct access to HR analytics and BI that supports workforce decision making.
3. More data sources regularly juxtaposed with workforce data.
4. More overall categories of HR metrics.

Sierra found that company size didn't matter, with successful companies in this area ranging in size from small (with workforces of just over 100) to very large (with workforces of more than 400,000). Many quantified HR organizations were also global, operating in an average of 29 different countries.[9]

The findings were clear. Quantified HR organizations outperformed even the top-performing organizations of the most recent Sierra study, achieving higher levels of financial performance, as well as positive HR and talent outcomes. However, the most dramatic difference in outcome analysis was in the return on equity.

There is more work to understand exactly how the quantified HR organization achieves results, as surely many factors have an impact on an organization's overall success. However, there is enough data from multiple sources to conclude that the data-driven HR organization is real, and that it isn't tied to a single type of technology, organizational makeup, or industry. Becoming an analytically driven HR function is achievable for any organization willing to take an honest look at its data and analytics and use that information to make workforce decisions.

 KEY TAKEAWAYS

- The future of People Analytics is bright, with opportunities in many areas.
- Certain trends will dramatically shape the field of People Analytics in the future.
- Employee tracking will proliferate in many forms.
- People Analytics insights will become more valuable.
- Predictive modeling will become the new de facto standard.
- Big Data will empower employee performance and development.
- Real-time data will advance People Analytics rapidly.
- Advances in automated analytics will make People Analytics more powerful.
- People analytical techniques will become more accessible to the nonanalyst.
- People Analytics will become a specialized department within the organization.
- An employee data privacy backlash will lead to rigorous attempts at individual employee control of one's own data.
- The quantified HR department will become the new standard.

NOTES

1. Thomas H. Davenport, Jeanne Harris, and Jeremy Shapiro, "Competing on Talent Analytics," *Harvard Business Review*, October 2010, https://hbr.org/2010/10/competing-on-talent-analytics.

2. Rebecca Greenfield, "So Now Your Boss Is Tracking You at Home," *Bangkok Post*, May 24, 2014, 21.

3. Zach Dennis, "Office ID Badges Could Track Employee Behavior and Production," *Palm Beach Post*, September 21, 2015, www.palmbeachpost.com/news/news/tech-science/office-id-badges-could-track-employee-behavior-and/nnj2f/.

4. Rachael King, "How Do Employees Really Feel about Their Companies?" *Wall Street Journal*, October 13, 2015, www.wsj.com/articles/how-do-employees-really-feel-about-their-companies-1444788408

5. Cyrus Sanati, "How Big Data Can Take the Pain out of Performance Reviews," *Fortune*, October 9, 2015, http://fortune.com/2015/10/09/big-data-performance-review/.

6. King, "How Do Employees Really Feel about Their Companies?"

7. Etienne Drouard, Ignasi Guardans, Samuel R. Castic, and Claude-Étienne Armingaud, "Did the ECJ Kill the Safe Harbor Framework on E.U.–U.S. Data Transfers?" K&L Gates, October 6, 2015, http://klgates.com/did-the-ecj-kill-the-safe-harbor-framework-on-eu-us-data-transfers-10-06-2015/.

8. Sierra-Cedar 2014–2015 HR Systems Survey: *HR Technologies, Deployment Approaches, Integration, Metrics, and Value, 17th Annual Edition*, Sierra-Cedar, 2014, http://www.sierra-cedar.com/wp-content/uploads/sites/12/2014/11/Sierra-Cedar_2014-2015_HRSystemsSurveyWhitePaper.pdf.

9. Ibid.

Index

Page numbers with *f* and *t* stand for figure and table.